Building High Performance Business Relationships

Building High Performance Business Relationships

Douglas M. Lambert
Fisher College of Business
The Ohio State University

A. Michael Knemeyer
Fisher College of Business
The Ohio State University

John T. Gardner
State University of New York

Supply Chain Management Institute
Sarasota, Florida
www.scm-institute.org

For information:

Supply Chain Management Institute
2425 Fruitville Road
Sarasota, FL 34237
Phone: (941) 957-1510
Fax: (941) 957-0900
www.scm-institute.org

For Order Information:
sales@scm-institute.org

For Training on the Partnership Model or the Collaboration Framework:
info@scm-institute.org

Printed in the United States of America.

Lambert, Douglas M.
Building High Performance Business Relationships
Douglas M. Lambert, A. Michael Knemeyer, John T. Gardner
        p. cm.
Includes bibliographical references and index.
    ISBN: 978-0-9759949-4-8

Project Manager: Nancy Bevier
Designer: Cynthia Klusmeyer
Printer: The Hartley Press, Inc.
                     4250 St. Augustine Road
                     Jacksonville, FL 32207

To the members of The Global Supply Chain Forum whose vision
and support guided us in the development of the Partnership Model

Contributing Authors

Douglas M. Lambert is the Raymond E. Mason Chair in Transportation and Logistics and Director of The Global Supply Chain Forum at The Ohio State University. He was the primary researcher for the project on partnerships that developed the Partnership Model and has facilitated numerous sessions using the model. Also, he was instrumental in the development of the Collaboration Framework. Dr. Lambert has served as a faculty member for over 500 executive development programs in North and South America, Europe, Asia and Australia. He is the author or co-author of seven books and more than 100 articles. In 1986, Dr. Lambert received the CLM Distinguished Service Award for his contributions to logistics management. He holds an honors BA and MBA from the University of Western Ontario and a Ph.D. from The Ohio State University.

A. Michael Knemeyer is an Associate Professor in the Department of Marketing and Logistics at The Ohio State University. His research focuses on developing and implementing collaborative business relationships. He was involved in the research to validate the Partnership Model and has been a facilitator for sessions using the model. One of these sessions resulted in the article, "We're in This Together," co-authored with Douglas M. Lambert that appeared in the *Harvard Business Review*, December, 2004. His work has been published in major academic journals and has been cited in leading practitioner journals. He received a BSBA in Business Logistics and Marketing from John Carroll University and a Ph.D. in Business Logistics from the University of Maryland.

John T. Gardner is a Professor of Marketing and Logistics at SUNY College of Brockport. He received his BS in Environmental Health and his MBA from East Carolina University, a MA and a Ph. D. in Marketing from The Ohio State University. His research interests include partnership formation and management in business-to-business relationships. He was a member of the research team that developed the Partnership Model and is a co-author of four articles published on the partnership research. In addition, he has facilitated a number of sessions using the model and has participated in executive programs on how to use the model in North America, Europe and Asia. Professor Gardner was the recipient of the CLM Dissertation Award in 1990.

Preface

In 1992, with the encouragement of Gary Ridenhower of 3M, I decided to take the steps to develop a research center that we had been talking about for a number of years. On April 23 and 24, 1992, executives from six companies accepted my invitation to meet and begin a research center which, in 1996 when I moved to The Ohio State University, became The Global Supply Chain Forum. The mission of the Forum is to provide the opportunity for leading practitioners and academics to pursue the critical issues related to achieving operational excellence. Membership in the Forum consists of representatives of firms recognized as industry leaders. Balance is maintained both as to the nature of the firms and the specific expertise of their representatives. The membership is targeted at fifteen firms. It is expected that members actively participate in Forum activities.

The members unanimously decided that the first research project funded by the Forum should be on partnerships. The objective was to determine how to develop and maintain close business relationships with key customers and suppliers. They agreed that their organizations were not good at this and they believed that partnerships would be critical for the long-term survival of their companies. It was their hope that if we studied 18 partnerships that they identified as good paartnerships from which we could learn, then we could help them replicate the successes and avoid the failures. In a progress report, the research team presented a description of characteristics of successful partnerships and the main reasons for failure. The members regarded the progress as positive, but they wanted a tool to determine when a partnership was appropriate and what form it should take as well as to set the right expectations for both partners.

In 1996, the first two articles on the Partnership Model were published. With the Partnership Model, managers have a tool to determine when a partnership is appropriate and what form the relationship should take. In a one and one-half day meeting using the Partnership Model, management from both organizations reach agreement on appropriate expectations for the relationship. In the years since 1996, we have facilitated more than 80 sessions using the Partnership Model. Since its beginning, the Partnership Model presented in this book has represented the combined knowledge and experience of the executives who are members of the Forum and the research team.

Douglas M. Lambert

Acknowledgements

A number of people have contributed to this work. First and foremost, the members of The Global Supply Chain Forum who guided us in the partnership research and helped us develop the material in this book. The friendship and guidance provided by the executives who represent the Forum member organizations is greatly appreciated. Representatives from the following companies contributed to the partnership research: 3M, Bob Evans Farms, Cargill, The Coca-Cola Company, Colgate-Palmolive Company, Defense Logistics Agency, The Goodyear Tire and Rubber Company, Hewlett-Packard Company, Imation, International Paper, Lucent Technologies (AT&T Network Systems), Limited Brands, Masterfoods USA, McDonald's Corporation, Shell Global Solutions International B.V., Sysco Corporation, TaylorMade-adidas Golf Company, Tyson Foods, Wendy's International, and Whirlpool Corporation.

Colleagues who contributed to the research that resulted in the development of the partnership model are Jay U. Sterling, Margaret A. Emmelhainz, Lisa Ellram and Sebastián J. García-Dastugue. Our colleague Keely Croxton offered valuable comments on chapters of this book. We would like to thank Yubei Hu, a graduate of the MBA and Master of Accounting programs at the Fisher College of Business, who now has a position in Global Channel Services at 3M, who read the manuscript and offered comments. Finally, we would like to thank Shirley Gaddis, assistant director of the Global Supply Chain Forum, for her support of Forum activities and research.

Provost Joseph A. Alutto, formerly Dean of the Fisher College of Business, deserves recognition for creating a productive research environment. Dean Christine A. Poon and Professor Robert Burnkrant, Chair of the Department of Marketing and Logistics, have provided encouragement. It is also important to recognize our outstanding colleagues in the Fisher College of Business.

Special thanks are given to General Raymond E. Mason and his wife, Margaret, who are generous supporters of the Fisher College of Business and great examples of what makes being a Buckeye something special.

Finally, we would like to thank our wives, Lynne, Stacey and Lynne, for their love and friendship.

Douglas M. Lambert
A. Michael Knemeyer
John T. Gardner

Contents

4. How to Use the Partnership Model

5. Sustaining the Relationship and Measuring Perfromance

6. Postscript: A Framework for Collaboration

Tools and Resources

Partnerships and Corporate Success

Developing and managing a partnership with a strategic customer or supplier as outlined in this book can provide you with a competitive edge and help tilt the playing field in your favor.

— Richard A. Locke

Vice President, Supply Chain, Food Packaging Americas
& Global Pharmaceutical Packaging, Alcan

Overview

Increasingly, corporate success will depend on the formation of mutually beneficial relationships with key customers and suppliers. While business leaders and academics have championed the value of partnerships for this purpose, the challenge is to find an effective method, which can be implemented and sustained, for forming these types of relationships. In this chapter, we describe why partnerships are so critical for corporate success, what a partnership involves, why management should seek partnership arrangements with key customers and suppliers, and a tool known as the partnership model. The Partnership Model provides management with a repeatable method to identify appropriate candidates for these increasingly critical relationships and determine how to appropriately resource and structure these relationships.

Why is Partnership Important?

In an environment characterized by scarce resources, increased competition, higher customer expectations, and faster rates of change, executives are turning to partnerships to strengthen supply chain integration and achieve a sustainable competitive advantage.

In an environment characterized by scarce resources, increased competition, higher customer expectations, and faster rates of change, executives are turning to partnerships to strengthen supply chain integration and achieve a sustainable competitive advantage. Partnering provides a way to leverage the unique skills and expertise of each partner and may also "lock out" competitors. According to Rosabeth Moss Kanter, "...being a good partner has become a key corporate asset...In the global economy, a well-developed ability to create and sustain fruitful collaborations gives companies a significant competitive leg up".[1] But exactly what is a partnership, when is one appropriate, and who should management target to form these relationships? At first glance, the answers to these questions may appear straight-forward, but they are not.

There is considerable confusion over the definition of partnership and when

[1] Kanter, Rosabeth M., "Collaborative Advantage: The Art of Alliances," *Harvard Business Review*, Vol. 72, No. 4 (1994), pp. 96-108.

this type of relationship is appropriate. As an example, one executive from a major manufacturer in the health care industry identified a relationship with a small-package express delivery company as a partnership. When analyzed in detail, it became apparent that the relationship was not a partnership; rather it was simply a single source contract with volume guarantees. The reason why managers from both firms believed that they were involved in a partnership was each firm was achieving the desired outcomes from the relationship. The transportation firm received a large revenue increase as the single-source provider of the service and the manufacturer achieved the service improvement and cost reductions that were promised. The initial reaction of an executive from the manufacturer, when she realized that this relationship was not a partnership, was that she ought to work to make it one. This executive's reaction is understandable and fairly common. A basic premise that seems to permeate business today is that partnerships are essential elements of business strategy and managers should strive to achieve such relationships with every customer and supplier. This is not only flawed thinking, it is dangerous thinking.

The lesson here is that a partnership is not necessarily a requirement for achieving business success with every customer and supplier. And, this is a good thing.[2] Partnerships, while beneficial, are costly in terms of the time and effort required to support them.[3] Consequently, a firm cannot and should not have partnerships with every supplier or customer. It is important to ensure that scarce resources are dedicated only to those relationships that will truly benefit from a partnership. Yet, many organizations become involved in relationships that do not meet management's expectations and/or which end in failure. How can managers determine, in advance, if a potential relationship is one that will result in competitive advantage, and is worthy of the time and resources needed to fully develop into a partnership? Further, all partnerships are not the same. How does management know what type of partnership would provide the best pay-off? These questions can be answered by using the partnership model presented in this book.

The Partnership Model presents a systematic process for developing, implementing and continuously improving the most important corporate relationships. Without effective relationships with key customers and suppliers, organizations are likely to be unsuccessful.[4] Partnering between firms is one way to find and maintain competitive advantage for both firms.[5] The partnership model that serves as the core of this book provides a structured and repeatable process to effectively and efficiently build and maintain tailored business relationships that might become an asset and a competitive advantage for the organization.

How can managers determine, in advance, if a potential relationship is one that will result in competitive advantage, and is worthy of the time and resources needed to fully develop into a partnership?

---

[2] Lambert, Douglas M., Margaret A. Emmelhainz and John T. Gardner, "Developing and Implementing Supply Chain Partnerships," *The International Journal of Logistics Management,* Vol. 7, No. 2 (1996), pp. 1-17.

[3] Gardner, John T., Martha C. Cooper and Tom Noordewier, "Understanding Shipper-Carrier and Shipper-Warehouser Relationships: Partnerships Revisted," *Journal of Business Logistics,* Vol. 15, No. 2 (1994), pp. 121-143.

[4] "Supply Chain Challenges: Building Relationships – A Conversation with Scott Beth, David N. Burt, William Copacino, Chris Gopal, Hau L. Lee, Robert Porter Lynch and Sandra Morris," *Harvard Business Review,* Vol. 81, No. 7 (2003), pp. 64-74.

[5] Mentzer, John T., Soonhong Min and Zach G. Zacharia, "The Nature of Interfirm Partnering in Supply Chain Management," *Journal of Retailing,* Vol. 76, No. 4 (2000), pp. 549-568.

What is a Partnership?

Relationships between organizations can range from arm's length relationships (consisting of either one-time exchanges or multiple transactions) to vertical integration of the two organizations, as shown in Figure 1-1. Traditionally, relationships between organizations have been at arm's length. Two organizations conduct business with each other, often over a long period of time and involving multiple exchanges. However, there is no sense of joint commitment or joint operations between the two companies. In arm's length relationships, a seller typically offers standard products/services to a wide range of customers who receive standard terms and conditions. When the exchanges end, the relationship ends. While arm's length represents an appropriate option in most situations, there are times when a closer, more integrated relationship, referred to as a partnership, would provide significant benefits to both firms.

While some have interpreted the word "partnership" to mean any business-to-business relationship, it should be reserved for closely integrated, mutually beneficial relationships that enhance the performance of both organizations. We believe that a partnership is most appropriately defined as follows:[6]

A partnership is a tailored business relationship based on mutual trust, openness, shared risk and shared rewards that results in business performance greater than would be achieved by the two firms working together in the absence of partnership.

> A partnership is a *tailored* business relationship based on mutual trust, openness, shared risk and shared rewards that results in business performance greater than would be achieved by the two firms working together in the absence of partnership.

A key point of this definition is that the relationship is customized. It is not standard fare, that is, something that would be done for any customer or supplier of a particular size or for a particular volume of business. Another key point is that incremental benefits must be gained from the tailoring effort. The tailoring process consumes managerial time and resources, thus it must yield measureable benefits that justify these costs.

A partnership is not the same as a joint venture that normally entails some degree of shared ownership across the two parties. Nor is it the same as vertical integration. Yet a partnership that is managed well can provide benefits similar to those found in joint ventures or vertical integration. For instance, when PepsiCo chose to acquire restaurants such as Taco Bell, Pizza Hut and KFC, a advantage was that Coca-Cola products would not be sold in those restaurants. The Coca-Cola

Figure 1-1
Types of Relationships

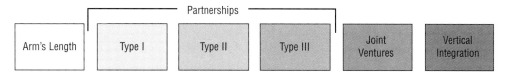

Source: Douglas M. Lambert, Margaret A. Emmelhainz and John T. Gardner, "Developing and Implementing Supply Partnerships," *The International Journal of Logistics Management*, Vol. 7, No. 2 (1996), p. 2.

[6] Lambert, Douglas M., Margaret A. Emmelhainz and John T. Gardner, "Building Successful Logistics Partnerships," *Journal of Business Logistics*, Vol. 20, No. 1 (1999), pp. 165-181; and, Douglas M. Lambert, A. Michael Knemeyer and John T. Gardner, "Supply Chain Partnerships: Model Validation and Implementation", *Journal of Business Logistics*, Vol. 23, No. 2 (2004), pp. 21-42.

Company achieved a similar result through its Type III partnership with McDonald's (see Figure 1-1). PepsiCo eventually divested of the restaurants stating that they distracted management's attention from the core businesses of snacks and beverages. Partnership provides the benefits of vertical integration without the cost of ownership.

While most partnerships share some common elements and characteristics, there is no one ideal or "benchmark" relationship which is appropriate in all situations. Because each relationship has its own set of motivating factors driving its development as well as its own unique operating environment, the duration, breadth, strength and closeness of the partnership will vary from case to case and over time. That is, there are degrees of partnering, a concept that is difficult for many to understand. The fact that there are degrees of partnership helps to explain how two managers can use the word partnership and see entirely different pictures. In order to make it easier to comprehend and implement, we have identified three types of partnerships (as shown in Figure 1-1):

- **Type I** - The organizations involved recognize each other as partners and, on a limited basis, coordinate activities and planning. Usually, the partnership is focused more on short-tem objectives and has less cross-functional and cross-division involvement.
- **Type II** - The organizations involved progress beyond coordination of activities to integration of activities. Although not expected to last "forever" the partnership has a long-term horizon. Multiple divisions and functions within the firm are involved in the partnership.
- **Type III** - The organizations share a significant level of strategic and operational integration. Each party views the other as an extension of their own firm. Typically no "end date" for the partnership exists.

Normally, a firm will have a wide range of relationships spanning the entire spectrum, the majority of which will not be partnerships at all but arm's length associations (see Figure 1-2). Figure 1-2 illustrates that for every 100 suppliers or customers that an organization may have, 70 percent do not need to be partnerships. The volume of business or the type of product/service involved should make it easy to determine the relationships that fall into this group (this will be dealt with in more detail in the next chapter). Of the relationships that are partnerships, the largest percentage will be Type I with only a limited number of Type III partnerships. Type III partnerships should be reserved for those suppliers or customers who are critical to an organization's long-term success. Criticality, ranging from low to strategic, is a function of: 1) impact on the firm if the relationship were to end; 2) volume of purchases from or sales to the organization; 3) involvement by the supplier/customer in support of the core competency or primary product line of the firm; 4) availability of other sources of supply, if the organization is a supplier; and, 5) percent of the firm's profitability that the other organization represents, if it is a customer.

Figure 1-3 illustrates the proportion of relationships that are likely to be strategic, high in criticality, medium and low in criticality, for traditional arm's length relationships and for Type I, Type II and Type III partnerships. For example, there is a small probability that a supplier of a critical item would be managed as an arm's-length relationship. This situation can occur because the supplier does not view the customer as profitable enough when compared to other customers to qualify for partnership. While the majority of Type III partnerships are with

Normally, a firm will have a wide range of relationships spanning the entire spectrum, the majority of which will not be partnerships at all but arm's length associations.

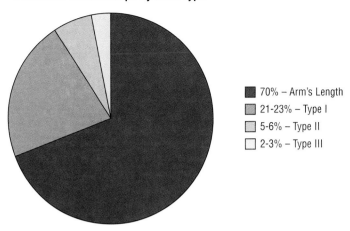

Figure 1-2
Relationship Segmentation Guide
Percent of Relationships by Each Type

- ■ 70% – Arm's Length
- ▨ 21-23% – Type I
- ▨ 5-6% – Type II
- □ 2-3% – Type III

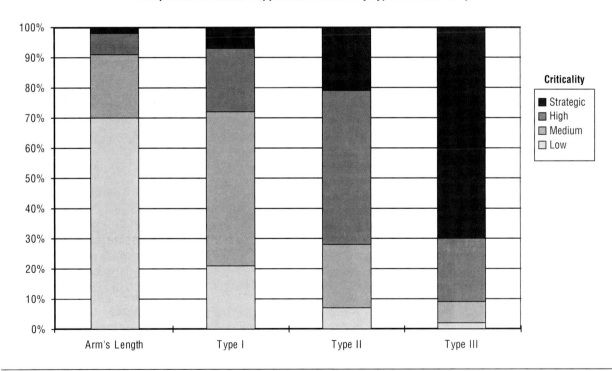

Figure 1-3
Relationship Segmentation Guide
Proportion of Critical Suppliers/Customers by Type of Relationship

Criticality
- ■ Strategic
- ▨ High
- ▨ Medium
- □ Low

suppliers of strategic commodities, there is a small probability that an organization would have a Type III partnership with a supplier of an item that is low in criticality. This might happen as a result of product shortages or the fact that the supplier sells the organization other items that are critical.

Why Partner?

The primary reasons for managers to seek partnership arrangements with key suppliers and customers are the following:

- To gain the advantages of vertical integration while maintaining organizational independence.
- To take advantage of best-in-class expertise of suppliers and customers. Closer relationships with key suppliers can lead to quality improvements, new product introductions and joint cost savings. Closer relationships with key customers can result in opportunities for joint marketing, joint development of new products and closer involvement with consumers.
- To achieve service improvements as a result of joint planning and process improvement.
- To gain operating efficiencies as a result of building trust, sharing information and working on process improvements.
- To respond to competitive pressures.

However, partnerships are costly to implement in terms of the management time involved. Because it is possible to have good win-win business relationships that are not partnerships, valuable senior management time is not required for such relationships. If management segments the firm's portfolio of relationships, management time can be made available for those relationships where incremental closeness in the relationship will lead to incremental benefits. Not all business relationships should be partnerships. Partnership strategy should be driven by corporate strategy. For example, it is more important for a restaurant chain to have a partnership with a beef and chicken supplier than a supplier of straws or napkins.

If management segments the firm's portfolio of relationships, management time can be made available for those relationships where incremental closeness in the relationship will lead to incremental benefits.

Based on our research, the characteristics of successful partnerships can be summarized as follows:

- Growth opportunities for both parties.
- Focus on service and not simply costs.
- Product development driven by customer needs.
- Access to critical information.
- Exclusive business arrangement.
- Willingness to share risk and rewards.
- Higher level of commitment.
- Employees empowered to solve problems.
- Willingness to work together.
- Openness between the parties.
- Trust between the parties.
- Genuine concern for the other party.
- Joint problem solving.

While the importance of partnerships has been widely recognized, most of the relationships that are called partnerships, at some point in time end up being disappointments to one or both of the parties involved. There are many reasons for these relationships failing, but the most common are:

- Unrealistic expectations on the part of one or both of the parties involved.
- Breakdowns in communication between the parties.
- Lack of competence to accomplish the desired goals.
- Corporate cultural differences.
- Failure to empower employees.
- Change in needs, corporate focus and people.

- Change in expectations by management in one or both organizations.
- Short-term focus by management.
- Lack of top management support.
- Imbalance of power.
- Lack of mutual benefit.
- Real or perceived unfairness from a cost and pricing standpoint.
- Lack of commitment.
- Lack of trust and openness.
- Lack of clearly defined goals and objectives.
- Changes in the market.
- Losing track of the goals for the relationship.

Partnerships may not meet expectations as a result of a number of problems. Our research has surfaced 11 problems that are associated with managing a partnership over time:

- Unclear definitions of expectations.
- Complete focus on cost.
- Perception of loss of control.
- The partnership runs counter to traditional business practice.
- Difficulty selling the "ease of doing business" as a benefit.
- Inability to gain the confidence of the sales organization regarding the partnership's ability to deliver the desired results.
- Distrust of financial people in one or both organizations.
- Lack of communication.
- Lack of time to focus on relationship issues.
- Union issues/job losses that impact the relationship.
- Legal issues that inhibit the partnership.

These potential problems can be mitigated by using the partnership model described in this book.

Importance of a Tool

When faced with allocating appropriate levels of resources (time and money) across a diverse set of business relationships, managers in resource-constrained companies need a tool to help them organize, simplify, and expedite decision making about the appropriate level of partnering.

When faced with allocating appropriate levels of resources (time and money) across a diverse set of business relationships, managers in resource-constrained companies need a tool to help them organize, simplify, and expedite decision making about the appropriate level of partnering. A tool is available to help management clarify the current state of a relationship, identify the value of the relationship for both parties, identify factors that influence the relationship, establish the importance of various potential activities in the relationship and provide guidance for moving forward with the relationship. The partnership model can be used by management to structure high performance business relationships. This book contains all of the resources that management needs to build and maintain high-performance business relationships.

The Partnership Model fulfills these needs by providing a systematic, repeatable and sustainable method for both parties to discuss their relationship using a common language. The model breaks down the complexity of a business relationship into its key components and provides a structured way for two parties to jointly determine the appropriate level of tailoring for their particular relationship. The major benefit of the model is its ability to guide managers in understanding and prioritizing both quantitative and qualitative information required for appropriately allocating resources to a relationship. As a consequence of using the model, the knowledge is shared among managers and the potential for personal bias towards the relationship is minimized. This is achieved by encouraging the managers involved in the relationship to focus on the potential of the relationship and how to calibrate their efforts to achieve this potential. Using the Partnership Model creates a collaborative environment for management to understand the key issues that are critical for success.

Overview of the Partnership Model

In response to executives from member companies of The Global Supply Chain Forum, who wanted a tool to structure business relationships, we developed the Partnership Model.[7] The model is based on in-depth study of 18 relationships that they identified as partnerships from which we could learn how to replicate the successes and avoid the failures. According to these executives, failures were much more frequent than successes. In-depth interviews with multiple individuals on each side of each relationship revealed that some of these "partnerships"" were not really "partnerships" at all, but were simply good business relationships. And, the ones that were partnerships were not the same. We discovered that there are degrees of partnering, which we classified as Type I, Type II and Type III (previously described). It is important to recognize that more partnering, a Type III versus a Type I or II, should not be the goal but rather to identify the correct type of partnership. That is, there must be increased benefits to justify the increased closeness in the relationship.

The Partnership Model separates the drivers of partnership, the facilitators of partnership, the components of partnership and the outcomes of partnership into four major areas for management attention (see Figure 1-4).

It is important to recognize that more partnering, a Type III versus a Type I or II, should not be the goal but rather to identify the correct type of partnership. That is, there must be increased benefits to justify the increased closeness in the relationship.

**Figure 1-4
The Partnership Model**

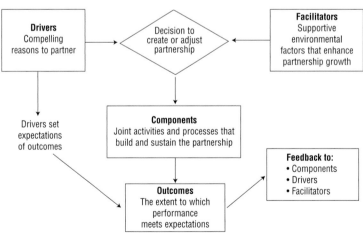

Source: Douglas M. Lambert, Margaret A. Emmelhainz, and John T. Gardner, "Developing and Implementing Supply Chain Partnerships," *The International Journal of Logistics Management*, Vol. 7, No. 2 (1996), p. 4.

---

[7] The Global Supply Chain Forum is a research center supported by 15 non-competing companies. For more information about The Global Supply Chain Forum see: http://fisher.osu.edu/centers/scm/

Drivers

Drivers are the compelling reasons to partner, and must be examined first when approaching a potential partner. Why add managerial complexity and commit resources to a business relationship if a good, long-term contract that is well specified will do? To the degree that business as usual will not deliver the efficiencies needed, partnership may be necessary. By looking for compelling reasons to partner, the drivers of partnership, management in two firms may find that they both have an interest in tailoring the relationship. The model separates the drivers into four categories: asset/cost efficiencies, customer service improvements, marketing advantage, and profit stability and growth. All businesses are concerned with these four issues, and the four can capture the goals of managers for their relationships.

Facilitators

Facilitators are characteristics of the two firms that will help or hinder the partnership development process. The nature of the two firms involved in partnership implementation will determine how easy or hard it will be to tailor the relationship. If the two firms mesh easily, the managerial effort and resources devoted to putting the correct relationship in place will be lower for the same results. The elements that make partnership implementation easy or hard are called facilitators. They represent the partnership environment; those aspects of the two firms that will help or hinder partnership activities. There are four major categories of facilitators: corporate compatibility, management philosophy and techniques, mutuality and symmetry.

Components

Components are the managerially controllable elements that can be implemented at various levels depending on the type of partnership. How the components are implemented will determine the type of partnership that is achieved. While drivers and facilitators determine the potential for partnership, the components are the building blocks of partnership. They are universal across firms and across business environments and unlike drivers and facilitators, are under the direct control of the managers involved. In other words, they are the activities that managers in two firms actually perform to implement the partnership. There are eight components of partnership: planning, joint operating controls, communications, risk/reward sharing, trust and commitment, contract style, scope and investment. The components are implemented differently for Type I, Type II and Type III partnerships. Action items are identified from the drivers and the components so that both parties' expectations are met.

Outcomes

A partnership, if appropriately established and effectively managed, should improve performance for both parties.

Outcomes measure the extent to which each firm achieves its drivers. A partnership, if appropriately established and effectively managed, should improve performance for both parties. Profit enhancement, process improvements, and increased competitive advantage are all likely outcomes of effective partnerships. Specific outcomes will vary depending upon the drivers that initially motivated the development of the partnership. It should be noted, however, that a partnership is not required to achieve satisfactory outcomes from a relationship. Typically, organizations will have multiple arm's length relationships which meet the needs of and provide benefits to both parties.

Together, drivers and facilitators determine the potential for partnership. The components are the actions management takes to implement the relationship and they vary by partnership type. The Partnership Model provides a structure for assessing the drivers and facilitators, and provides component descriptions for the prescribed type of partnership.

Together, drivers and facilitators determine the potential for partnership. The components are the actions management takes to implement the relationship and they vary by partnership type.

The Partnership Building Meeting

Using the Partnership Model to tailor a relationship requires that the correct team from each firm be identified and committed to a one and one-half day session. The teams should include top executives, functional managers and the individuals who must interact day-to-day across the organizations. The broad mix of management levels and functional expertise is necessary to ensure that all perspectives are considered and that cross-functional and cross-firm support is developed.

The success of the partnership building meeting depends on the openness and creativity brought to the session. The decision is not whether or not to have a business relationship but rather to determine the appropriate type of relationship? The partnership building session is the first step in tailoring the business relationship for enhanced results.

When to Use the Partnership Model

The model was designed primarily as a tool to identify and develop partnerships with key suppliers and customers. It can be used to establish a new partnership, assess an existing relationship, resolve conflicts in a relationship and to create a common vision of partnership within the organization.

Establishing a New Partnership with a Customer or Supplier

When a major transportation company conducted a partnership meeting with a key customer, two very positive results emerged. First, using the partnership model clearly indicated to the parties the difference between a partnership and a long-term contract with volume and price guarantees (which is often mistakenly thought of as a partnership). According to one manager, "…the partnership model identified eight or nine behaviors which we needed to change, as well as eight or nine behaviors we thought they could change."

Second, in a multi-division firm it is difficult to put a single-face forward. The partnership meeting helped the transportation company coordinate the response of different business units to a partnership opportunity. In the words of a manager, "If we are looking at a corporate solution for the customer, one unit might have to do something that in the short run will be suboptimal, but in the long run will be positive for the corporation as a whole as a result of positive gains made by other units. Or we may have to gamble and set rates and service commitments, which we know the competitor will match; and we will have to rely on the customer's integrity to deliver on their promise."

Assessing an Existing Relationship

The Partnership Model can be used as a tool for assessing an existing relationship. It works as an excellent check to ensure that a relationship is being

The Partnership Model can be used as a tool for assessing an existing relationship.

implemented as the appropriate type. By jointly working through the model, managers can determine if the relationship needs to be recalibrated.

For example, Colgate Palmolive and APL had a strong relationship for a number of years and they closely coordinated efforts and participated in numerous joint activities for logistics services. Although no problems existed in the relationship, managers at Colgate decided to evaluate the relationship using the model. The assessment of the drivers and facilitators confirmed that a Type II partnership was appropriate. The components were reviewed and managers from both firms believed that working through the model strengthened the partnership and helped management identify areas for improvement.

Resolving Conflicts in a Relationship

Texas Instruments used the model to strengthen its relationship with Photronics, a key supplier of photomask. Texas Instruments purchased 99 percent of its domestic market photomask requirements from Photronics, which represented about 36 percent of Phonotronics' sales. Photronics had five facilities in the U.S., including one in Texas dedicated to Texas Instruments.

Realizing the importance of the relationship, the two firms used the model to determine how the partnership might more effectively be managed. Considerable time was spent in joint meetings agreeing upon the meanings of each element of the drivers, facilitators, and components. Then each party independently assessed the drivers. Ten individuals from Photronics and 25 people from Texas Instruments conducted these assessments. After assessing both drivers and facilitators, the firms agreed that the most appropriate type of relationship was a Type II. In a meeting attended by vice-presidents from Texas Instruments, the president, the chairman and vice-presidents from Photronics, and numerous operational personnel from both firms, agreement was reached on the specific implementation of the components. The team prioritized the components and developed a detailed action plan outlining what each party would do to ensure successful implementation. Over a four month period, the teams held approximately five to six hours of meetings per week, involving eight to 10 people from each firm. After a short time, management from both firms became more satisfied with the direction of the partnership and its working arrangement. They shared and meshed five year plans and each has made a commitment to the other. Even though their existing contract expired, they chose to move forward with no contract.

Creating a Common Partnership Vision

The model is also useful in harmonizing the partnership process throughout an organization. Executives from The Coca-Cola Company used the model with key suppliers such as Cargill and Graham Packaging as part of implementing a supplier relationship management process. The common language of drivers, facilitators, and components helped executives see the importance and potential of partnerships.

Executives from The Coca-Cola Company used the model with key suppliers such as Cargill and Graham Packaging as part of implementing a supplier relationship management process.

The model also serves as a screening tool in deciding where to allocate scarce resources. A firm can have a Type III partnership with only a limited number of partners. This limitation makes it critical that the correct relationship style is used in each business-to-business link. The model can be used to identify which relationships offer the best potential pay-back and should be given the most attention and resources.

Conclusions

Increasingly, partnerships with key customers and suppliers are being viewed as a way to achieve business success in a complex environment. However, every business relationship is not a candidate for partnership. Management needs to direct scarce resources to those relationships where incremental effort results in incremental performance. In Chapter 2, we describe how to identify potential candidates for partnership. In Chapter 3, we describe the Partnership Model in more detail and explain how it was developed. Chapter 4 provides a detailed description of how to use the Partnership Model. In Chapter 5, you are shown how to sustain and measure the performance of the partnerships that you establish using the model. In Chapter 6, a collaboration framework is presented. It is based on insights gained from more than 80 sessions with the Partnership Model and it can be used to increase collaboration with suppliers and customers who are for one reason or another are not candidates for a partnership session. Finally, we have included a set of "Resources and Tools" to help managers build high performance business relationships for their organizations.

Management needs to direct scarce resources to those relationships where incremental effort results in incremental performance.

CHAPTER 2 Identifying Potential Partners

At The Coca-Cola Company, we use supplier segmentation as the foundation of our global supplier relationship management process. Partnership sessions are held with suppliers categorized as strategic during the segmentation.
— Martha Buffington

Director, Supply Chain Strategy and Program Management
The Coca-Cola Company

Overview

Partnerships are developed with a small set of key customers and suppliers based on their potential for co-creation of value.

The development of a partnership strategy begins with a determination of which customers and suppliers are key to the organization's success now and in the future. The goal is to segment customers and suppliers based on their value over time and develop product and service agreements that improve the profitability of both parties. Partnerships are developed with a small set of key customers and suppliers based on their potential for co-creation of value. In this chapter we will describe methods of segmentation that form the basis of the organization's partnership strategy.

Introduction

Partnerships require significant resource commitments on the part of both parties involved. For this reason, it is not practical to partner with every customer or supplier. Management must identify those customers and suppliers who are potential candidates for successful partnerships. This segmentation usually takes place as part of implementation of the customer relationship management and the supplier relationship management processes.

Customer Relationship Management

Typically, large sums of money are spent to attract new customers; yet management is often complacent when it comes to nurturing existing customers to build and strengthen relationships with them.[1] However, for most companies, existing customers represent the best opportunities for profitable growth. There are direct and strong relationships between profit growth; customer loyalty; customer

---

[1] Berry, Leonard L. and A. Parasuraman, "Marketing to Existing Customers" in *Marketing Services: Competing Through Quality*, New York, NY: The Free Press, 1991, p.132.

satisfaction; and, the value of goods delivered to customers.[2] "Relationship marketing concerns attracting, developing, and retaining customer relationships".[3]

In a business-to-business environment, customer relationship management is the business process that provides the structure for how relationships with customers are developed and maintained. Management identifies key customers and customer groups to be targeted as part of the firm's business mission. It is within this group of key customers that candidates for partnerships will be identified. The decision regarding who represents key customers requires evaluation of the profitability and potential profitability of individual customers. Often it is assumed that the marketing function is responsible for creating, maintaining and strengthening relationships with business-to-business customers because it does this with consumers. However, for two large organizations to be able to coordinate their complex operations, all corporate functions must be involved and actively participate in the relationship. This is necessary in order to align corporate resources with the profit potential of each relationship.

The customer teams tailor product and service agreements (PSAs) to meet the needs of key accounts and segments of other customers.[4] PSAs come in many forms, both formal and informal, and may be referred to by different names from company to company. However, for best results they should be formalized as written documents. The goal is to develop PSAs that address the major business drivers of the two organizations involved. Teams work with key accounts to improve processes, enhance quality and eliminate demand variability and non-value-added activities. Performance reports are designed to measure the profitability of individual customers as well as the firm's financial impact on those customers.

While there are a great number of software products that are being marketed as customer relationship management, these technology tools should not be confused with the relationship-focused business process. Customer relationship management software has the potential to enable management to gather customer data quickly, identify the most valuable customers over time, and provide the customized products and services that should increase customer loyalty. When it works, the costs to serve customers can be reduced making it easier to acquire more, similar customers. However, according to Gartner Group, 55% of all customer relationship management (software solutions) projects do not produce results.[5] There are four major reasons for the failure of customer relationship management software projects: (1) implementing software solutions before creating a customer strategy; (2) rolling out software before changing the organization; (3) assuming that more technology is better; and, (4) trying to build relationships with the wrong customers.[6] To be successful, management must place its primary focus on the customer relationship management process and the

> *...customer relationship management is the business process that provides the structure for how relationships with customers are developed and maintained.*

---

[2] Heskett, James L., W. Earl Sasser, Fr. and Leonard A. Schlesinger, *The Service Profit Chain*, New York, NY: The Free Press, 1997, p.11.

[3] Berry, Leonard L. and A. Parasuraman, "Marketing to Existing Customers" in *Marketing Services: Competing Through Quality*, New York, NY: The Free Press, 1991, p.133.

[4] Seybold, Patrica B., "Get Inside the Lives of Your Customers", *Harvard Business Review*, Vol. 78, No. 5 (2001), pp. 81-89.

[5] Rigby, Darrell K., Frederick F. Reichheld and Phil Scheffer, "Avoid the Four Perils of CRM," *Harvard Business Review*, Vol. 80, No. 2 (2002), pp. 101-109.

[6] Rigby, Darrell K., Frederick F. Reichheld and Phil Scheffer, "Avoid the Four Perils of CRM," *Harvard Business Review*, Vol. 80, No. 2 (2002), pp. 101-109.

people and the procedures that make the technology effective. Relying on the technology by itself will most often lead to failure.[7]

Unfortunately, there are a wide range of views as to what constitutes customer relationship management. At one extreme, it is about the implementation of a specific technology solution and at the other, it is a holistic approach to selectively managing relationships to create shareholder value.[8] It is the former perspective that results in so many failures. In order to develop mutually beneficial business relationships, customer relationship management should be positioned in a broad strategic context and be consistently implemented throughout the organization.[9] According to Payne and Frow, customer relationship management must be viewed as strategic, cross-functional and process-based in order to avoid the potential problems associated with a narrow technology oriented definition.[10] However, the functions that they included appear to be limited to executives working in sales, marketing and information technology. There was no indication that managers from finance, research and development, production/operations, purchasing, logistics or other functions had been included or even considered. It is imperative that all corporate functions are involved in complex, high-value business relationships. As identified in *The Service-Dominant Logic of Marketing*, knowledge is the fundamental source of competitive advantage, the customer is a co-producer, and a service-centered view is customer oriented and relational.[11] In order to generate knowledge of the customer that will lead to the co-production of value, all business functions should be involved in the relationship. The more business functions that are involved in key customer relationships, the more useful the knowledge that will be generated.

Customer relationship management has become a critical business process do to a number of factors. These factors include: competitive pressures; the need to achieve cost efficiency in order to be a low-cost, high-quality supplier; a recognition of the fact that customers are not equal in terms of their profitability; and, knowledge that customer retention can significantly affect profitability.

Supplier Relationship Management

Supplier relationship management is the business process that provides the structure for how relationships with suppliers are developed and maintained. As the name suggests, it is similar to customer relationship management. Just as close relationships need to be developed with key customers, management should forge close cross-functional relationships with a small number of key suppliers, and

Supplier relationship management involves developing partnership relationships with key suppliers to reduce costs, innovate with new products and create value for both parties based on a mutual commitment to long-term collaboration and shared success.

[7] Turchan, Mark P. and Paula Mateus, "The Value of Relationships," *Journal of Business Strategy*, Vol. 22, No. 6 (2001), pp. 29-32.

[8] Payne, Adrian and Pennie Frow, "A Strategic Framework for Customer Relationship Management," *Journal of Marketing*, Vol. 69, No. 4 (2005), pp. 167-176.

[9] Swift, Ronald S., *Accelerating Customer Relationships - Using CRM and Relationship Technologies*, Upper Saddle River, New Jersey: Prentice Hall, 2000; and Atul Parvatiyar and Jagdish N. Sheth, "Customer Relationship Management: Emerging Practice, Process and Discipline," *Journal of Economic and Social Research*, Vol. 3, No. 2 (2001), pp. 1-34.

[10] Payne, Adrian and Pennie Frow, "A Strategic Framework for Customer Relationship Management," *Journal of Marketing*, Vol. 69, No. 4 (2005), pp. 167-176.

[11] Lusch, Robert F. and Stephen L. Vargo, *The Service-Dominant Logic of Marketing*, Armonk, New York: M.E. Sharpe, Inc., 2006.

maintain more traditional buyer and salesperson relationships with the others.[12] Management identifies those suppliers and supplier groups to be targeted as part of the firm's business mission. Supplier relationship management teams work with key suppliers to tailor PSAs to meet the organization's needs, as well as those of the selected suppliers. Standard PSAs are crafted for segments of other suppliers. Supplier relationship management is about developing and managing the PSAs. Teams work with key suppliers to improve processes, increase quality, and eliminate variability and non-value-added activities. The goal is to develop PSAs that address the major business drivers of both the organization and the supplier. Performance reports are designed to measure the profit impact of individual suppliers as well as the firm's impact on the profitability of suppliers.

Supplier relationship management involves developing partnership relationships with key suppliers to reduce costs, innovate with new products and create value for both parties based on a mutual commitment to long-term collaboration and shared success. For complex relationships such as the one between The Coca-Cola Company and Cargill, Inc., it is necessary to coordinate multiple divisions spread across multiple geographic areas. Coca-Cola and Cargill both have revenue in excess of $80 billion per year, one represents the largest beverage and bottling system and the other the largest ingredient and nutritional company. Cross-functional teams from each of the companies meet on a regular basis to identify projects that will create joint value in areas such as new markets, new products, productivity and sustainability. The relationship involves the CEOs of both companies.

Supplier relationship management has become a critical business process for a number of reasons. These include: competitive pressures; the need to achieve cost efficiency in order to be cost competitive; and, the need to develop closer relationships with key suppliers who can provide the expertise necessary to develop innovative new products and successfully bring them to market.

Customer Relationship Management and Supplier Relationship Management Form the Critical Business-to-Business Linkages

Together, customer relationship management and supplier relationship management provide the critical linkages throughout the supply chain (see Figure 2-1). For each supplier, the ultimate measure of success for the customer relationship management process is the change in profitability of an individual customer or segment of customers. For each customer, the most comprehensive measure of success for the supplier relationship management process is the impact that a supplier or supplier segment has on the firm's profitability. For key relationships, the goal is to increase the joint profitability by developing the relationship and reaching agreement on how to split the gains that are made through joint process improvement efforts. The overall performance of a buyer-seller relationship is determined by the combined improvement in profitability of both parties from one year to the next.

Each firm in the supply chain should perform segmentation to determine which customers and/or suppliers are key to the organization's success and

...the goal is to increase the joint profitability by developing the relationship and reaching agreement on how to split the gains that are made through joint process improvement efforts.

---

[12] Dyer, Jeffery H., Dong Sung Cho and Wujin Wu, "Strategic Supplier Segmentation: The Next 'Best Practice' in Supply Chain Management," *California Management Review*, Vol. 40, No. 2 (1998), pp. 57-77.

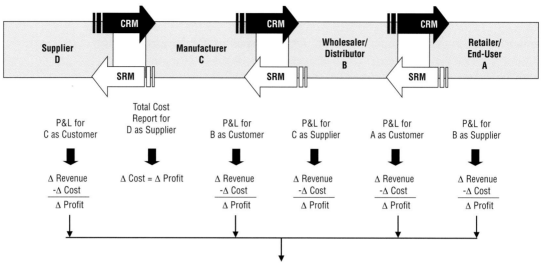

Supply Chain Performance = Increase in Profit for A, B, C, and D

Source: Adapted from Douglas M. Lambert and Terrance L. Pohlen, "Supply Chain Metrics," *The International Journal of Logistics Management,* Vol. 12, No. 1 (2001), p. 14.

therefore candidates for partnership. In order for a partnership to be appropriate, both the buyer and seller must view the other as important for long-term success. In the remainder of this chapter, we will describe methods for segmenting customers and suppliers in order to identify candidates for partnership.

Segmenting Customers and Identifying Candidates for Partnership

It is necessary for management to identify the criteria that will be used to segment customers. For example, grocery retail may be viewed as an important segment, but all grocery retailers will not be of equal importance to the organization's success. This segmentation provides guidelines for determining which customers qualify for tailored PSAs and which customers will be grouped into segments and offered a standard PSA that is developed to provide value to the segment. It is through segmentation that candidates for partnership are identified. Potential segmentation criteria include:

It is through segmentation that candidates for partnership are identified.

- Profitability.
- Growth potential.
- Volume.
- Competitive positioning issues.
- Access to market knowledge.
- Market share goals.
- Margin levels.
- Level of technology.
- Resources and capabilities.
- Compatibility of strategies.

- Channel of distribution.
- Buying behavior (what drives their buying decision).

In the absence of a reason for using another basis for segmentation, current profitability and potential for profit growth are excellent choices. Figure 2-2 illustrates the output of such a segmentation exercise. The candidates for partnership are the firms that are in the top right hand corner of the matrix. These customers will deliver long-term profitable growth if the relationships are managed correctly. They require executive level involvement and the Partnership Model that is described in this book can be used to align strategies.

In addition to their role in customer segmentation, customer profitability reports enable management to track performance of the relationship over time. If calculated as shown in Table 2-1, these reports reflect all of the cost and revenue implications of the relationship. Variable manufacturing costs are deducted from net sales to calculate a manufacturing contribution. Next, variable marketing and logistics costs, such as sales commissions, transportation, warehouse handling, special packaging, order processing and a charge for accounts receivable, are deducted to calculate a contribution margin. Assignable nonvariable costs, such as salaries, customer related advertising expenditures, slotting allowances and inventory carrying costs, are subtracted to obtain a segment controllable margin. The net margin is obtained after deducting a charge for dedicated assets. These statements contain opportunity costs for investment in receivables and inventory and a charge for dedicated assets. Consequently, they are much closer to cash flow statements than a traditional profit and loss statement. They contain revenues minus the costs (avoidable costs) that disappear if the revenue disappears.

At Sysco, a $23.4 billion food distributor, profitability reports by customer were implemented in 1999. These reports enabled management to make strategic decisions about the allocation of resources to accounts including which customers

Figure 2-2
Segmenting Customers Based on Profitability and Potential for Growth

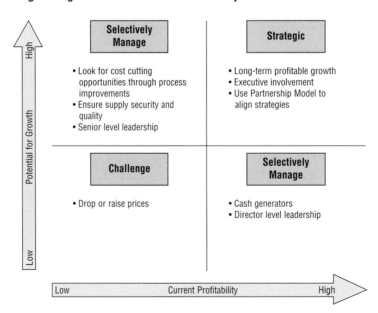

Table 2-1
Customer Profitability Analysis:
A Contribution Approach with Charge for Assets Employed

	Customer A	Customer B	Customer C	Customer D
Net Sales				
Cost of Goods Sold (Variable Manufacturing Cost)	——	——	——	——
Manufacturing Contribution				
Variable Marketing and Logistics Costs:				
Sales Commissions				
Transportation				
Warehousing (Handling in and out)				
Special Packaging				
Order Processing				
Charge for Investment in Accounts Receivable	——	——	——	——
Contribution Margin				
Assignable Nonvariable Costs:				
Salaries				
Segment Related Advertising				
Slotting Allowances				
Inventory Carrying Costs				
Controllable Margin				
Charge for Dedicated Assets Used				
Net Margin	═══	═══	═══	═══

Source: Douglas M. Lambert, Editor, *Supply Chain Management: Processes, Partnerships, Performance*, Third Edition, Sarasota, FL: Supply Chain Management Institute, 2008, p. 34.

receive the preferred delivery times and which customers must pay for value added services if they want to receive them. The results are illustrated in Figure 2-3. The five year cumulative annual growth rate for the period 1999 to 2003 was 11.3% for sales and 19.1% for net earnings. As shown in Figure 2-3, net earnings growth improved sharply after the profitability reports were implemented.

These reports also can be used to track the profitability of customers over time and to generate pro-forma statements that estimate the impact of potential process improvement projects. Decision analysis can be performed to consider what-if scenarios such as best case, worst case and the most likely outcome.

All customers do not contribute equally to the firm's success

All customers do not contribute equally to the firm's success and a key measure is the current profitability of each customer measured as shown in Table 2-1. Table 2-2 shows how one major corporation has segmented customers based on profitability. The most profitable customers were classified as Platinum followed by Gold, Silver, Bronze and Lead (unprofitable). Platinum customers only represented 8.36% of the accounts but they produced 65% of the pretax earnings. At the other extreme, unprofitable customers represented 34.29% of the accounts and actually reduced overall pretax earnings by 6%. Management must determine which of the unprofitable customers have the potential to become profitable and which ones will likely remain unprofitable. Table 2-3 shows how the profitability and thus segments can change from year to year. Not only did some Platinum customers turn to Gold, Silver, Bronze and Lead in 2003, but unprofitable customers became profitable with some even becoming Platinum. The goal is to understand what is driving the numbers and reassign resources on that basis.

Figure 2-3
Sysco Sales and Earnings History

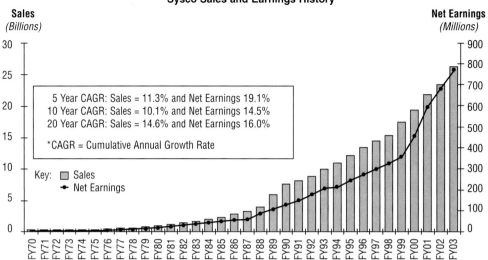

Source: Douglas M. Lambert, Editor, *Supply Chain Management: Processes, Partnerships, Performance*, Third Edition, Sarasota, FL: Supply Chain Management Institute, 2008, p. 35.

Table 2-2
Customer Segmentation Based on Pretax Profit Contribution

Segment	Percentage of Accounts	Percentage of Pretax Earnings
Platinum	8.36%	65%
Gold	17.13%	25%
Silver	18.23%	11%
Bronze	21.99%	5%
Lead (Unprofitable)	34.29%	-6%
Total	100%	100%

Source: Douglas M. Lambert, Editor, *Supply Chain Management: Processes, Partnerships, Performance*, Third Edition, Sarasota, FL: Supply Chain Management Institute, 2008, p. 38.

Table 2-3
A Comparison of Customer Segmentation for Two Years

	First Year Segmentation	Second Year Segmentation					
Mix		Platinum	Gold	Silver	Bronze	Lead (Unprofitable)	Total
Platinum	7.71%	5.89%	1.35%	0.21%	0.09%	0.15%	7.71%
Gold	16.49%	1.74%	10.44%	2.82%	0.79%	0.70%	16.49%
Silver	17.90%	0.26%	3.61%	8.79%	3.47%	1.77%	17.90%
Bronze	22.05%	0.15%	0.93%	4.37%	11.59%	5.02%	22.05%
Lead (Unprofitable)	35.85%	0.32%	0.80%	2.04%	6.06%	26.04%	35.85%
Total	100%	8.36%	17.13%	18.23%	21.99%	34.29%	100%

Source: Douglas M. Lambert, Editor, *Supply Chain Management: Processes, Partnerships, Performance*, Third Edition, Sarasota, FL: Supply Chain Management Institute, 2008, p. 38.

Segmenting Suppliers and Identifying Candidates for Partnership

Just as with customers, the results of the supplier segmentation are used to determine with which suppliers the firm should develop tailored PSAs and which suppliers should be grouped and offered a standard PSA that meets the firm's goals as well as generates a reasonable profit for the suppliers. The segmentation also enables management to identify the suppliers with which the organization will conduct partnership sessions. Potential criteria include:

- Profitability.
- Growth and stability.
- Criticality of the service level necessary.
- Sophistication and compatibility of the supplier's processes.
- Supplier's technology capability and compatibility.
- Volume purchased from the supplier.
- Capacity available from the supplier.
- Culture of innovation at the supplier.
- Supplier's anticipated quality levels.[13]

At Wendy's International, a matrix is used to categorize commodities purchased on the basis of the complexity of the commodity for Wendy's and the volume of the spend (see Figure 2-4). Items that are low in complexity and low in terms of the expenditure are non-critical items such as straws. Leverage items are those for which Wendy's spend is high but the items are not complex or strategic to the business. The goal for these items is to improve service by such things as reducing lead times. For non-critical and leverage items, it is not necessary to have

Figure 2-4
Comparing Suppliers on Complexity and Volume

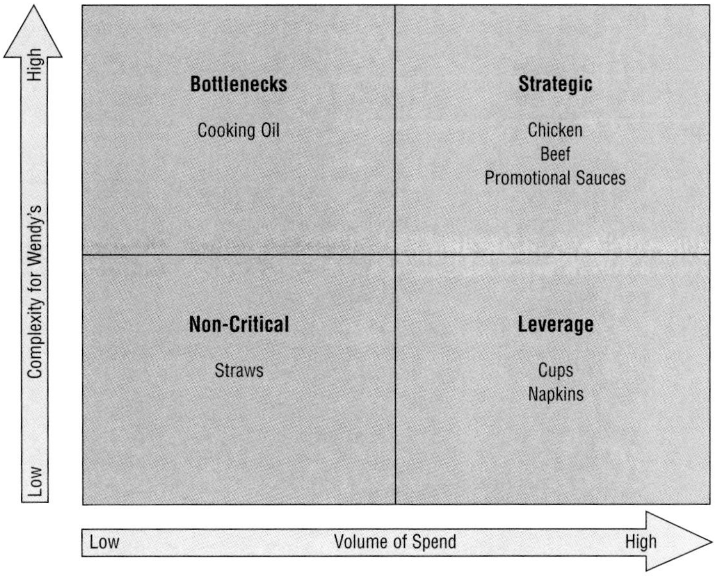

Source: Douglas M. Lambert, Editor, *Supply Chain Management: Processes, Partnerships, Performance*, Third Edition, Sarasota, FL: Supply Chain Management Institute, 2008, p. 57.

---

[13] Burt, David, N., Donald W. Dobler and Stephen L. Starling, *World Class Supply Management*, New York, NY: McGraw-Hill/Irwin, 2003.

cross-functional teams interacting with the supplier. Salespeople from companies providing these commodities call on buyers as they traditionally have done and buyers select suppliers based on price and service. Bottleneck items are those for which Wendy's spend is low but they are very complex such as cooking oil. Finally, strategic items are those that are both high in complexity and high in the amount spent per year. These items for Wendy's include chicken, beef and promotional sauces. Generally, Wendy's management tries to move items from the bottleneck quadrant to the non-critical or to the leverage quadrant. Management's goal was to move cooking oil from the bottleneck segment to the leverage segment, but it was actually moved to the strategic segment as a result of a product innovation with Cargill, a key supplier. Suppliers of strategic items are candidates for partnership relationships. Cross-functional teams from the supplier and Wendy's pursue initiatives that will increase revenues and reduce costs thereby improving the financial performance of both firms.

Suppliers of strategic items are candidates for partnership relationships.

Masterfoods USA developed a matrix that is similar to Wendy's, but uses "supply risk" and "contribution potential" as the two axes. The fewer the number of suppliers, the more these suppliers move up on the low to high scale for supply risk. The mid point on the low to high "contribution potential" scale is $500,000. The savings potential must exceed $500,000 for the supplier to be in either of the segments on the right side of the matrix (Strategic and Leverage quadrants).

Figure 2-5 shows the supplier segmentation matrix used by management of The Coca-Cola Company. At Coca-Cola the supplier relationship management

Figure 2-5
Supplier Segmentation Matrix for The Coca-Cola Company

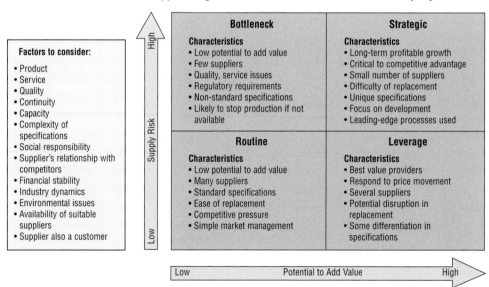

Factors to consider:

- Product
- Service
- Quality
- Continuity
- Capacity
- Complexity of specifications
- Social responsibility
- Supplier's relationship with competitors
- Financial stability
- Industry dynamics
- Environmental issues
- Availability of suitable suppliers
- Supplier also a customer

Supply Risk (Low → High)

Bottleneck

Characteristics
- Low potential to add value
- Few suppliers
- Quality, service issues
- Regulatory requirements
- Non-standard specifications
- Likely to stop production if not available

Strategic

Characteristics
- Long-term profitable growth
- Critical to competitive advantage
- Small number of suppliers
- Difficulty of replacement
- Unique specifications
- Focus on development
- Leading-edge processes used

Routine

Characteristics
- Low potential to add value
- Many suppliers
- Standard specifications
- Ease of replacement
- Competitive pressure
- Simple market management

Leverage

Characteristics
- Best value providers
- Respond to price movement
- Several suppliers
- Potential disruption in replacement
- Some differentiation in specifications

Potential to Add Value (Low → High)

Factors to consider:

- Innovation and technology
- Intellectual property
- Supply chain process integration
- Minority/women-owned business
- Global presence
- Competitive pricing
- Cost management
- Volume/spend
- Compatibility/strategic alignment
- Access to assets and capabilities
- Impact on cost, quality, delivery, profitability
- Our attractiveness as a customer

Source: Douglas M. Lambert, Editor, *Supply Chain Management: Processes, Partnerships, Performance*, Third Edition, Sarasota, FL: Supply Chain Management Institute, 2008, p. 58.

(SRM) team decided that supply risk and potential to add value would be used as the segmentation criteria. Under supply risk there are 13 factors to consider and under potential to add value there are 12 factors. It is possible to rate suppliers on each of the factors and then based on the relative importance of each factor, develop two scores for each supplier that are used to position the supplier on the matrix. The team also specified the characteristics of firms for each of the four quadrants of the matrix (see Figure 2-5). For example, suppliers in the strategic category had the following characteristics:

- Long-term profitable growth.
- Critical to competitive advantage.
- One of a small number of suppliers.
- Difficult to replace.
- Unique specifications.
- Focus on development.
- Leading-edge processes.

In contrast, the characteristics of the routine category of suppliers were:

- Low potential to add value.
- Many suppliers.
- Standard specifications.
- Ease of replacement.
- Competitive pressure.
- Simple market management.

Suppliers in this category are dealt with in a traditional buyer-seller relationship.

In addition, management at Coca-Cola defined business objectives for each segment of suppliers as well as the expected results from achieving these objectives (see Figure 2-6). For example, the business objectives for the strategic segment are:

Figure 2-6
Business Objectives by Segment

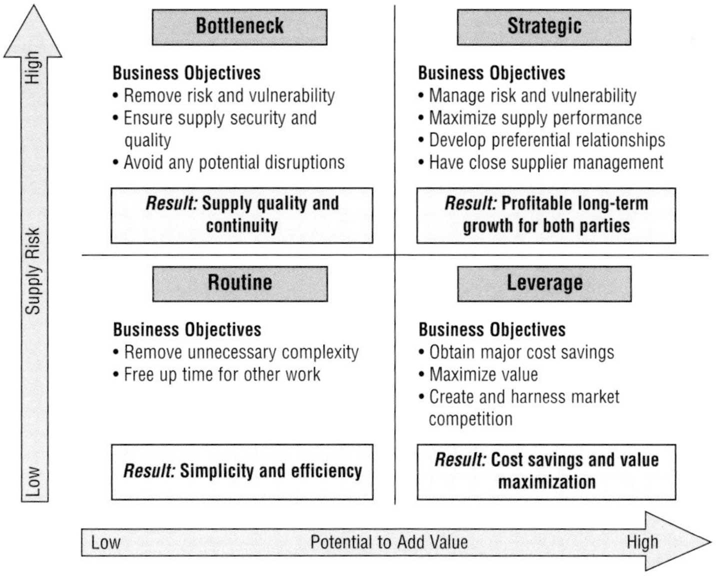

Source: Douglas M. Lambert, Editor, *Supply Chain Management: Processes, Partnerships, Performance*, Third Edition, Sarasota, FL: Supply Chain Management Institute, 2008, p. 59.

- Manage risk and vulnerability.
- Maximize supply performance.
- Develop preferential relationships.
- Have close supplier management.

The result of managing these strategic relationships as partnerships (see Figure 2-6) is profitable long-term growth for both parties.

The Coca-Cola supplier relationship management team also identified relationship implication guidelines for each of the four segments that specify the level of engagement, the amount of resources necessary, the depth of involvement and how the relationship should be measured (see Figure 2-7). For example, the resources committed to the strategic category of suppliers include vice president or higher leadership, a dedicated relationship manager, quarterly business reviews, top-to-top executive meetings and on-site or dedicated supplier resources. The organizations mesh strategic plans and the supplier is linked into The Coca-Cola Company's sales and operations planning (S&OP) process. These suppliers are also involved in new product development. Metrics are customized for the relationship and are two-way in nature. Finally, The Coca-Cola Company uses the partnership model described in this book to structure relationships with these suppliers.

The result of managing these strategic relationships as partnerships (see Figure 2-7) is profitable long-term growth for both parties.

Figure 2-7
Relationship Implication Guidelines by Segment

Bottleneck

Resources	• Director or senior level leadership • Non-dedicated relationship manager • Semi-annual business review meetings • Dedicated quality or technical resources
Strategic Planning	• Semi-annual business planning • Share forecasts and demand plans
Customer/ Market	• Effort to change specifications or develop substitutes to reduce supply risk
Measurement/ Knowledge	• Standard supplier metrics (one-way) • Some strategic information sharing

Strategic

Resources	• VP up to Executive level leadership • Dedicated relationship manager • Quarterly reviews; top-to-top meetings • On-site or dedicated supplier resources
Strategic Planning	• Extensive business planning • Direct linkage to S&OP process
Customer/ Market	• Involvement in new product development • Knowledge of our business strategy
Measurement/ Knowledge	• Customized supplier metrics (two-way) • Use **Partnership Model** to align strategies

Tactical

Resources	• Tactical management resources
Strategic Planning	• Transactional focus to planning
Customer/ Market	• May or may not be opportunities for product or service development
Measurement/ Knowledge	• Transactional supplier metrics • Commercial information sharing

Leverage

Resources	• Director level leadership • Non-dedicated relationship manager • Use cross-functional commodity councils • Annual business review meetings
Strategic Planning	• Annual business planning • Standard volume forecasts
Customer/ Market	• May or may not be opportunities for product development
Measurement/ Knowledge	• Standard supplier metrics (one-way) • Some strategic information sharing

Supply Risk: High → Low

Potential to Add Value: Low → High

Note: These implications show the level of engagement, amount of resources, and depth of involvement focused on managing the performance of suppliers in each quadrant.

Source: Douglas M. Lambert, Editor, *Supply Chain Management: Processes, Partnerships, Performance*, Third Edition, Sarasota, FL: Supply Chain Management Institute, 2008, p. 60.

In order to provide employees of The Coca-Cola Company with details on the progress that is being made implementing supplier relationship management and the results that are being achieved, the Global Supplier Relationship Management (SRM) Program Manager at The Coca-Cola Company produces a newsletter on a quarterly basis. Topics covered in the newsletter include the supplier relationship management framework, updates on activities and results, supplier relationship management tools, and how success is measured. The newsletter also contains reports on partnership sessions that were held with key suppliers identified as strategic in the segmentation activity previously described.

For each relationship, it is necessary to measure performance. At the wholesale and retail level, the development of supplier profitability reports enables the process team to track performance over time. If calculated as shown in Table 2-4, these reports reflect all of the cost and revenue implications of the relationship. The cost of goods sold is deducted from net sales to calculate a gross margin. Then, revenue adjustments such as discounts and allowances, market development funds, slotting allowances and co-operative advertising allowances must be added to achieve a net margin. Next, variable marketing and logistics costs are deducted to calculate a contribution margin. Assignable non-variable costs, such as salaries, advertising, and inventory carrying costs less a charge for accounts payable, are subtracted to obtain a segment controllable margin. These statements contain opportunity costs for investment in inventory. Consequently, they are much closer to cash flow statements than a traditional profit and loss statement. They contain revenues minus the costs (avoidable costs) that disappear if the revenue disappears.

Table 2-4
Supplier Profitability Analysis:
A Contribution Approach with Charge for Assets Employed

	Supplier A	Supplier B	Supplier C	Supplier D
Sales				
Cost of Goods Sold				
Gross Margin				
Plus: Discounts and Allowances				
Market Development Funds				
Slotting Allowances				
Co-operative Advertising Allowances				
Net Margin				
Variable Marketing and Logistics Costs:				
Transportation				
Receiving				
Order Processing				
Order Costs (will depend on situation)				
Controllable Margin				
Assignable Nonvariable Costs				
Salaries				
Advertising				
Inventory Carrying Costs Less:				
Charge for Accounts Payable				
Other Costs (will depend on situation)				
Segment Controllable Margin				

Source: Douglas M. Lambert, Editor, *Supply Chain Management: Processes, Partnerships, Performance*, Third Edition, Sarasota, FL: Supply Chain Management Institute, 2008, p. 62.

Supplier profitability reports can be constructed by wholesalers and retailers but it is not possible for manufacturers to develop these reports for the suppliers of undifferentiated components and materials. In this case, total cost reports are used along with calculations of the total delivered cost per unit purchased. Total cost reports should include the purchase price plus transportation costs, inventory carrying costs, financial impact of terms of sale, ordering costs, receiving costs, quality costs and administrative costs. At the end of the day, it is the change in profits or costs (in the case of total cost reports) that measures the impact of the relationship on earnings per share and this is what management should focus on.

Conclusions

Partnerships are costly to implement in terms of the management time involved. For this reason, it is necessary to segment customers and suppliers to identify those that are candidates for partnership. In this chapter, you were shown how to segment customers and suppliers. In the next chapter, the Partnership Model will be described. It is a tool that can be used to structure relationships with the key organizations identified during the segmentation. In Chapter 4, you will be shown how to use the model to conduct a partnership meeting. In Chapter 5 we describe a framework that can be used: to implement the partnership plan that results from the partnership meeting; to sustain the relationship overtime; and, to monitor performance on an on-going basis.

Partnerships are costly to implement in terms of the management time involved. For this reason, it is necessary to segment customers and suppliers to identify those that are candidates for partnership.

CHAPTER 3

The Partnership Model

The partnership model described in this book provides the structure to be successful.

> — Don Klock
> Former Vice President,
> Chief Procurement Officer, Colgate-Palmolive

Overview

...there is a need for a tool for determining when a partnership is warranted and if so how it should be structured.

While practitioners and academics have championed the value of partnerships to improve business performance, there is a need for a tool for determining when a partnership is warranted and if so how it should be structured. In this chapter, we describe a model that can be used to structure business relationships and how it was developed.[1]

Introduction

The Partnership Model was developed based upon detailed case studies of 18 relationships which members of The Global Supply Chain Forum said reflected successful partnerships. They believed that by studying these relationships, it would be possible to learn how to replicate the successes and minimize the failures (see Table 3-1). The experience of these executives was that most of the relationships between their firms and customers and suppliers that both sides initially referred to as "partnerships" turned out to be "bad marriages that ended in divorce."

In-depth interviews, ranging from one to four hours were conducted with managers at various levels and functions in both firms involved in each relationship. The interviews were conducted using a comprehensive, pre-tested interview guide of 45 questions, which had been developed based upon an extensive literature review. The interviews were conducted in-person and recorded. The interviews were transcribed resulting in over 2000 pages of text. After a light editing, the transcripts were returned to each interviewee for review.

---

[1] This chapter is based on Douglas M. Lambert, Margaret A. Emmelhainz and John T. Gardner, "Developing and Implementing Supply Chain Partnerships," *The International Journal of Logistics Management*, Vol. 7, No. 2 (1996), pp. 1-17; Douglas M. Lambert, Margaret A. Emmelhainz and John T. Gardner, "Building Successful Logistics Partnerships," *Journal of Business Logistics*, Vol. 20, No. 1 (1999), pp. 165-181; Douglas M. Lambert, A. Michael Knemeyer and John T. Gardner, "Supply Chain Partnerships: Model Validation and Implementation," *Journal of Business Logistics*, Vol. 23, No. 2 (2004), pp. 21-42; and, Douglas M. Lambert and A. Michael Knemeyer, "We're in This Together," *Harvard Business Review*, Vol. 82, No. 12 (2004), pp. 114-122.

Table 3-1
Relationship Cases Used to Develop the Partnership Model

Lucent Technologies (formerly known as AT&T Network Systems) and Panalpina for freight forwarding services of telecommunications equipment in the South American Market. Lucent Technologies manufactured and installed telecommunications systems, high-tech fibers, and switching technologies. The systems were shipped in the form of component parts with final assembly and installation in-country. As Lucent entered the Latin America market, it found customs documentation requirements to be particularly burdensome. For instance, the Brazilian government required that the documentation describe every separate part and item. For large systems this was equivalent to taking an automobile apart and shipping it by every nut, bolt, screw, fender, and bumper. Panalpina was a forwarder with offices in facilities in Central and South America and with a well established in-country infrastructure.

A small package express delivery company and a manufacturer for national distribution of healthcare products. This involved an offering of both air and ground transportation on the part of the carrier and a guaranteed volume on the part of the manufacturer.

McDonald's and Martin-Brower for the distribution of products and supplies to franchisees and company stores Martin-Brower was the largest of McDonald's six distributors, handling approximately 40% of McDonald's locations. Martin-Brower

distributed a complete range of products from food supplier to paper items.

McDonald's and OSI for the supply of hamburger patties to McDonald's restaurants. OSI was a manufacturer of beef patties, supplying approximately 25% of McDonald's volume. McDonald's was OSI's only customer.

McDonald's and Coca-Cola for the supply of beverages to McDonald's restaurants. McDonald's was Coke's largest customer and Coke was McDonald's largest supplier. Coca-Cola was the only cola beverage sold in any McDonald's store.

Xerox and Ryder for the delivery, installation, and removal of copiers. In this relationship, Ryder truck drivers delivered, set-up, tested, and demonstrated copiers for Xerox. In addition, the drivers performed initial customer training and removed the old equipment.

Xerox and Ryder for inbound transportation services to Xerox's manufacturing locations. Xerox depended upon Ryder Dedicated Logistics to manage the Xerox in-bound network so that JIT requirements were met.

Whirlpool and ERX for the warehousing an distribution of Whirlpool appliances to dealers and customers within 24-48 hours of order placement. Quality Express was a program through which Whirlpool sought to improve its customer service levels by

partnering with third party providers. ERX was a joint venture between MARK VII, a transportation company, and Elston-Richards, a warehousing company, and operated six of eight Quality Express programs.

Whirlpool and IP Logistics for the warehousing and distribution of Whirlpool appliances to dealers and customers in one of eight Quality Express programs. KP Logistics was a partnership between Kenco, a warehousing company, and Premier Transportation.

Whirlpool and TRMTI (Leaseway) for the warehousing and distribution of appliances to dealers and customers from one of eight Quality Express locations. TRMTI was a division of Leaseway Transportation and had been providing delivery services to builders in Florida for Whirlpool prior to the initiation of Quality Express.

3M and Yellow Freight for less-than-truckload outbound transportation services. This was a relationship which extended from 1981 until 1993 and evolved from a one-year contract to a long-term based arrangement.

Target and 3M for a wide range of consumer products. This arrangement involved seven distinct relationships: one between the two corporations and six others between 3M divisions and Target departments.

Source: Douglas M. Lambert, Margaret A. Emmelhainz and John T. Gardner, "Developing and Implementing Supply Chain Partnerships," *The International Journal of Logistics Management*, Vol. 7, No. 2 (1996), p. 3.

Based upon the approved transcripts, a case study of each relationship was developed. The cases were sent to the involved Forum members for comments and a final review.

The approved case studies, along with the literature review, were used as a basis for the development of the Partnership Model. Then, each case relationship was analyzed using the model and ranked by degree of partnering present. It was determined that not only were the relationships studied not the same, not all of them were partnerships. A detailed implementation guide for the model was developed and provided to executives from member companies. Management in these companies is using the model and the guide to develop and manage relationships.

The methodology used to develop and validate the model addresses a number of frequently cited criticisms of partnership research. For instance, Baba complained that most partnership research was based only on a limited number of interviews, often with just one executive, from only one party to the partnership.[2] Another concern is that much partnership research is based upon mail surveys.

The methodology used to develop and validate the model addresses a number of frequently cited criticisms of partnership research.

---

[2] Baba, Maretta L., "Two Sides to Every Story: An Ethnohistorical Approach to Organizational Partnerships", *City and Society*, Vol. 2, No. 2 (1988), pp. 71-104.

While mail surveys allow for gathering large amounts of data from numerous sources, the richness of the data collected are limited. Also, with a mail survey, there is no assurance that all participants are interpreting questions in the same way.

"While case studies of partnerships do provide a fuller picture at the micro organizational level, such studies have not followed a unified research framework that would permit replication and generalization of findings. Partnership studies would benefit from research designs aimed at identification and explication of integrative processes that serve to bond partners and strengthen interorganizational relationships. Future research on partnerships must have the partnership dyad as the minimum unit of analysis. Investigations that capture only from one side of a given partnership will fail to reflect accurately the dynamic forces that bond or break partnerships in the long run."[3]

The Partnership Model

Both parties must believe that they will receive significant benefits in one or more areas and that these benefits would not be possible without a partnership.

The Partnership Model has four major elements: drivers, facilitators, components, and outcomes, as shown in Figure 3-1. Drivers are the compelling reasons to partner. Facilitators are supportive corporate environmental factors that enhance partnership growth and development. Components are joint activities and processes used to build and sustain the partnership. Outcomes reflect the performance of the partnership.

Drivers

Both parties must believe that they will receive significant benefits in one or more areas and that these benefits would not be possible without a partnership.

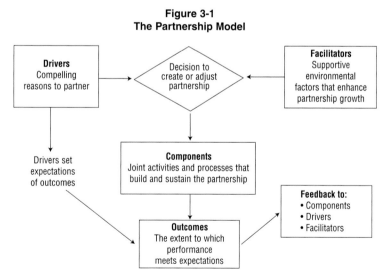

Figure 3-1
The Partnership Model

Source: Douglas M. Lambert, Margaret A. Emmelhainz, and John T. Gardner, "Developing and Implementing Supply Chain Partnerships," *The International Journal of Logistics Management*, Vol. 7, No. 2 (1996), p. 4.

---

[3] Baba, Maretta L., "Two Sides to Every Story: An Ethnohistorical Approach to Organizational Partnerships", *City and Society*, Vol. 2, No. 2 (1988), p. 75.

The primary potential benefits which drive the desire to partner are: asset/cost efficiencies, customer service improvements, marketing advantages, and profit stability/growth.

Asset/Cost Efficiencies. A potential for cost reduction provides a strong reason to partner. Closer integration of activities may lead to reductions in transportation costs, handling costs, packaging costs, information costs, or product costs and may increase managerial efficiencies. A partnership may also enhance the development and use of specialized equipment and processes between the parties, without fear of technology transfer to a competitor.[4] For example, McDonald's found that by establishing partnerships with regional distributors who serve as the single distributor for all products to all stores within a region, that warehousing, delivery and ordering costs were reduced.

Customer Service. Integrating activities in the supply chain through partnerships can often lead to service improvement for customers in the form of reduced inventory, shorter cycle times, and more timely and accurate information.[5] After discovering that they were significantly slower in deliveries to dealers and had more damage than competitors, Whirlpool developed a Type III partnership, termed Quality Express with ERX. ERX, a logistics service provider, was a joint venture between MARK VII Transportation Company and Elston-Richards, a warehousing company, created specifically for this partnership. According to a Whirlpool executive, "Our original goal was to be 95% on-time, within the first year. By the fourth month, we were at 99% on-time."

Marketing Advantage. A third reason for entering into a partnership is to gain a marketing advantage. A stronger integration between two organizations can: (1) enhance an organization's marketing mix; (2) ease entry into new markets, and (3) provide better access to technology and innovation.[6] Through its partnership with Ryder for delivery and installation of copiers, Xerox was able to reduce its costs and thus become more price competitive. Target chose to partner with 3M in order to gain access to special packaging, creative promotional strategies and product innovations.

Profit Stability/Growth. A potential for profit growth or stability in profits is a strong driver for most partnerships. Strengthening of a relationship often leads to long-term volume and price commitments, reduced variability in sales, joint use of assets, and other improvements that enhance profitability.[7]

While the presence of strong drivers is necessary for successful partnerships, the drivers by themselves do not ensure success.

While the presence of strong drivers is necessary for successful partnerships, the drivers by themselves do not ensure success. The benefits derived from the drivers must be sustainable over the long term. If, for instance, a competitor can easily match the marketing advantage or cost efficiencies resulting from the relationship, the probability of long-term partnership success is reduced.

[4] Williamson, Oliver E., *Markets and Hierarchies: Analysis and Antitrust Implications*, New York: The Free Press, 1975.

[5] Weitz, Barton and Sandy Jap, "Relationship Marketing and Distribution Channels", *Journal of the Academy of Marketing Science*, Vol. 23, No. 4 (1995), pp. 305-320.

[6] Oliver, Christine, "Determinants of Inter-organizational Relationships: Integration and Future Directions", *Academy of Management Review*, Vol. 15, No. 2 (1990), pp. 241-265.

[7] Noordeweir, Thomas G., George John and John R. Nevin, "Performance Outcomes of Purchasing Arrangements in Industrial Buyer-Vendor Relationships", *Journal of Marketing*, Vol. 54, No. 4 (1990), pp. 80-93.

Assessing Drivers

In evaluating a relationship, how does a manager know if there are enough drivers to pursue a partnership? First, drivers must exist for each party. It is unlikely that the drivers will be the same for both parties, but they need to be strong for both. For instance, in the Whirlpool/ERX partnership, improved service was the driver for Whirlpool, while stable, guaranteed volume was the strongest driver for ERX. Second, the drivers must be strong enough to provide each party with a realistic expectation of significant benefits through a strengthening of the relationship.

The representatives from each organization should independently assess the strength of their specific drivers by using the assessment guide shown in Table 3-2. The guide lists the four drivers and provides examples of each. These examples are not meant to be all-inclusive, but rather should be used only as a starting point. It is important for each group to develop and agree upon specific descriptors of each driver that are appropriate for the relationship. Further, parameters for measuring each descriptor must be developed. For instance, under Asset/Cost Efficiencies, management must decide whether product cost reduction is a driver. The description and metrics for each driver should be specified in detail, for example, 7% cost reductions each year, and agreed upon because the success of the partnership will be measured based upon whether the desired improvements are actually achieved.

The guide provides a rating scheme with a maximum score of 24. A very low score (below 8) indicates that the potential pay-off from a partnership is so low that it should not be pursued, and therefore it is not necessary to proceed with an evaluation of the facilitators. A score of 8 or above indicates that facilitators should be examined. A high score (16 or above) indicates a potential for significant benefits and suggests that a partnership should be pursued.

The Primary Facilitators

Drivers provide the motivation to partner. But even with strong drivers, the probability of partnership success is reduced if both corporate environments are not supportive of a close relationship.

Drivers provide the motivation to partner. But even with strong drivers, the probability of partnership success is reduced if both corporate environments are not supportive of a close relationship. On the other hand, a supportive environment that enhances integration of the two parties will increase the likelihood of partnership success.

Facilitators are elements of a corporate environment that allow a partnership to grow and strengthen. They serve as a foundation for a good relationship. In the short run, facilitators cannot be developed. They either exist or they do not. And the degree to which they exist often determines whether a partnership succeeds or fails. Facilitators include: corporate compatibility, similar managerial philosophy and techniques, mutuality, and symmetry.

Corporate Compatibility. For an integrated relationship to succeed partners must share compatible values. The cultures and business objectives of the two firms must mesh. They do not have to be identical, but they cannot clash. For instance, the value placed on strategic planning and the approaches used for planning should be similar. The more similar the culture and objectives, the more comfortable the partners are likely to feel, and the higher the chance of partnership success.[8]

---

[8] Deshpande, Rohit, and Fedrick E. Webster, "Organizational Culture and Marketing: Defining a Research Agenda", *Journal of Marketing*, Vol. 53, No. 1 (1989), pp. 3-15.

Table 3-2
Assessment of Drivers

Drivers are strategic factors which result in a competitive advantage and which help to determine the appropriate level of a business relationship. For each driver, circle the boxed number which reflects the probability of your organization **realistically** achieving a benefit **through forming a tighter relationship**.

	Probability				
ASSET/COST EFFICIENCY	No Chance 0%	25%	50%	75%	Certain 100%
1. *What is the probability that this relationship will substantially reduce channel costs or improve asset utilization?*	1	2	3	4	5

-product cost savings
-distribution cost savings, handling cost savings
-packaging cost savings, information handling cost savings
-managerial efficiencies
-assets to the relationship

If you rated efficiencies in the shaded area and if the advantage is either a sustainable competitive advantage or it allows your firm to match benchmark standards in your industry, circle the I to the right.   [1]

	Probability				
CUSTOMER SERVICE	No Chance 0%	25%	50%	75%	Certain 100%
2. *What is the probability that this relationship will substantially improve the customer service level as measured by the customer?*	1	2	3	4	5

-improved on-time delivery
-better tracking of movement
-paperless order processing
-accurate order deliveries
-improved cycle times
-improved fill rates
-customer survey results
-process improvements

If you rated customer service in the shaded area and if the advantage is either a sustainable competitive advantage or if it allows your firm to match benchmark standards in your industry, circle the I to the right.   [1]

	Probability				
MARKETING ADVANTAGE	No Chance 0%	25%	50%	75%	Certain 100%
3. *What is the probability that this relationship will lead to substantial marketing advantages?*	1	2	3	4	5

-new market entry
-promotion (joint advertising, sales promotion)
-price (reduced price advantage)
-product (jointly developed product Innovation, branding opportunities)
-place (expanded geographic coverage, market saturation)
-access to technology
-innovation potential

It you rated marketing advantage in the shaded area and it the advantage is either a sustainable competitive advantage or if it allows your firm to match benchmark standards in your industry, circle the I to the right.   [1]

	Probability				
PROFIT STABILITY/GROWTH	No Chance 0%	25%	50%	75%	Certain 100%
4. *What is the probability that this relationship will result in profit growth or reduced variability in profit?*	1	2	3	4	5

-growth
-cyclical leveling
-seasonal leveling
-market share stability
-sales volume
-assurance of supply

It you rated profit stability/growth in the shaded area and if the advantage is either a sustainable competitive advantage or if it allows your firm to match benchmark standards in your industry, circle the 1 to the right.   [1]

Add all the boxed numbers which you have circled and place the total in the box to the right. This represents the strength of your motivation to partner.   [ ]

Source: Douglas M. Lambert, Margaret A. Emmelhainz and John T. Gardner, "Developing and Implementing Supply Chain Partnerships," *The International Journal of Logistics Management*, Vol. 7, No. 2 (1996), p. 6.

Managerial Philosophy and Techniques. Another important facilitator is the compatibility of management philosophy and techniques between the two firms. While corporate culture changes very slowly and business objectives are set at the top, operational level managers implement the objectives through their managerial philosophy and techniques. Such things as organizational structure, attitude toward employee empowerment, the relative importance of teamwork and the commitment to continuous improvement are examples of management philosophies.[9] The strong similarities in basic values as well as operating styles between McDonald's and Coca-Cola provides a strong foundation for an highly integrated Type III partnership.

Mutuality. The ability of a management team to put themselves in their partner's shoes and take a long-term perspective is critical in partnering. This ability is usually expressed as a willingness to develop joint goals, share sensitive information, and take a long-term perspective.[10] If management is under pressure to achieve quarterly financial goals, it will be difficult to be a good partner. As soon as the company experiences a bad quarter, managers will revert to short-term goals. An executive expressed mutuality this way. "A partnership has to benefit both parties. It cannot be a one way relationship because if you are going to weaken the other side, eventually you are going to weaken the whole operation."

"A partnership has to benefit both parties. It cannot be a one way relationship because if you are going to weaken the other side, eventually you are going to weaken the whole operation."

Symmetry. The probability for success is enhanced when the partners are "demographically" similar. Symmetry in terms of importance of each firm to the other's success, relative size, market share, financial strength, productivity, brand image, company reputation, and level of technological sophistication will make a stronger relationship. When firms are relatively symmetrical, there is no junior partner and therefore none of the insecurity, defensiveness and fear that is often found in an unequal relationship.[11] The partnership between McDonald's and Coca-Cola is enhanced by the fact that both have strong brand images and each is the number one firm in its industry. Further, McDonald's is Coca-Cola's largest customer and Coca-Cola is McDonald's largest supplier, adding more symmetry to the relationship.

Additional Facilitators

The four facilitators previously described are universal in that they should exist in any relationship. Their presence strengthens the probability of success and their absence increases the chance of failure. In addition, situation-specific facilitators may be present. While the presence of these facilitators is likely to increase the probability of success, their absence does not spell failure. The additional facilitators include shared competitors, physical proximity, exclusivity, a prior history of working with the partner, and a shared high value end user.

---

[9] Mohr, Jakki and Robert Spekman, "Characteristic of Partnership Success: Partnership Attributes, Communication Behavior, and Conflict Resolution Techniques", *Strategic Management Journal*, Vol. 15, No. 2 (1994), pp. 135-152.

[10] Cooper, Martha C., and John T. Gardner, "Good Business Relationships: More than Just Partnerships or Strategic Alliances", *International Journal of Physical Distribution and Logistics Management*, Vol. 23, No. 6 (1993), pp. 14-36.

[11] Langley, John C. and Mary C. Holcomb, "Creating Logistics Customer Value", *Journal of Business Logistics*, Vol. 13, No. 2 (1992), pp. 1-27.

Shared Competitors. In the relatively rare case when both parties face a common competitor, the partnership is likely to have a stronger foundation. An excellent example of this was the McDonald's and Coca-Cola relationship when Pepsi owned Kentucky Fried Chicken, Pizza Hut and Taco Bell restaurants. Both McDonald's and Coca-Cola faced Pepsi as a competitor. "Now that Pepsi is in the hamburger business… it has given us a synergy that has added to the partnership," stated a McDonald's executive at the time.

Close Proximity. If key players from both firms are located near each other, this can enhance the relationship. The relationship between Target and 3M reflects the influence of proximity. According to a 3M representative, "[the relationship] developed over time since both companies are based in the Twin cities." Also, the fact that Marzetti and Wendy's are both located in the Columbus, Ohio metropolitan area enabled Marzetti R&D personnel to take samples of new products to Wendy's for trial in a matter of minutes. Kraft, which is located in Chicago, Illinois, is not able to provide this timely response, thus giving Marzetti an advantage.

Exclusivity. When managers of both firms are willing to entertain the possibility of exclusivity, then the opportunities for and the likely advantages of the partnership are broadened. In the case of a branded product where exclusivity would not be possible, exclusivity can be addressed by segregating customer contact employees or by establishing a separate division that deals solely with the partner, as Coca-Cola has done for McDonald's, or by providing unique packaging for a customer.

Prior History. Firms with a prior history of positive interaction will have an advantage when building partnerships. Having worked closely and successfully with a partner in the past strengthens the chance of future successful interactions.[12]

Shared End User. In the case where both partners are serving the same end user, and that end user is of particularly high value, the partnership is likely to be strengthened. For example, both McDonald's and Coca-Cola place emphasis on the young consumer market and this strengthens their relationship.

Assessing Facilitators

Facilitators apply to the combined environment of the two potential partners. Therefore, unlike drivers that are assessed by managers in each firm independently, facilitators should be assessed jointly. The discussion of corporate values, philosophies, and objectives often leads to an improved relationship even if no further steps toward building a partnership are taken. The strength of facilitators can be assessed using a 25 point rating scheme shown in Table 3-3. The higher the facilitators score, the better the chance of partnership success. A very low score (below 8) would suggest that even with strong drivers, a partnership is likely to fail because of a hostile environment. Conversely, very high facilitators (16 or above) could lead to partnership success even in the face of a low drivers score (8 to 11 points).

Facilitators apply to the combined environment of the two potential partners. Therefore, unlike drivers that are assessed by managers in each firm independently, facilitators should be assessed jointly.

---

[12] Graham, T. Scott, Patricia J. Daugherty and William N. Dudley, "The Long-term Strategic Impact of Purchasing Partnerships", *International Journal of Purchasing and Material Management*, Vol. 30, No. 4 (1994), pp. 13-18.

Table 3-3
Assessment of Facilitators

Facilitators are factors which provide a supportive environment for the growth and maintenance of a partnership. For each facilitator, indicate the probability of it being a factor in this relationship, by circling one of the boxed numbers.

	Probability				
CORPORATE COMPATIBILITY	**No Chance** 0%	25%	50%	75%	**Certain** 100%
1. *What is the probability that the two organizations will mesh smoothly in terms of.,*	1	2	3	4	5

(a) CULTURE?
-Both firms place a value on keeping commitments
-Constancy of purpose
-Employees viewed as long term assets
-External stakeholders considered important

(b) BUSINESS?
-Strategic plans and objectives consistent
-Commitment to partnership ideas
-Willingness to change

	Probability				
MANAGEMENT PHILOSOPHY AND TECHNIQUES	**No Chance** 0%	25%	50%	75%	**Certain** 100%
2. *What is the probability that the management philosophy and techniques of the two companies will match smoothly?*	1	2	3	4	5

-Organizational structure
-Commitment to continuous improvement
-Degree of top management support
-Types of motivation used
-Importance of teamwork
-Attitudes toward "personnel churning"
-Degree of employee empowerment

	Probability				
MUTUALITY	**No Chance** 0%	25%	50%	75%	**Certain** 100%
3. *What is the probability both parties have the skills and predisposition needed for mutual relationship building?*	1	2	3	4	5

Management skilled at:
-two-sided thinking and action
-taking the perspective of the other company
-expressing goals and sharing expectations
-taking a longer term view
-mutual respect

Management willing to:
-share financial information
-integrate systems

	Probability				
SYMMETRY	**No Chance** 0%	25%	50%	75%	**Certain** 100%
4. *What Is the probability that the parties are similar on the following important factors that will affect the success of the relationship:*	1	2	3	4	5

-Relative size in terms of sales
-Relative market share in their respective industries
-Financial strength
-Productivity
-Brand image/reputation
-Technological sophistication

ADDITIONAL FACTORS (BONUS POINTS)

	Yes	No
5. *Do you have shared competitors which will tend to unite your efforts?*	1	0
6. *Are the key players in the two parties in close physical proximity to each other?*	1	0
7. *Is there a willingness to deal exclusively with your partner?*	1	0
8. *Do both parties have prior experience with successful partnerships?*	1	0
9. *Do both parties share a high value end user?*	1	0

Add all the boxed numbers which you have circled on this page and place the total in the box to the right. This represents the strength/ability to sustain and grow the partnership.

Source: Douglas M. Lambert, Margaret A. Emmelhainz and John T. Gardner, "Developing and Implementing Supply Chain Partnerships," *The International Journal of Logistics Management*, Vol. 7, No. 2 (1996), p. 9.

Partnership Types

If both parties realistically expect benefits from a partnership and if the corporate environments appear supportive, then a partnership is warranted. However, not all partnerships are the same. Three types of partnering exist, each with different degrees of integration. The appropriateness of any one type of partnership is a function of the combined strength of the drivers and facilitators. A combination of strong drivers and strong facilitators would suggest a Type III partnership while low drivers and low facilitators suggest an arm's length relationship, as shown in Table 3-4.

While it might seem, from all of the press on the importance of integrated relationships and alliances, that managers should attempt to turn all of their corporate relationships into Type III partnerships, this is not the case. In partnering, more is not always better. Implementing the appropriate type of partnership is better. The objective in establishing a partnership should not be to have a Type III partnership rather it should be to have the most appropriate type of partnership given the specific drivers and facilitators. In fact, in situations with low drivers and/or low facilitators, trying to achieve a Type III partnership is likely to be counterproductive. The necessary foundation is just not there. Having determined that a partnership, of a specific type, is warranted and should be pursued, the next step is to actually put the partnership into place. This is done through the components.

In partnering, more is not always better. Implementing the appropriate type of partnership is better.

In summary, the assessment of the drivers and facilitators is used to determine the potential for a partnership. That is, should a partnership be implemented and if so what type of partnership is appropriate? However, it is the management components and how they are implemented which determines the type of relationship that is actually achieved.

Components

Components are the activities that management uses throughout the life of the partnership to implement the relationship. Components make the relationship operational and help managers create the benefits of partnering. Every partnership has the same basic components, but the way in which the components are implemented and managed varies. Components include: planning, joint operating controls, communications, risk/reward sharing, trust and commitment, contract style, scope, and financial investment.[13]

Table 3-4
Propensity to Partner Matrix

		DRIVER POINTS		
		8-11 Points	12-15 Points	16-24 Points
FACILITATOR POINTS	8-11 Points	Arm's Length	Type I	Type II
	12-15 Points	Type I	Type II	Type III
	16-25 Points	Type II	Type III	Type III

Source: Douglas M. Lambert, Margaret A. Emmelhainz and John T. Gardner, "Developing and Implementing Supply Chain Partnerships," *The International Journal of Logistics Management*, Vol. 7, No. 2 (1996), p. 10.

---

[13] Macnell, Ian R., *The New Social Contract, an Inquiry into Modern Contractual Relations*, New Heaven, CT: Yale University Press, 1980; and, Robert Dwyer, Paul H. Schurr and Sejo Oh, "Developing Buyer-Seller Relationships", *Journal of Marketing*, Vol. 51, No. 2 (1987), pp. 11-27.

Joint planning, a key component of effective partnerships, can range from the sharing of existing plans to the joint development of strategic objectives.

Planning. Joint planning, a key component of effective partnerships, can range from the sharing of existing plans to the joint development of strategic objectives. Effective joint planning adds both flexibility and strength to a relationship. In the McDonald's and Coca-Cola relationship, joint planning is done at multiple levels, on both a periodic and continual basis.[14]

Joint Operating Controls. Joint operating controls include the metrics that are used to evaluate performance and the ability to make changes. In a partnership, either party should be able to change the operations of the other for the good of the partnership. The ability to make changes can range from being encouraged to suggest changes to being empowered to implement a change without needing prior approval or notification from the partner.[15] Within the Whirlpool Quality Express partnership, ERX could change the delivery schedule to a customer, without first obtaining approval, or even notifying Whirlpool.

Communications. Effective communication, on both a day-to-day and a non-routine basis, is a key component of successful partnerships. Integrated E-mail systems, regularly scheduled meetings and phone calls, and the willingness to share both good and bad news, as well as communication systems such EDI, all contribute to the success of a partnership. The more breadth and depth that exists in communication patterns, the stronger the partnership is likely to be. Communication links should be across all levels of the organizations.[16]

Risk/Reward Sharing. At the core of a partnership is the concept of "shared destiny". Mechanisms need to be in place to ensure that not only are the benefits and rewards of the partnership shared, but that the costs and risks are also shared.[17] A strong commitment to shared risk is evident when either party is willing to take a short-term "hit" in order to help out the partner and to strengthen the partnership over the long-term. In one of our cases, a firm deliberately delayed a planned price increase because its partner was not meeting its financial goals due to competitive pressures. In another case, productivity gains above a stated level were shared 50/50.

Trust and Commitment. No partnership can exist without trust and commitment. Loyalty to each other, loyalty to the partnership, and a long-term focus are all elements of trust and commitment. True partners do not have to constantly worry about being replaced. While most executives involved in partnerships found it difficult to precisely define trust, they all intuitively knew when it existed.

Contract Style. The type of contract that governs a partnership speaks volumes about the relationship.[18] The strongest partnerships generally have the shortest and least specific agreements or no written agreement at all. A one or two-page

---

[14] La Londe, Bernard J. and Martha C. Cooper, *Partnerships in Providing Customer Service: A Third Party Perspective*, Oak Brook, IL: Council of Logistics Management, 1989.

[15] Gardner, John T., Martha C. Cooper and Thomas G. Noodewier, "Understanding Shipper-Carrier and Shipper-Warehouser Relationships: Partnerships Revised", *Journal of Business Logistics*, Vol. 15, No. 2 (1994), pp. 121-143.

[16] Ellram, Lisa M., "A Managerial Guideline for the Development and Implementation of Purchasing Partnerships", *Journal of Purchasing and Materials Management*, Vol. 27, No. 3 (1991), pp. 2-8.

[17] Cooper, Martha C. and Lisa M. Ellram, "Characteristics of Supply Chain Management and the Implications for Purchasing and Logistics Strategy", *The International Journal of Logistics Management*, Vol. 4, No. 2 (1993), pp. 13-24.

[18] Gundlatch, Gregory T. and Patrick C. Murphy, "Ethical and Legal Foundations of Relational Marketing Exchanges", *Journal of Marketing*, Vol. 57, No. 4 (1993), pp. 36-46.

document, outlining the basic philosophy and vision for the partnership, is all that is needed when the parties are truly integrated. The partnership contract for the Quality Express program was only about three pages long, and most managers who operated under the contract had not seen it and were not aware that it existed. The "contract" between McDonald's and Coca-Cola was not in writing. It was an agreement based on trust and sealed with a handshake.

Scope. A partnership is made stronger by including more of the economic activities of each firm within the relationship. The number and complexity of the value-added steps covered and the amount of business involved are key elements of a partnership.[19] The strength of the partnership between Xerox and Ryder resulted in Ryder performing light assembly and testing of equipment and Ryder truck drivers delivering the new machines, setting them up, demonstrating them for customers, and taking away the old equipment.

Financial Investment. Firm's sharing financial resources across the relationship can strengthen a partnership. Shared assets, joint investment in technology, exchange of key personnel, and joint research and development reflect a high degree of financial interdependence. Such interdependence leads to a stronger partnership.[20]

Levels of Components

Each of the eight components will be evident in every partnership, regardless of type. However, the amount of each component, ranging from low to high, and the way in which the component is managed will vary depending upon the type of partnership. For instance, while every partnership will have some degree of joint planning, that planning can range from infrequent, ad-hoc sharing of individual plans (low) to systematic, multi-level, joint strategic planning (high). Table 3-5 shows the various levels of implementation of the components.

Implementing the Components

After having determined the appropriate type of partnership and the associated level of component implementation, the parties must agree on how each component is specifically going to be implemented and managed. For instance, if it is determined that a Type III partnership is appropriate, this means that the majority, but not necessarily all, of the components should be implemented at a high level. Therefore decisions must be made on which of the components will be implemented at a high level, and which may be more appropriately implemented at a medium level, as well as a timetable for implementation and the resources needed.

At Texas Instruments, this model was used with a major supplier. After deciding that a Type II partnership was appropriate, the parties agreed to specifics on how communications were to take place, what type of joint planning was to be done, the operations that would be jointly managed and other aspects of the components. Each partner then determined what resources were necessary in

After having determined the appropriate type of partnership and the associated level of component implementation, the parties must agree on how each component is specifically going to be implemented and managed.

---

[19] Harrigan, Kathryn Rudie, "Matching Vertical Integration Strategies to Competitive Conditions", *Strategic Management Journal*, Vol. 7. No. 4 (1996), pp. 535-555.

[20] Heide, Jan B. and George John, "The Role of Dependence Balancing in Safeguarding Transaction-Specific Assets in Conventional Channels", *Journal of Marketing*, Vol. 52, No. 1 (1988), pp. 20-35.

Table 3-5
Management Component Levels

Component		Low	Medium	High
PLANNING	• Style	• On ad-hoc basis	• Regularly scheduled	• Systematic: Both scheduled and ad hoc
	• Level	• Focus on projects or tasks	• Focus is on process	• Focus is on relationship
	• Content	• Sharing of existing plans	• Performed jointly, eliminating conflicts in strategies	• Performed jointly and at multiple levels, including top management; objective is to mesh strategies; each party participates in other's business planning
JOINT OPERATING CONTROLS	• Measurement	• Performance measures are developed independently and results are shared	• Measures are jointly developed and shared; focused on individual firm's performance	• Measures are jointly developed and shared; focused on relationship and joint performance
	• Ability to make changes	• Parties may suggest changes to other's system	• Parties may make changes to other's system after getting approval	• Parties may make changes to other's system without getting approval
COMMUNICATIONS	NON-ROUTINE	• Very limited, usually just critical issues at the task or project level	• Conducted more regularly, done at multiple levels; generally open and honest	• Planned as part of the relationship; occurs at all levels; sharing of both praise and criticism; parties "speak the same language"
	DAY-TO-DAY • Organization	• Conducted on ad-hoc basis, between individuals	• Limited number of scheduled communications; some routinization	• Systematized method of communication; may be manual or electronic; communication systems are linked
	• Balance	• Primarily one-way	• Two-way but unbalanced	• Balanced two-way communications flow
	• Electronic	• Use of individual system	• Joint modification of individual systems	• Joint development of customized electronic communications
RISK/REWARD SHARING	• Loss tolerance	• Very low tolerance for loss	• Some tolerance for short-term loss	• High tolerance for short-term loss
	• Gain commitment	• Limited willingness to help the other gain	• Willingness to help the other gain	• Desire to help other party gain
	• Commitment to fairness	• Fairness is evaluated by transaction	• Fairness is tracked year to year	• Fairness is measured over life of relationship
TRUST AND COMMITMENT	• Trust	• Trust is limited to belief that each partner will perform honestly and ethically	• Partner is given more trust than others, viewed as "most favored" supplier	• There is implicit, total trust; trust does not have to be earned
	• Commitment to each other's success	• Commitment of each party is to specific transaction or project; trust must be constantly "re-earned"	• Commitment is to a longer-term relationship	• Commitment is to partner's long-term success; commitment prevails across functions and levels in both organizations
CONTRACT STYLE	• Timeframe	• Covers a short time frame	• Covers a longer time frame	• Contracts are very general in nature and are evergreen, or alternatively the entire relationship is on a handshake basis
	• Coverage	• Contracts are specific in nature	• Contracts are more general in nature	• Contract does not specify duties or responsibilities; rather, it only outlines the basic philosophy guiding the relationship
SCOPE	• Share	• Activity of partnership represents a very small share of business for each partner	• Activity represents a modest share of business for at least one partner	• Activity covered by relationship represents significant business to both parties
	• Value-added	• Relationship covers only one or a few value-added steps (functions)	• Multiple functions, units are involved in the relationship	• Multiple functions and units are involved; partnership extends to all levels in both organizations
	• Critical activities	• Only activities which are relatively unimportant for partner's success	• Activities that are important for each partner's success are included	• Activities that are critical for each partner's success are included
INVESTMENT	• Financial	• There is low or no investment between the two parties	• May jointly own low value assets	• High value assets may be jointly owned
	• Technology	• No joint development of products/technology	• There is some joint design effort and there may be some joint R&D planning	• There is significant joint development; regular and significant joint R&D activity
	• People	• Limited personnel exchange	• Extensive exchange of personnel	• Participation on other party's board

Source: Douglas M. Lambert, Margaret A. Emmelhainz and John T. Gardner, "Developing and Implementing Supply Chain Partnerships," *The International Journal of Logistics Management*, Vol. 7, No. 2 (1996), p. 12.

terms of dollars, time and personnel; and commitments were obtained from top management for those resources. As a result, both parties understood and accepted the expectations and requirements of the partnership.

Outcomes

A partnership, if appropriately established and effectively managed, should improve performance for both parties. Profit enhancement, process improvements, and increased competitive advantage are all likely outcomes of effective partnerships. Specific outcomes will vary depending upon the drivers that initially motivated the development of the partnership. It should be noted, however, that a partnership is not required for both organizations to achieve satisfactory outcomes from a relationship. Typically, organizations will have multiple arm's length relationships which meet the needs of and provide benefits to both parties. One of our case study relationships, between an express delivery company and a national manufacturer, was viewed by both parties at the beginning of the research as a partnership, since both parties were receiving their desired outcomes: a service improvement and cost reduction for the manufacturer and a revenue increase for the delivery company. At the completion of the research, it was clear to management in the manufacturing firm and the researchers that this relationship was not a partnership. The components of a partnership were not present. The desired benefits were achieved because the parties involved were appropriately using an effective arm's length relationship. It was a single source contract with volume and service guarantees.

A partnership, if appropriately established and effectively managed, should improve performance for both parties.

Validation of the Model

Validation of the model was achieved by analyzing 20 partnership meetings where the model was used (representing 20 distinct business relationships). Each lasted one and one-half days with participants that represented various levels and functions in both firms involved in the relationship. A comprehensive note-taking instrument was developed in order to systematically collect observations about the meeting. The notes from the meeting along with an open-ended meeting evaluation form were consolidated and content analyzed to develop findings related to the use of the partnership model. Content analysis is an objective and systematic research technique suitable for replicable and valid interfaces from data to their context.[21] The method is advantageous for understanding social communication and interactions and relationships.[22] In particular, we analyzed participant observations and evaluations after each meeting and consulted with participants if any clarification was required.

The use of ethnographic case studies to contribute to the solution of practical problems has been defined as action research.[23] The core idea of action research is that the researcher is involved with the subject of investigation. When

---

[21] Kolbe, Richard H, and Melissa S. Burnett, "Content Analysis Research: An Examination of Applications with Directives for Improving Research Reliability and Objectivity," *Journal of Consumer Research*. Vol. 18, No. 1 (1991), pp. 243-250.

[22] McAlister, Debbie T. and Robert C. Erffmeyer, "A Content Analysis of Outcomes and Responsibilities for Consumer Complaints to Third-Party Organizations," *Journal of Business Research*, Vol. 56, No. 4 (2003), pp. 341-351

[23] Naslund, Dag "Logistics Needs Qualitative Research - Especially Action Research," *International Journal of Physical Distribution & Logistics Management*, Vol. 32, No. 5 (2002), pp. 321-338.

undertaking action research, the researcher should actively participate in the project.[24] The goal of action research is to advance both science and practice.[25]

Our research methodology addressed a number of frequently cited criticisms of partnership research. As previously described, Baba[26] complained that most partnership research was based only on a limited number of interviews, often with just one executive, from only one side of the partnership. Another weakness of previous partnership research is the over-dependence on surveys. While mail surveys allow for the collection of large amounts of data from numerous respondents, the extent and richness of the data collected are limited. They typically involve only one individual within an organization and with few exceptions only collect data from one side of the relationship.[27] While some of these partnership surveys provide statistically significant results, they tend to provide limited amounts of information that could be used by managers to develop business relationships.

The cut-off point of 20 cases was determined during the course of the study based on the flow of new information out of the meetings. The actual number of cases is not as important as reaching a saturation or "redundancy" point. The primary goal was to facilitate meetings until the flow of new ideas and/or findings was minimal. Although there is no set heuristic as to the number of cases needed to reach saturation, previous research suggests 12 to 20 for a heterogeneous sample such as the one in this study.[28]

Of the 20 partnership meetings, a major retailer provided an opportunity to use the model with nine product and service suppliers that involved a diverse set of relationships.

Of the 20 partnership meetings, a major retailer provided an opportunity to use the model with nine product and service suppliers that involved a diverse set of relationships. Both critical component suppliers and support product suppliers were included in the sample. Seven of the meetings took place at the retailer's facilities and two were conducted at the supplier's facilities.

Another nine partnership cases were completed with three companies in the consumer goods sector and their suppliers. The nine relationships included suppliers of raw materials and packaging materials as well as a vertically integrated internal relationship between two wholly owned subsidiaries of the same company who also conducted business with companies outside of the relationship. Six of

---

[24] Checkland, Peter, *Systems Thinking. Systems Practice*. New York, NY: John Wiley & Sons, 1993.

[25] Foote-Whyte, W., *Participatory Action Research*. London, England: Sage, 1991; and James McKeman, Curriculum Action Research: *A Handbook of Methods and Resources for the Reflective Practitioner*. London, England: Kogan Page, 1991.

[26] Baba, Marietta. "Two Sides to Every Story: An Ethnohistorical Approach to Organizational Partnerships," *City and Society*, Vol. 2, No. 2 (1988), pp. 71-106.

[27] Boyson, Sandor, Thomas Corsi, Martin Dresner, and Elliot Rabinovich, "Managing Effective Third Party Logistics Partnerships: What Does It Take?" *Journal of Business Logistics*, Vol. 20, No. 1 (1999), pp. 73-100; John L. Kent and John T. Mentzer, "The Effect of Investment in Interorganizational Information Technology in a Retail Supply Chain," *Journal of Business Logistics*, Vol. 24. No. 2 (2003), pp. 155-176; Michael Maloni and W. C. Benton, "Power Influences in the Supply Chain," *Journal of Business Logistics*, Vol. 21, No. 1 (2000), pp. 49-73; and, Christopher R. Moberg and Thomas W. Speh, "Evaluating the Relationship Between Questionable Business Practices and the Strength of Supply Chain Relationships," *Journal of Business Logistics*, Vol. 24, No. 2 (2003), pp. 1-20.

[28] Carter, Craig R. and Marianne M. Jennings, "Logistics Social Responsibility: An Integrative Framework," *Journal of Business Logistics*, Vol. 23, No. 1(2002), pp. 145-180.; Barney G. Glaser and Anselm L. Strauss, *The Discovery of Grounded Theory*, New York, NY, 1967.; Aldine De Gruyter; Yvonna S. Lincoln and Egon G. Guba, *Naturalistic Inquiry*, Beverly Hills, CA: Sage, 1985; Grant D. McCracken, *The Long Interview*, Newbury Park, CA: Sage, 1988; and, Michael Q. Patton, *Qualitative Evaluation Methods*. Beverly Hills, CA: Sage, 1990.

the meetings took place at the customer's facilities and three were conducted at a neutral site.

The final two cases involved a major company in the technology sector. The cases involved service suppliers. One of the associated meetings was conducted at the customer's facilities and the other was at a neutral site.

All 20 validation cases supported the original driver classifications. Each of the compelling reasons for developing a more tailored relationship identified by participants could be captured by one of the four drivers. The compelling reasons also had a specific driver that was the best fit; however this required a careful explanation of the drivers by the meeting facilitator. Thus, the research supports the idea that the original drivers were mutually exclusive and collectively exhaustive. The drivers were seen by the participants as being conceptually distinct from the facilitators and components. Also, the cases supported the mutually exclusive and collectively exhaustive nature of the facilitators. In all of the case studies used to validate the model, managers were able to connect their action plans to the managerial components within the model. All of the action items from the 20 cases could be expressed through various components of the model.

Conclusions

In a highly competitive business environment with leaner organizations, it is necessary to form closer relationships with key customers and suppliers in order to maintain a leadership position and to grow. But the same forces that provide the benefits of partnering make it impossible to develop these relationships with everyone. Trying to develop a partnership where one is not warranted will waste valuable resources while providing minimal return. Not having a partnership when one is appropriate squanders an opportunity for competitive advantage. The Partnership Model is a tool that management can use to determine when a partnership is appropriate as well as the type of partnership that should be implemented. In the next chapter, you will be shown how to use the partnership model to structure relationships with key customers and suppliers.

The Partnership Model is a tool that management can use to determine when a partnership is appropriate as well as the type of partnership that should be implemented.

How to Use the Partnership Model

I think the model is invaluable and I have seen it work with all types of relationships.

— Joe Gordon
Vice President of Supply Chain
Noodles & Company

Overview

In this chapter we describe how to use the Partnership Model to identify the potential for a partnership between two organizations. Implementation issues are documented and guidance is provided for managers who want to use this tool to structure business relationships with key customers and suppliers.

Introduction

The Partnership Model has been used successfully to structure buyer - seller relationships, to encourage divisions of the same corporation with separate financial statements to work for the common shareholder, with government and non-government organizations, and in domestic and international settings.

The Partnership Model has been used successfully to structure buyer - seller relationships, to encourage divisions of the same corporation with separate financial statements to work for the common shareholder, with government and non-government organizations, and in domestic and international settings. Managers consistently report that they would not have considered as many issues and would not have done so as holistically without the structure provided by the model. Some of the outcomes have surprised the users. A retailer used the model with a supplier who subsequently acquired a west coast manufacturing capability to provide full national coverage. The investment had been resisted before the partnership meeting. In another example, a consumer products manufacturer used the model in order to increase the flow of innovation opportunities from key suppliers. During one partnership meeting, a supplier committed to assigning a dedicated salesperson as well as an employee in their research and development department to this manufacturer. This commitment was made because the partnership meeting identified the concerns of the vice president of research and development of the manufacturer about how the confidentiality of joint innovations between the companies would be handled.

The managers who participated in the more than 80 meetings using the model have quantified the value of using the model. Executives from a consumer products manufacturer identified that one of the outcomes of using the model was implementation of vendor managed supply that produced $4.3 million in annual savings. Another case involving this manufacturer resulted in $2.8 million in annual savings by identifying an opportunity to work with the supplier to restructure its network. In another company, management attributed the acceleration of a key plant opening (a reduction of 2 months) to the partnership session. Thus, both qualitative and quantitative measures provided by managers support the value of using the model to tailor relationships with key customers and suppliers.

Preparation for Meeting

All parties involved in the process have activities that should be completed prior to the meeting. These activities include participant selection decisions, meeting scheduling, meeting planning issues and groundwork issues.

Once management has made the decision to use the model, it must determine which business relationship(s) are candidates. Our findings suggest that managers go through a learning curve with the model. It is beneficial to begin with an important relationship but not a critical relationship in order to gain experience. Once a comfort level with the model has been developed, more critical relationships can be addressed. Additionally, management should consider the word-of-mouth issues associated with the decision to use the model with specific companies. In particular, what might be the reaction within a supplier or customer organization when it is discovered that a competitor has gone through the process and they have not? During several of our facilitations, managers from the company invited to participate in the meeting asked who else had gone through the process.

The partnership meetings are greatly enhanced by the presence of individuals from multiple levels within the organizations and with diverse functional expertise. We have found that the make-up of the group sends a message to those in the other firm about the importance of the relationship to the party proposing the meeting. Also, it is important to involve the highest-level executives possible and still have the meeting. The more levels of management above the people in the room, the more difficult it may be to successfully implement the commitments that are made in the partnership meeting.

The partnership meetings are greatly enhanced by the presence of individuals from multiple levels within the organizations and with diverse functional expertise.

The need to have the involvement of multiple levels of employees with diverse functional expertise makes scheduling difficult. As was stated by one participant, "this is the first time all of these people have been together in the same room." The best way to address this challenge is to have a high-level executive in each organization state that the meeting is a priority and also attend the meeting. In many of the partnership sessions that we have conducted, the president of the firm attended the entire meeting.

Additional recommendations for the preparation for a partnership meeting can be summed up as follows:

- A detailed agenda should be prepared to establish expectations and maintain the focus in the meeting.
- A partnership meeting requires one and a half days and back-to-back partnership meetings are not recommended because of the intensity of these sessions and overlap of participants.
- A dinner should be scheduled at the end of the first day to enable networking and clarification of the prior discussions.
- The model should be reviewed in advance to ensure that all participants are prepared for the session. We assign the *Harvard Business Review* article, "We're in This Together," to be read by all participants prior to the meeting (it is included in the Resources and Tools section of this book and reprints are available from HBR).

- The individuals leading the meeting should be conversant in the business situation and be independent of the relationship.
- A neutral location, spacious rooms, and proper supplies for recording and communicating are necessary.
- An agenda, a list of participants, and copies of materials should be prepared for each participant.

While the preparation details appear to be intuitive, some meetings were hampered by a lack of attention to these issues.

The Partnership Meeting

With the preparatory work done, the partnership meeting can be held. This meeting is a complex, multi-session process in which expectations are set, the environment is examined, and action plans with timelines are developed and responsibilities assigned. Descriptions of the introduction and expectation setting session, drivers session, facilitators session, targeting session, managerial components session, and wrap-up session follow.

Introduction and Expectation Setting Session

The partnership meeting should begin with an introduction that reinforces the motivations for undertaking the process, a review of the model, and a discussion about expectations.

The partnership meeting should begin with an introduction that reinforces the motivations for undertaking the process, a review of the model, and a discussion about expectations. For example, the vice president of one company detailed the corporate goals of increased innovation and profit margin growth as the underlying reason for using the model to build more structure into their relationships with key suppliers. In another firm, the vice president stated that the motivation for using the model was to achieve a structured and consistent approach to relationship management. Whatever the reason, it is critical for those in attendance to understand that the business is not at risk.

It is common for participants from one of the companies to want more partnership because they feel that somehow it relates to the security of the business. It is important to establish from the very beginning of the session that the goal is to tailor the partnership to the most efficient and effective type. It should be made clear that the goal is NOT to have a Type III partnership. The goal is to determine the most appropriate type of partnership, that is, obtain the desired business results for the least amount of effort. Incremental benefits must accrue to both firms, if management is going to invest incremental effort. This point should be reinforced throughout the meeting. The managerial time wasted on an unneeded Type III partnership would have large opportunity costs.

Some additional issues concerning the critical role of the meeting facilitators are:
- Two individuals from outside the relationship are needed for the session that develops the drivers for each company.
- These individuals serve as the lead trainers and pace setters for the process.
- The individuals must be skilled in building consensus, probing for more information, assuring closure, and reinforcing agreements on action plans.

These recommendations were drawn from multiple cases. For instance, during a meeting at their customer's location, executives from a supplier stated that the driver session felt like it was taking place back at their own headquarters. This comfort level would be difficult to achieve without unbiased facilitation.

Drivers Session

A critical part of the Partnership Model is the drivers, the compelling reasons to partner. It is necessary to ensure that the two parties objectively analyze their potential drivers of partnership. Representatives of the two firms should evaluate drivers separately and the evaluation must be from a selfish perspective. There are a number of issues that need to be addressed to make this session actionable and effective.

Representatives of the two firms should evaluate drivers separately and the evaluation must be from a selfish perspective.

The most fundamental issue is the potential for double counting. Since profits are a function of costs, service and marketing, there is a possibility for double counting. For example, cost reductions and better asset utilization will lead to higher profits. Customer service improvements should lead to higher sales volume that should lead to higher profits. If a supplier hopes to gain a marketing advantage as a result of increased partnership, they will also expect higher profit. Consequently, it is necessary to admonish the participants not to double count. They should use the first three drivers whenever they are appropriate. Only those potential drivers of profit that cannot be included in any one of the others should be included in profit stability and growth. If a customer service improvement by the seller yields lower inventories for the buyer, this is asset/cost efficiency for the buyer. If it yields better customer service to the buyer's customers, then it should be counted as a customer service improvement for the buyer. If a joint effort can level volumes, then it should be in profit stability and growth. Wendy's management believed that a closer relationship with Tyson Foods would reduce the volatility in chicken prices and this would result in increased stability in profits.

Another difficulty with identifying and scoring drivers comes from the need to consider only the incremental gains possible through partnership. Thus, if a cost savings could be gained through hard bargaining or competitive bidding, it should not be scored high as a driver. If a savings due to deploying a new technology could be contemplated only in the context of a close, long-term cooperative relationship, then it should be counted. Making this distinction is often difficult.

It is often challenging for suppliers to think in terms of their own self-interest particularly if the buyer initiated the partnership meeting. Since they respond to the customer in a customer-oriented way in most discussions, taking a selfish perspective is sometimes difficult.

Customer service poses a consistent problem for sellers. Representatives from the supplier organization want to score as a driver, customer service improvements to the potential partner. While these are advantages to the potential partner, they are not compelling reasons for the seller to want a closer relationship. In order for the evaluation to be selfish on the part of the seller, only customer service improvements that can be offered to other customers as a result of more closeness in this relationship should be counted. If a firm, through partnership, can develop a customer service delivery approach that can later be rolled out to other customer accounts, then the seller can score customer service as a compelling reason to partner.

When evaluating a driver each side should define specific bullets that apply to their business situation. It is important to put measurable goals on each specific bullet identified by the participants. An example for cost efficiency could be to reduce controllable costs in the component parts by five percent per year. A marketing advantage that would be harder to quantify in dollars would be to come up with at least five new product ideas over a two-year period, one of which would reach commercialization. After the group comes up with drivers specific to the relationship, they should be challenged to come up with measurable goals.

For each driver of partnership, the managers must decide on a probability that it will be achieved. For the first driver, the question is "What is the probability that this relationship will substantially reduce channel costs or improve asset utilization?" The scoring is on a five-point basis from 1 to 5 ranging from zero percent chance to 100 percent chance. Thus, in the scoring process the managers for each firm will determine four driver scores based on the probability of making substantial gains for their firm. There is no expectation that the drivers will be in the same categories for each firm, nor will the total scores be the same. Each side must assess their own self-interest independently and honestly, which is why the business should not be at risk.

Drivers are assessed on "the probability that this relationship will substantially…" with the key word being substantially. If the driver bullets within one of the four drivers are collectively weak on substantiality, then a probability of getting a substantial advantage should be low, before factoring uncertainty into the judgment. When one buyer organization assessed the potential for cost avoidance through partnership, they found a large number of potential savings. However, the total savings would only amount to a small part of one percent of the overall costs for the firm, therefore the rating had to be a low score even though managers thought achieving the savings was relatively certain.

It is important to use the blank driver forms provided with this book for each of the four drivers (see Table 4-1) when recording the driver elements specific to the relationship rather than use the generalized bullet points in the original model. The group should develop an exhaustive list of descriptors for each specific driver and then through discussion reduce it to a parsimonious list that can be summarized in a few bullet points. Each of the four driver categories should be evaluated and scored as a group. Evaluating each and weighting each, then coming up with a probability for each may add a false sense of accuracy, slow the process, and/or defy consensus. The participants should seek consensus for the final number for each of the four drivers. It is not reasonable to average the numbers, since one person's reason to choose a low or high probability may not have been factored into others' thinking. Talking about differences and coming to consensus is very useful in encouraging communication among the participants and facilitating implementation later. Issues come out in the defense of specific ratings that otherwise would not emerge. Also, there needs to be buy-in from the participants if the drivers are to be achieved.

Drivers for the supplier and the buyer will rarely match up in strength by category. It is important to emphasize this to the seller, as they often feel that their score on a particular driver should match their counterpart's score. In fact, often sellers have low customer service scores while buyers often have high customer service scores. It is not important that the scores match, just that both sides have compelling reasons to commit more resources to the relationship than is typical of an arm's-length relationship. In addition to completing each of the driver sections shown in Table 4-1, each group should complete the summary sheet showing the total drivers score (see Table 4-2).

Table 4-1
Driver Forms for a Partnership Session

Drivers are strategic factors which result in a competitive advantage and which help to determine the appropriate level of a business relationship. For each driver, identify specific bullets, appropriate metrics and circle the boxed number which reflects the probability of your organization **realistically** achieving a benefit **through forming a tighter relationship**.

		Probability			
ASSET/COST EFFICIENCY	No Chance 0%	25%	50%	75%	Certain 100%

1. *What is the probability that this relationship will substantially reduce channel costs or improve asset utilization?*

[1] [2] [3] [4] [5]

- _____
- _____
- _____
- _____
- _____
- _____
- _____

If you rated efficiencies in the shaded area and if the advantage is either a sustainable competitive advantage or it allows your firm to match benchmark standards in your industry, circle the I to the right.   [1]

		Probability			
CUSTOMER SERVICE	No Chance 0%	25%	50%	75%	Certain 100%

2. *What is the probability that this relationship will substantially improve the customer service level as measured by the customer?*

[1] [2] [3] [4] [5]

- _____
- _____
- _____
- _____
- _____
- _____
- _____

If you rated customer service in the shaded area and if the advantage is either a sustainable competitive advantage or if it allows your firm to match benchmark standards in your industry, circle the I to the right.   [1]

		Probability			
MARKETING ADVANTAGE	No Chance 0%	25%	50%	75%	Certain 100%

3. *What is the probability that this relationship will lead to substantial marketing advantages?*

[1] [2] [3] [4] [5]

- _____
- _____
- _____
- _____
- _____
- _____
- _____

It you rated marketing advantage in the shaded area and it the advantage is either a sustainable competitive advantage or if it allows your firm to match benchmark standards in your industry, circle the I to the right.   [1]

		Probability			
PROFIT STABILITY/GROWTH	No Chance 0%	25%	50%	75%	Certain 100%

4. *What is the probability that this relationship will result in profit growth or reduced variability in profit?*

[1] [2] [3] [4] [5]

- _____
- _____
- _____
- _____
- _____
- _____
- _____

It you rated profit stability/growth in the shaded area and if the advantage is either a sustainable competitive advantage or if it allows your firm to match benchmark standards in your industry, circle the 1 to the right.   [1]

Add all the boxed numbers which you have circled and place the total in the box to the right. This represents the strength of your motivation to partner. [ ]

Source: Adapted from Douglas M. Lambert, Margaret A. Emmelhainz and John T. Gardner, "Developing and Implementing Supply Chain Partnerships," *The International Journal of Logistics Management*, Vol. 7, No. 2 (1996), p. 6.

Table 4-2
Assessment of Drivers: Summary Sheet

Driver	Score
Asset/Cost Efficiency	
Customer Service	
Marketing Advantage	
Profit Stability/Growth	
Total Driver Score	

Once each side has scored their drivers, the next step is to come together and present these drivers to the other side. It is important for each side to explain why the drivers were selected and how they were scored.

Once each side has scored their drivers, the next step is to come together and present these drivers to the other side. It is important for each side to explain why the drivers were selected and how they were scored. This represents an expectations-setting session that is critical for partnership success. One of the reasons that partnerships fail is the existence of unrealistic expectations by the parties involved in the relationship. What each bullet point means as well as the score for the overall driver and the thinking behind that score needs to be understood by both sides of the relationship. If the representatives of the other firm indicate that they cannot or will not help achieve a particular driver, the driver should be reevaluated. If no-one objects to the other side's drivers, then management is obligated to help the other firm achieve its drivers as the partnership is implemented.

There is a direct connection between drivers and outcomes. If the drivers are quantified in the driver assessment session, then the evaluation of the partnership over time is made much easier. An example for asset/cost efficiency would be the reduction of product costs by 7% per year over the next three years. By knowing the exact expectation there is more realistic buy-in and better tracking of progress when outcomes are measured over time.

Facilitators Session

Facilitators are the environmental factors that make implementing partnership easy or difficult and they are assessed in a joint session.

Facilitators are the environmental factors that make implementing partnership easy or difficult and they are assessed in a joint session. The evaluation process should focus on the potential for the two firms to mesh easily, so the fit rather than each firm's individual characteristics is the issue to be addressed. The focus of the session is to identify the degree to which the four major environmental factors and the five additional facilitators in the model are present (see Table 4-3). Unlike drivers, it is not necessary to develop a new list of facilitators but rather, to use the facilitators identified in Table 4-3 as the basis for discussion.

The facilitators should not be examined at the outset of a relationship. After a period of working together, managers in the two firms will have a much easier time assessing each facilitator. In a new relationship, a logistics service provider and a large telecommunications manufacturer went through a partnership session too soon. Managers in both organizations felt it was not possible to complete the facilitators because they lacked experience working together and decided to wait

Table 4-3
Assessment of Facilitators

Facilitators are factors which provide a supportive environment for the growth and maintenance of a partnership. For each facilitator, indicate the probability of it being a factor in this relationship, by circling one of the boxed numbers.

	Probability				
CORPORATE COMPATIBILITY	**No Chance** 0%	25%	50%	75%	**Certain** 100%
1. *What is the probability that the two organizations will mesh smoothly in terms of.,*	1	2	3	4	5

   (a) CULTURE?
     -Both firms place a value on keeping commitments
     -Constancy of purpose
     -Employees viewed as long term assets
     -External stakeholders considered important

   (b) BUSINESS?
     -Strategic plans and objectives consistent
     -Commitment to partnership ideas
     -Willingness to change

	Probability				
MANAGEMENT PHILOSOPHY AND TECHNIQUES	**No Chance** 0%	25%	50%	75%	**Certain** 100%
2. *What is the probability that the management philosophy and techniques of the two companies will match smoothly?*	1	2	3	4	5

     -Organizational structure
     -Commitment to continuous improvement
     -Degree of top management support
     -Types of motivation used
     -Importance of teamwork
     -Attitudes toward "personnel churning"
     -Degree of employee empowerment

	Probability				
MUTUALITY	**No Chance** 0%	25%	50%	75%	**Certain** 100%
3. *What is the probability both parties have the skills and predisposition needed for mutual relationship building?*	1	2	3	4	5

   Management skilled at:
     -two-sided thinking and action
     -taking the perspective of the other company
     -expressing goals and sharing expectations
     -taking a longer term view
     -mutual respect

   Management willing to:
     -share financial information
     -integrate systems

	Probability				
SYMMETRY	**No Chance** 0%	25%	50%	75%	**Certain** 100%
4. *What Is the probability that the parties are similar on the following important factors that will affect the success of the relationship:*	1	2	3	4	5

     -Relative size in terms of sales
     -Relative market share in their respective industries
     -Financial strength
     -Productivity
     -Brand image/reputation
     -Technological sophistication

ADDITIONAL FACTORS (BONUS POINTS)

	Yes	No
5. *Do you have shared competitors which will tend to unite your efforts?*	1	0
6. *Are the key players in the two parties in close physical proximity to each other?*	1	0
7. *Is there a willingness to deal exclusively with your partner?*	1	0
8. *Do both parties have prior experience with successful partnerships?*	1	0
9. *Do both parties share a high value end user?*	1	0

Add all the boxed numbers which you have circled on this page and place the total in the box to the right. This represents the strength/ability to sustain and grow the partnership. ☐

Source: Douglas M. Lambert, Margaret A. Emmelhainz and John T. Gardner, "Developing and Implementing Supply Chain Partnerships," *The International Journal of Logistics Management*, Vol. 7, No. 2 (1996), p. 9.

six months before finishing the process. The experience gained over these months sharpened the managers' views about how well the two firms would mesh.

It is critical that the person leading the session emphasize the disfunctional nature of painting an overly positive picture of the environment. The result will be to move the firms into more partnership than the situation demands and consume more managerial resources than necessary. The participants should be challenged to give examples of each claim and to relate each example to how it might result in a partnership being easier to implement. If both sides claim employee empowerment, then a concrete example of empowered decision-making is in order. In one case, both sides were indicating a strong quality focus, but one was a six sigma supporter and the other was focused on relationships not process. Both firms were very strong and successful with their approach, but these differences could make joint work more difficult.

Within mutuality, the sharing of financial information is a key indicator. Openness in sharing sensitive information is a key to building partnership. Challenging the participants to give examples of taking a longer-term view is also a good practice. The discussion on symmetry should focus on the concept that there should not be a junior partner.

Bonus points are given for environmental factors that cannot be reasonably expected in every relationship but when they are present they strengthen the relationship. For example, if two firms are headquartered in the same city, this proximity increases the ability of employees at all levels in both firms to interact more frequently. However, managers regularly want to claim close proximity based on something other than the two headquarters being in the same metropolitan area. A field office for one firm located close to the headquarters of the other or an on-site account manager is not close proximity as defined by the model. It is hard to have informal and social contacts between top management and others up and down both organizations if they are not closely co-located. When claims of prior experience with partnership are made, they should be based on the style of relationship described previously. As was the case with drivers, it is important to gain consensus on the facilitator scores and summarize them on the summary sheet provided (see Table 4-4).

Targeting Session

The next step is to target the type of partnership using the Propensity to Partner matrix (see Table 4-5). Because the model uses a three-by-three matrix to prescribe partnership types, it is subject to the difficulties present with any grid approach. The person leading the session needs to be sensitive to the fact that a single point change on either drivers or facilitators can move a relationship from a Type II partnership to a Type III or to a Type I. The prescriptions near the intersections of the boxes need to be evaluated with care. If a Type III partnership is indicated, but no joint investment is demanded to achieve the drivers, a low target for the financial component is fine. The goal is to tailor the relationship to fit the drivers and the environment not to match the grid.

Since the drivers are being assessed independently, it is possible for the firms to have driver scores that fall into two different categories (low, medium, or high). When one firm has a driver score in a higher category than the other, the low driver score is used to type the relationship. Like any relationship the party that wants it

> *It is critical that the person leading the session emphasize the disfunctional nature of painting an overly positive picture of the environment. The result will be to move the firms into more partnership than the situation demands and consume more managerial resources than necessary.*

Table 4-4
Assessment of Facilitators: Summary Sheet

Facilitators	Score
Corporate Compatibility	☐
Management Philosophy and Techniques	☐
Mutuality	☐
Symmetry	☐
Bonus points (zero or one)	☐
Shared Competitors	☐
Close Proximity	☐
Exclusivity	☐
Prior Experience	☐
Share End User	☐
Total Facilitator Score	☐

Table 4-5
Propensity to Partner Matrix

		DRIVER POINTS		
		8-11 Points	12-15 Points	16-24 Points
FACILITATOR POINTS	8-11 Points	Arm's Length	Type I	Type II
	12-15 Points	Type I	Type II	Type III
	16-25 Points	Type II	Type III	Type III

Source: Douglas M. Lambert, Margaret A. Emmelhainz and John T. Gardner, "Developing and Implementing Supply Chain Partnerships," *The International Journal of Logistics Management*, Vol. 7, No. 2 (1996), p. 10.

the least determines the outcome. The relationship is only as strong as the weakest commitment. There will be only one facilitator score since facilitators are evaluated jointly.

It is important to understand how to handle a mismatch in driver scores. There might be considerable concern about a disparity in driver scores. After experiencing two cases in which there were a large disparity in scores, it appears that this situation need not damage an otherwise good business relationship. It is important for the meeting facilitator to note the disparity as it emerges and encourage the representatives of the lower-scoring organization to emphasize how their drivers were scored. It should be reinforced that the reason for using the lowest driver score is because the firm with the least amount to gain will determine the level of effort that goes into the relationship.

By the end of the targeting session, both parties should have a clearer understanding of the joint expectations of their relationship. This is critical for partnership success and is also useful if a partnership is not indicated. In the latter case, both parties benefit from a better understanding of why an arm's length relationship is the best fit.

Components Session

While the drivers and facilitators determine the potential for partnership, implementation of the management components determines the type of partnership that is actually achieved. The components session is critical since it involves developing the action plan. The first three components, planning, joint operating controls, and communications, are the keys to a successful relationship. Setting these three at the appropriate position typically takes the most time. To help the process along each participant should have the table of management components available (see Table 4-6) as well as a note page to record the current and the desired state as well as action items, timelines and responsible parties (see Table 4-7).

The first step is to assess the current relationship component by component. In fact, the level of the analysis should be bullet by bullet within the components, as each component can be implemented in a tailored fashion. Thus, a relationship can entail joint planning on a regularly scheduled basis but focusing on tasks. A typical review of the current state of management components found many of them with bullet points in different columns. The current implementation of the management components reveals the amount of partnership that has been implemented in the relationship to this point in time. This provides initial guidance on managerial components that need more or less focus depending on the desired level of partnership. The bold type in the shaded boxes in Table 4-8 shows how the relationship was currently implemented.

The eight components should be reviewed again to determine the target level of implementation based on the targeted partnership type. In the relationship shown as an example in Table 4-8, the goal was to implement a Type II partnership which meant that the majority of the components must be implemented at a medium level. Table 4-8 shows the components that need to be improved. Next, the participants must determine action items such as forming a task force to set up communications links that support the attainment of the targeted partnership. In one relationship, management chose to form a steering committee charged with developing a vision for the relationship. This committee was responsible for ensuring that progress was made towards reaching the desired levels of implementation of the management components.

If specific actions are properly identified, then responsibility can be placed on individuals and due dates established. It is not enough to say that metrics for a particular hard-to-measure driver should be jointly developed. The parties need to determine who should be involved, who leads, when the work will be completed, and to whom they will report. If this level of detail is achieved in the managerial components session, the outcomes assessment to be done later will be that much easier and the probability of the relationship staying on track is higher. The action items from the components session need to become part of the ongoing planning activities, such as a quarterly business review.

The final, but very important, step in the components session is to review the drivers to ensure that each has been addressed. Drivers from each side should be available to all participants. If a driver for the seller (as is often the case) is to gain access to other business units within the parent company, then the trust and commitment components need to have specific action items. An example item would be to communicate examples of the level of commitment and trust in the relationship within their respective company newsletters. This was an action item

Table 4-6
Management Components Overview

Component		Low	Medium	High
PLANNING	• Style	• On ad-hoc basis	• Regularly scheduled	• Systematic: Both scheduled and ad hoc
	• Level	• Focus on projects or tasks	• Focus is on process	• Focus is on relationship
	• Content	• Sharing of existing plans	• Performed jointly, eliminating conflicts in strategies	• Performed jointly and at multiple levels, including top management; objective is to mesh strategies; each party participates in other's business planning
JOINT OPERATING CONTROLS	• Measurement	• Performance measures are developed independently and results are shared	• Measures are jointly developed and shared; focused on individual firm's performance	• Measures are jointly developed and shared; focused on relationship and joint performance
	• Ability to make changes	• Parties may suggest changes to other's system	• Parties may make changes to other's system after getting approval	• Parties may make changes to other's system without getting approval
COMMUNICATIONS	NON-ROUTINE	• Very limited, usually just critical issues at the task or project level	• Conducted more regularly, done at multiple levels; generally open and honest	• Planned as part of the relationship; occurs at all levels; sharing of both praise and criticism; parties "speak the same language"
	DAY-TO-DAY • Organization	• Conducted on ad-hoc basis, between individuals	• Limited number of scheduled communications; some routinization	• Systematized method of communication; may be manual or electronic; communication systems are linked
	• Balance	• Primarily one-way	• Two-way but unbalanced	• Balanced two-way communications flow
	• Electronic	• Use of individual system	• Joint modification of individual systems	• Joint development of customized electronic communications
RISK/REWARD SHARING	• Loss tolerance	• Very low tolerance for loss	• Some tolerance for short-term loss	• High tolerance for short-term loss
	• Gain commitment	• Limited willingness to help the other gain	• Willingness to help the other gain	• Desire to help other party gain
	• Commitment to fairness	• Fairness is evaluated by transaction	• Fairness is tracked year to year	• Fairness is measured over life of relationship
TRUST AND COMMITMENT	• Trust	• Trust is limited to belief that each partner will perform honestly and ethically	• Partner is given more trust than others, viewed as "most favored" supplier	• There is implicit, total trust; trust does not have to be earned
	• Commitment to each other's success	• Commitment of each party is to specific transaction or project; trust must be constantly "re-earned"	• Commitment is to a longer-term relationship	• Commitment is to partner's long-term success; commitment prevails across functions and levels in both organizations
CONTRACT STYLE	• Timeframe	• Covers a short time frame	• Covers a longer time frame	• Contracts are very general in nature and are evergreen, or alternatively the entire relationship is on a handshake basis
	• Coverage	• Contracts are specific in nature	• Contracts are more general in nature	• Contract does not specify duties or responsibilities; rather, it only outlines the basic philosophy guiding the relationship
SCOPE	• Share	• Activity of partnership represents a very small share of business for each partner	• Activity represents a modest share of business for at least one partner	• Activity covered by relationship represents significant business to both parties
	• Value-added	• Relationship covers only one or a few value-added steps (functions)	• Multiple functions, units are involved in the relationship	• Multiple functions and units are involved; partnership extends to all levels in both organizations
	• Critical activities	• Only activities which are relatively unimportant for partner's success	• Activities that are important for each partner's success are included	• Activities that are critical for each partner's success are included
INVESTMENT	• Financial	• There is low or no investment between the two parties	• May jointly own low value assets	• High value assets may be jointly owned
	• Technology	• No joint development of products/technology	• There is some joint design effort and there may be some joint R&D planning	• There is significant joint development; regular and significant joint R&D activity
	• People	• Limited personnel exchange	• Extensive exchange of personnel	• Participation on other party's board

Source: Douglas M. Lambert, Margaret A. Emmelhainz and John T. Gardner, "Developing and Implementing Supply Chain Partnerships," *The International Journal of Logistics Management*, Vol. 7, No. 2 (1996), p. 12.

Table 4-7
Action Plan Template

From the drivers for each side of the relationship an action plan needs to be developed. Action items should include a brief description (what), who from each side are responsible for the item (who), and the date when the next action is planned (when).

What	Who	When

in one relationship which was only added after a review of the drivers indicated that the marketing driver of the seller was not fully covered in the components after the first pass at setting an action plan.

For each specific managerial component, we have some additional suggestions based on our experiences:

- Planning – Participants often have difficulty with the distinction between process and relationship as the focus of planning. An example of a process focus would be the development of a method for making changes to the partner's delivery parameters, while a relationship focus would institutionalize the partnership by putting the maintenance of the relationship within the job responsibilities of a leadership level executive.
- Joint operating controls – Participants should be clear that this component refers to the operations at the interface between the firms. It is unlikely that management would allow a key value-adding step to be modified by a partner independently. It is important to give realistic examples. The distinction between suggesting changes and making changes after approval is subtle.
- Communications – The electronic component remains an important consideration, however it is becoming less of a question about whether electronic communication is used or not. The new differentiator is the types of electronic communication taking place between the organizations and the degree of tailoring of these tools to the specific relationship.
- Risk and reward sharing – When addressing this item the managers should be challenged to provide examples of what sharing will take place and how it will take place. Will there be a gain-sharing program developed? How would management in each firm react to some fairly realistic hypothetical scenarios regarding the sharing of the potential costs and benefits of jointly developed initiatives?

Table 4-8
Example of Management Components Targeting

Component		Low	Medium	High
PLANNING	• Style • Level • Content	• On ad-hoc basis • Focus on projects or tasks • **Sharing of existing plans**	• **Regularly scheduled** • **Focus is on process** • Performed jointly, eliminating conflicts in strategies	• Systematic: Both scheduled and ad hoc • Focus is on relationship • Performed jointly and at multiple levels, including top management; objective is to mesh strategies; each party participates in other's business planning
JOINT OPERATING CONTROLS	• Measurement • Ability to make changes	• **Performance measures are developed independently and results are shared** • **Parties may suggest changes to other's system**	• Measures are jointly developed and shared; focused on individual firm's performance • Parties may make changes to other's system after getting approval	• Measures are jointly developed and shared; focused on relationship and joint performance • Parties may make changes to other's system without getting approval
COMMUNICATIONS	NON-ROUTINE DAY-TO-DAY • Organization • Balance • Electronic	• Very limited, usually just critical issues at the task or project level • **Conducted on ad-hoc basis, between individuals** • **Primarily one-way** • **Use of individual system**	• **Conducted more regularly, done at multiple levels; generally open and honest** • Limited number of scheduled communications; some routinization • Two-way but unbalanced • Joint modification of individual systems	• Planned as part of the relationship; occurs at all levels; sharing of both praise and criticism; parties "speak the same language" • Systematized method of communication; may be manual or electronic; communication systems are linked • Balanced two-way communications flow • Joint development of customized electronic communications
RISK/REWARD SHARING	• Loss tolerance • Gain commitment • Commitment to fairness	• Very low tolerance for loss • Limited willingness to help the other gain • **Fairness is evaluated by transaction**	• **Some tolerance for short-term loss** • **Willingness to help the other gain** • Fairness is tracked year to year	• High tolerance for short-term loss • Desire to help other party gain • Fairness is measured over life of relationship
TRUST AND COMMITMENT	• Trust • Commitment to each other's success	• Trust is limited to belief that each partner will perform honestly and ethically • Commitment of each party is to specific transaction or project; trust must be constantly "re-earned"	• **Partner is given more trust than others, viewed as "most favored" supplier** • **Commitment is to a longer-term relationship**	• There is implicit, total trust; trust does not have to be earned • Commitment is to partner's long-term success; commitment prevails across functions and levels in both organizations
CONTRACT STYLE	• Timeframe • Coverage	• **Covers a short time frame** • **Contracts are specific in nature**	• Covers a longer time frame • Contracts are more general in nature	• Contracts are very general in nature and are evergreen, or alternatively the entire relationship is on a handshake basis • Contract does not specify duties or responsibilities; rather, it only outlines the basic philosophy guiding the relationship
SCOPE	• Share • Value-added • Critical activities	• Activity of partnership represents a very small share of business for each partner • Relationship covers only one or a few value-added steps (functions) • **Only activities which are relatively unimportant for partner's success**	• **Activity represents a modest share of business for at least one partner** • **Multiple functions, units are involved in the relationship** • Activities that are important for each partner's success are included	• Activity covered by relationship represents significant business to both parties • Multiple functions and units are involved; partnership extends to all levels in both organizations • Activities that are critical for each partner's success are included
INVESTMENT	• Financial • Technology • People	• **There is low or no investment between the two parties** • **No joint development of products/technology** • **Limited personnel exchange**	• May jointly own low value assets • There is some joint design effort and there may be some joint R&D planning • Extensive exchange of personnel	• High value assets may be jointly owned • There is significant joint development; regular and significant joint R&D activity • Participation on other party's board

Source: Douglas M. Lambert, Margaret A. Emmelhainz and John T. Gardner, "Developing and Implementing Supply Chain Partnerships," *The International Journal of Logistics Management,* Vol. 7, No. 2 (1996), p. 12.

- Trust and commitment – This should be distinguished from the mutuality construct in the facilitator portion of the model. Where mutuality is a propensity in general to care about the other side of a relationship, here it is specific to the two firms going through the session. Trust is managerially built as a spiral of commitment, performance, and communications of the trust building activities throughout the organizations. These three are repeated as the spiral raises the level of trust. Each of these three is under managerial control and should be considered.
- Contract style – Business as usual does not make it a partnership. If no supplier or no customer operates on a contract, then the absence of a contract should not be interpreted as a Type III partnership. Conversely, if the legal department requires every customer or supplier to sign a detailed contract, but the parties do not use it to manage the relationship, then the existence of the contract is not the issue either. The key is the amount of tailoring of the business relationship.
- Scope – Including more value-added steps in the relationship typically makes the bonds tighter. The key issue to be considered is what would happen if this partner disappeared. How would the loss of the partner affect the business unit or the corporation?
- Investment – As mentioned above, financial commitment only makes sense if there is a need to make an investment in order to achieve relationship drivers.

Components need to be examined three times, each with a different goal: 1) to determine the current state; 2) to determine desired state; and 3) to make sure nothing was omitted.

Wrap-up Session

A key aspect of the wrap-up session is to reinforce to the participants that the business outcomes should result directly from the drivers, which is why it is so important to articulate in detail each organization's drivers. The partnership will be viewed as a success when both parties are achieving their drivers. Therefore, during the components session, it is important to bring back the drivers and establish a specific action plan for achieving the drivers. The most common approach was to establish a set of action items with assignment of responsibility and due dates. This is needed in order to maintain the momentum gained in the meeting.

The partnership will be viewed as a success when both parties are achieving their drivers. Therefore, during the components session, it is important to bring back the drivers and establish a specific action plan for achieving the drivers.

In one partnership meeting, the participants failed to develop an action plan before ending the meeting. Their plan was to follow-up the partnership meeting with a video conference focused on developing the action plan and assigning time frames and responsibilities for achieving the drivers. The follow-up video conference failed to demonstrate the same level of focus and energy that existed during the partnership meeting. According to one of the managers, "we had to schedule an additional team building meeting in order to regain the momentum that was lost by waiting to establish an action plan." Thus, an action plan, time frames and responsibilities should be developed before the meeting ends.

The key takeaways related to the facilitation of a partnership meeting are summarized in Table 4-9, which shows the key points to remember for each of the seven stages as well as the challenges that are likely to be faced at each stage from preparation for the meeting to the wrap-up session. In addition, we have found that it is beneficial to provide all participants with an overview document that highlights the results of the partnership session. The information contained in this document serves as both a review and reinforcement of the results of the meeting and thus provides a consistent base from which to move forward with the relationship. An example of this document is provided in the Appendix of this chapter.

Table 4-9
Partnership Facilitation - Key Takeaways

Stage	Key Points	Challenges
Preparation for Meeting	- read the *Harvard Business Review* article, "We're in This Together," one more time prior to the meeting - invite appropriate participants to include multiple levels and functions - consider a pre-meeting conference call to review expectations and deal with any concerns	- scheduling difficulties
Introduction and Expectation Setting Session	- communicate that the business is not at risk - establish expectations of the process - ask each team to make a short presentation about how this relationship fits with their firm's strategy	- ensuring candid discussion
Drivers Session	- communicate the need to be selfish when establishing drivers - ensure confidentiality of session - be prepared to present ideas to the other party	- establishing solid driver metrics - explaining the customer service driver to the supplier - learning how to score the drivers
Facilitators Session	- explain how the facilitators will be jointly evaluated - ensure that all participants express their views - require that participants provide concrete examples to support their scoring	- ensuring candid discussion - establishing the need to provide examples of past behavior
Targeting Session	- explain the need to use the lowest driver score when determining the partnership type	- communicating to the parties that the goal is to identify the appropriate type of partnership, not to have the highest type (Type III)
Components Session	- connect components to drivers and prescribed level of partnership - formulate an action plan that addresses managerial components and drivers - assign timelines and responsibilities	- connecting action items to drivers - prioritizing action items - incorporating driver metrics
Wrap-up Session	- establish appropriate follow-up schedule - evaluate meeting	- maintaining momentum - ensuring the allocation of managerial resources in order to execute plans

Source: Adapted from Douglas M. Lambert, A. Michael Knemeyer and John T. Gardner, "Supply Chain Partnerships: Model Validation and Implementation," *Journal of Business Logistics*, Vol. 23, No. 2 (2004), p. 26.

Conclusions

Partnerships are an important aspect of successful business development. A well-designed facilitation process for establishing the appropriate level of partnership with key customers and suppliers has substantial benefits. The Partnership Model provides a systematic method for ensuring that business relationships are developed and managed in the most beneficial way for both firms. Users have found that the most helpful aspect of the model is not the specific scores obtained, but rather that the partnership session leads to a disclosure of the important issues. However, the Partnership Model alone is not sufficient to guarantee effective relationship management. Business will continue "as usual" unless managers are rewarded for building and maintaining effective partnerships. Top management must not only embrace partnership ideals, they must recognize and reward the necessary behavior.

In order to keep the partnership on track, there needs to be regular reporting and communication about the relationship and its progress both within each firm and across the organizations. This reporting can be done at joint team meetings, through internal newsletters, and/or managerial reports. For example, at The Coca-Cola Company, Martha Buffington, the Global SRM Program Manager, prepared and distributed a supplier relationship management newsletter that kept other employees aware of developments with key suppliers such as Cargill. How to sustain the relationship and measure performance are dealt with in the next chapter.

APPENDIX: **Partnership Meeting Report**

Meeting participants: Alpha Company and Beta Company

Desired Outcome: Conduct a partnership session to evaluate current relationship and ensure that we continuously set expectations, track progress and meet our shared goals and objectives.

Facilitators: Douglas Lambert and Michael Knemeyer

Location/Date: Columbus, Ohio on April 21 & 22, 2008

Attendees

Alpha:		
	Mike Smith	President
	Richard Johnson	Vice President
	Bob Gold	Director of Purchasing
	Paul Shay	Purchasing Manager
	Pat Dwight	Director, Marketing
	Jeff Tracki	Research Associate,
	Chris Jones	Operations Planning Manager
	Bob Blum	Director - Materials & Process Technology
	Roop Nan	Marketing Manager
	Scott Carlson	Technical Manager - Production/Manufacturing, R&D/Technology

Beta:		
	Scott Sam	Sr. Technology, Service & Development Leader
	Rob Cotter	Technology Leader
	Bernie Kuzar	Sr. Product Manager
	Paul Nevitt	Sales Director
	Kelly Nor	Customer Service Rep
	Doug Spanos	Account Executive
	Trina Pena	Sales Support Manager
	Doug Croxton	Supply Chain Planner
	Kip Toms	Sr. Market Manager
	Glenn Sander	Vice President

Session Outcome: It was decided that Alpha Company and Beta Company had the potential for a Type II partnership and a number of areas of opportunity for both companies were identified. An action plan for pursuing these opportunities is included in the next section, Summary of Meeting Results.

Summary of Meeting Results

Driver Assessment – an identification of the compelling reasons to partner

- *Alpha Driver Session* (13 total driver points):
  - Asset/Cost Efficiency (3 points plus 1 point = 4 total points)
    - Goal to reduce non-market costs by at least 3% each year (improving payment terms, VMI, consignment, inventory reduction)
    - Technical service/development shared resources at Alpha plants (identify faster running products, labeling, waste reductions)
    - Help improve internal processes (paperless, cycle time)
    - Long-term commitment for more competitive supply
    - Extend favorable pricing on new products (special pricing)
  - Customer Service (1 point)
    - Nothing directly applicable, connections with other drivers recognized
  - Marketing Advantage (3 points plus 1 point = 4 total points)
    - Share more market intelligence/knowledge/dynamics
    - Most favored nations' clause (new or existing business)
    - Sustainability objectives (joint projects, shared resources)
    - Innovation objectives (new resin within 12 months, co-innovate)
    - Exclusivity on new product development
    - Utilize three party meetings (Alpha, Beta and Strategic Customer) for product development and cost reduction
  - Profit Stability/Growth (3 points plus 1 point = 4 total points)
    - Expand price locks for less price volatility
    - 100% assurance of long-term supply
    - Help us shorten development lead time (time-to-market)
    - Develop a relationship scorecard
- *Beta Driver Session* (15 total driver points):
  - Asset/Cost Efficiency (3 points)
    - Reduction of supply chain costs / optimize working capital (e.g., need on-time payment, accurate forecasting, especially during ramp up, faster return of rail cars, self-service regarding receivables, no pre-buy, look at total value of our offering)
  - Customer Service (1 point)
    - Nothing directly applicable, connections with other drivers recognized
  - Marketing Advantage (5 points plus 1 point = 6 total points)
    - Become the development partner of choice for new projects
    - Establish timelines and milestones for all resourced projects that are mutually acceptable by all functions and levels
    - Establish a steering team that jointly manages the development and innovation process - serves as conduit to build cross-functional relationships
    - Access to new ideas on emerging trends and performance requirements
    - Enhance relationship with Alpha marketing - access to Alpha customers' current and future needs
    - Rapidly evaluate and provide meaningful feedback on new Beta technology
    - Achieve more effective project management

- Jointly promote Beta/Alpha successes - case studies - sustainability and flexible packaging – for example, Gama in Latin America
- Voice of customers on next generation resins for improved films
- Advance project opportunities:
  - Growth of core business
  - Evaluation of new opportunities
  - Evaluation of water packaging in Epsilon type packages
  - Want to be development partner of choice for next generation products
  - Profit Stability/Growth (4 points plus 1 point = 5 total points)
    - Volume growth
    - 100% of growth in new projects
    - Want opportunity to participate/evaluate core businesses when openings occur
    - Maintain our gross margin on a per pound basis or offset via volume
    - Enter into long-term commitment (3 to 5 years - full business cycle)
    - Mutually establish a formal agreement of price programs and parameters - need a signed contract
    - Better and timely understanding of Alpha priorities and strategies
    - Better understand functional scorecards
    - Definition of an ideal supplier

Facilitator Assessment (13 total facilitator points)
- Corporate compatibility (3 points) – good match in terms of culture, but differences exist in the business related items
- Management philosophy and techniques (3 points) – changes in management at Beta has caused some challenges, Alpha less cross-functional in nature and differences exist between the levels of management
- Mutuality (3 points) – good long-term view, both sides have mutual respect and there is a willingness to share as long as it is justified
- Symmetry (4 points) – similar in many ways, differences exist in the % of buy and % of sales
- Additional Factors (0 points)

Relationship scored a Type II partnership – (Medium Level Drivers – 13/15 points and Medium Level Facilitators – 13 points)

Management Component Assessment – expectation is that a majority of the components are implemented at a medium level
- Planning – currently the style of planning was regularly scheduled which is appropriate for a Type II partnership. However, the participants indicated that the focus was on projects and a sharing of existing plans, which indicates there is an opportunity for improvement. The focus should shift to process and more planning should be performed jointly, eliminating conflicts. Both sides agreed that a relationship steering committee should be formed to support improvements in this area.
- Joint operating controls – measurement and ability to make changes are currently implemented at a low level. In order to move to a medium level of implementation that is recommended for a Type II partnership, the performance measures should be jointly developed although the focus will still remain on the performance of each firm.

- Communications – non-routine and day-to-day communication currently implemented between the low and medium level – both parties agree that there is a need to communicate timely information to the other side regarding issues related to the relationship and that particular attention should be focused on enhancing communication between the organizations by scheduling regular meetings. The use of electronic communication was viewed as being implemented at a low level, but both sides are interested in exploring opportunities to enhance this type of communication by modifying individual systems to support better communication.
- Risk/Reward sharing – loss tolerance, gain commitment and commitment to fairness are currently implemented at a medium level and thus require no changes. Both sides described how these components have been demonstrated over the past few years.
- Trust and commitment – the consensus opinion was that trust and commitment were currently implemented at a low level. Extensive discussion occurred regarding the level of confidence in each other, both parties felt that particular attention should be paid to enhancing this component. While this component was seen as a challenge, both sides felt that there was an opportunity to move to the medium level based on the conversation at the meeting.
- Contract style – timeframe was implemented at a medium level and coverage at a low level – Alpha and Beta traditionally work in a contract environment, the parties are going through the process of implementing a new long-term contract with the desire to have it completed soon.
- Scope – it was agreed that the share of business represented by the relationshop was at a medium level and thus required no change. Value-added and critical activities were rated at a low level. Value-added and critical activities may change with progression to a more cross-functional perspective and by including more activities that are critically to each partner's success.
- Investment – the financial and people aspects of investment are implemented at a low level and technology is implemented at a medium level. It was agreed that there may be an opportunity to have some additional exchange of personnel to support enhancements to processes and identify cost savings opportunities.

Action Planning Items
- Establish a relationship steering committee (Richard Johnson and Paul Nevitt)
  - Determine participants and frequency of meetings
  - Establish milestones and timelines by the end of Q2
- Establish a team to focus on cost reduction initiatives (Paul Shay and Doug Spanos)
  - Supply chain analysis
  - Establish cost savings targets consistent with stated drivers for both sides regarding cost reduction targets (Alpha - 3%) and maintaining gross margins (Beta)
  - Use six sigma methodology
  - Establish framework by end of Q2
- Establish/Sign long-term contractual agreement (Bob Gold and Doug Spanos)
  - Feedback to Beta in 30 days
  - Goal to be done with legal by the end of 2008
- Establish a technical review team to improve efficiency in planning and plant operations (Scott Sam and Rob Cotter)
  - Establish plan within the next 30 days
- Establish a list of existing R&D projects (Rob Cotter and Bob Blum)
  - Innovation
  - Sustainability
  - Goal to shorten lead time
  - Complete by end of May, 2008
- Conduct customer research on next generation film (Rob Cotter and Scott Sam)
  - Initial conference call followed by a meeting in May, 2008

- Have an executive level meeting (Paul Nevitt and Richard Johnson)
    - Schedule by end of Q2
- Conduct a SKU Review (Paul Schabow and Trina Pena)
    - Examine Tier 2 supply risk for items
    - Identify capacity issues
    - Determine risk exposure for loss of supply
    - Prepare first draft within 45 days

CHAPTER 5

Sustaining the Relationship and Measuring Performance

It is easy to put the commitments on paper, but it is more difficult to put them into action.

— Judy Hollis
President, Judith L. Hollis LLC
Former Senior Vice President, Wendy's International, Inc.

Overview

In order to achieve the desired outcomes made possible through partnership, it is critical to leave the partnership session with a jointly developed implementation plan and sustainable management routines that help ensure that the agreed upon goals are achieved.

The Partnership Model should be used only with a company's most important customers and suppliers. Successful partnerships with these customers and suppliers require trust and collaboration to work on joint value creation opportunities. In order to achieve the desired outcomes made possible through partnership, it is critical to leave the partnership session with a jointly developed implementation plan and sustainable management routines that help ensure that the agreed upon goals are achieved. In this chapter, we describe a partnership maintenance framework that can be used to sustain the relationship and monitor performance over time. The framework also provides direction regarding when the partnership should be reexamined due to driver achievement and/or a significant change in the environment surrounding the relationship.

Partnership Development and Maintenance Framework

As we have described throughout this book, a partnership is a tailored business relationship based on mutual trust, openness, shared risk and shared rewards that results in business performance greater than would be achieved by two firms working together in the absence of partnership. This enhanced business performance can only be achieved if the partnership is managed appropriately within and across both organizations. Otherwise, an imbalance in the relationship will arise and one or both parties will become disenchanted with the partnership.

The Partnership Model is a tool that can be used to structure business relationships. What remains to be addressed is how to maintain these partnerships over time. While the Partnership Model provides a repeatable process for identifying the potential of a given relationship and helps calibrate the management components needed to pursue this potential, using it only requires a one and one-half day meeting. In order to sustain the momentum gained during the meeting over the days, months and years to follow, managers must continually measure progress, identify gaps in desired outcomes, address these gaps as well as monitor the relationship for potential changes that could affect the partnership and/or new action items that emerge.

Figure 5-1 contains the steps in partnership development and highlights an approach for relationship maintenance. We use this framework to show how a partnership can be implemented and institutionalized within and across organizations. There is a focus on establishing an on-going system for assessing performance that ensures that the initial action plan established during the partnership session is efficiently and effectively implemented and updated. Additionally, situations when firms should consider reexamining the partnership are described to provide guidance regarding when it is appropriate to hold another partnership meeting. Examples of company activities related to partnership maintenance are then provided. The chapter ends with conclusions concerning the importance of these maintenance activities.

Review of Partnership Development

The first four activities shown in Figure 5-1 take us up through the partnership meeting and can be viewed as the relationship development portion of the framework. Chapters 2 to 4 have provided a description of the activities managers can take to correctly structure key business relationships. Relationship development begins with the determination of which customers and suppliers are key to the organization's success now and in the future (see Chapter 2 for details). The goal is to segment customers and suppliers based on their value over time and develop product and service agreements that improve the profitability of both parties. Partnerships are developed with a small set of key customers and suppliers based on their potential for co-creation of value. Chapters 3, The Partnership Model, provided a description of a tool that can be used to structure business relationships, as well as a description of how it was developed and validated using actual business relationships. In Chapter 4, we addressed a number of implementation issues including the importance of identifying an executive sponsor, relationship manager and team members that will be charged with using this tool to structure the key relationships that have been identified through segmentation. These key individuals will also serve as participants in a meeting using the model. Chapter 4 explained how to use the Partnership Model as a systematic method for ensuring that business relationships are developed and managed in the most beneficial way for both firms. The chapter described how users have found that the most helpful aspect of using the model is not the specific scores obtained, but rather that the process leads to a disclosure of the important issues between the parties. The chapter concludes by pointing out that the Partnership Model alone is not sufficient to guarantee effective relationship management. Managers must take the information and momentum gained by using the model to help develop a plan for the partnership. This plan will help ensure that the benefits of using the model are sustainable.

Managers must take the information and momentum gained by using the model to help develop a plan for the partnership.

Achieving the targeted type of partnership is dependent on setting objectives, identifying specific initiatives, implementing the appropriate plans, and targeting the levels of management actions (the management components). The management components provide the roadmap to successfully manage the relationship in pursuit of jointly agreed upon objectives. Management should not have too many objectives at one time. Targeting three to four objectives with the

Figure 5-1
Partnership Development and Maintenance Framework

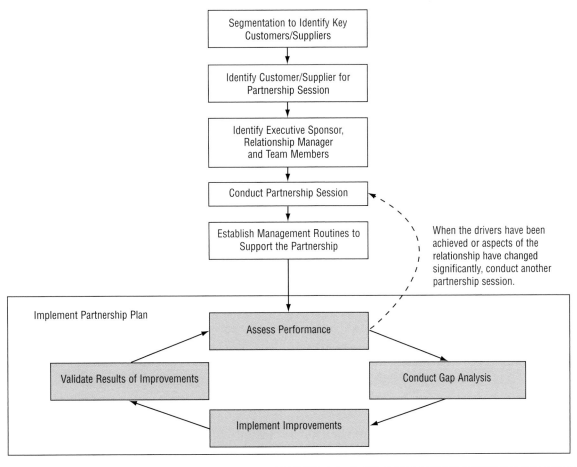

idea that as one is completed another can be started is advisable in order to maximize the likelihood of achieving the full set of objectives. It is important that some goals are achieved early on to gain traction. Reflecting on the more than 80 partnership meetings we have facilitated, one of the potential implementation problems occurs when managers pursue too many initiatives. While progress can be made on several of them, there typically is not enough focus to drive any one to a conclusion. Thus, the partnership plan must provide the needed prioritization of effort to get the partnership off to a good start.

Reflecting on the more than 80 partnership meetings we have facilitated, one of the potential implementation problems occurs when managers pursue too many initiatives.

The relationship managers for each organization must collaborate with other key members of the two organizations to develop a list of key partnership objectives. The drivers identified in the partnership meeting provide the basis for these objectives which must be clear and both organizations must agree on the measures of success. It is necessary to review the objectives carefully and ensure that the prioritized drivers established during the partnership meeting have yielded appropriate objectives. This is also an important time to jointly review the business objectives of each company and determine if any of the drivers have been missed in the development of objectives.

After the objectives are agreed upon by both organizations, the group needs to move to the development of the initiatives to achieve the stated partnership objectives. Some initiatives may rest with only one organization, but others will be the shared responsibility of both. Since both kinds of initiatives are typically necessary to achieve the overall objectives, both should be monitored jointly. Ownership needs to be established for each initiative in each organization. Many initiatives will require joint implementation teams and joint leadership. The assignment of team members is very important for the implementation of the initiatives and the achievement of the desired objectives. There should not be too much overlap in team members and leadership so that it is possible to make progress on a number of initiatives at the same time. It is also important to establish plans for each initiative that include timelines, assignment of responsibilities and success metrics (see Table 5-1). Metrics should be established for each of the initiatives. For example, it is not enough to indicate that the partners will work to reduce packaging costs. The parties must establish clear

Table 5-1
Partnership Plan Example

Driver	Objective	Initiative	Timeline	Team Leaders	Goal
Asset/Cost Efficiencies *Buyer* **Profit Stability and Growth** *Seller*	**Cost reduction while maintaining supplier margins**	Specification simplification	New functional specifications by Q2	Smith and Jones	5%/year product spend reduction
		Quality assurance alignment	New single, joint quality process by Q4	Roberts and Carlson	
		Joint forecasting	Shared forecasting by Q3	Hines and West	
Customer Service *Buyer* **Asset /Cost Efficiencies** *Seller*	**Maintain continuity of supply**	Advanced notice/early commitment by buyer	Beginning of next fiscal year	Owens and Lee	100% in stock when within 20% of forecast
		Joint forecasting	See above	Owens and Lee	
Marketing Advantage *Buyer/Seller*	**Reduction of new product development timeline**	Digital printing of packaging	Testing – by Q2, Implementation by Q4	Joyce and Meyer	Changeover for LTO (limited time offers) to three weeks
		Shared graphic systems	Six weeks to testing, Q2 to changeover	Lance and Miller	
Profit Stability and Growth *Buyer/Seller*	**Reducing variability in profit**	Joint price ceiling and floor multi-year agreement	Outline by next quarter, approval by Q2	Wells and Pryor	Limit price shocks to each party by percent TBD

metrics such as a 5% reduction of packaging costs, to ensure both sides can judge how successful the partnership has been in achieving their joint initiatives.

Establish Management Routines to Support the Partnership

It is the responsibility of relationship managers for each organization to establish management routines to ensure that the partnership initiatives are successfully completed. The management routines include:

- Ensure necessary resources are available.
- Monitor status on all initiatives.
- Communicate regularly between organizations.
- Report to executive sponsors in a timely fashion.

Commitments to providing the necessary resources to support the tailoring of the relationship are agreed to in the partnership meeting. However, often these agreements are general in nature and may require buy-in or cooperation of functional areas or individuals who were not present in the partnership meeting. Resource issues include management time, information systems modifications and potential financial commitments. An example of the need to establish the resource requirements for building partnership-sustaining routines would be the involvement of individuals from information technology (IT) in joint efforts to tailor communications across firm boundaries. IT services may be necessary in order to obtain data for reports that track progress in achieving objectives and individual initiatives. Usually, IT services are in short supply and project staffing can be a difficult issue.

The owners of each initiative should submit a joint status report to the relationship managers at least each quarter and inform them of important events as appropriate. After evaluating the reports, the relationship managers should summarize progress made on each initiative and prepare a status report for the executive sponsors who will use this information to modify priorities, eliminate barriers to implementation and allocate resources as needed.

At least once each year, the executive sponsors and relationship managers from both organizations should meet to review progress and make adjustments to priorities, if necessary. Some companies have used this meeting to conduct a modified driver session that only focuses on identifying new opportunities. Some companies hold these meetings as part of their annual planning process to allow examination of important relationships with respect to their newly developed annual operating plans. During this meeting it is important for the executive sponsors to visibly demonstrate their commitment to the relationship so that people in both organizations understand the benefits of the relationship to their company as well as the value that is being co-created. Another reason to reexamine drivers at the end of the first year is that by then all players have a much better understanding of the Partnership Model, its power and the potential of the driver session to help identify initiatives. A new look could conceivably come up with more out-of-the -box ideas that the partnership could undertake.

After the management routines have been established, the focus moves to a continuous cycle that is meant to institutionalize the partnership.

Implement Partnership Plan

After the management routines have been established, the focus moves to a continuous cycle that is meant to institutionalize the partnership. This partnership maintenance cycle is made up of four steps: 1) assess performance; 2) gap analysis;

3) implement improvements; and 4) validate (see Figure 5-1). Depending on the type of partnership that has been formed, the cycle may vary in timing. At the operational level, the relationship team might repeat the cycle every month or every quarter to ensure progress towards driver achievement.

Step 1: Assess Performance. Assessing performance must be part of the partnership maintenance cycle. To ensure sustained commitment to the partnership, it is important to track progress on the initiatives that have been jointly established. The first step in the partnership maintenance cycle is to assess if the desired outcomes are being realized. In this step, management uses various control methods to ensure the desired goals are being met. The relationship team reviews performance using the metrics that have been established during the driver session and/or during the components session. Managers assess partnership outcomes at regular intervals using the appropriate metrics. While the relationship team will determine appropriate timing for assessing performance, repeating the cycle for partnership maintenance on a monthly or quarterly basis is typical.

While the team is monitoring each initiative for progress and completion, each driver must also have its own metrics that best defines its successful achievement. The metrics must be tracked over time to ensure the driver is being achieved and that it is adding the expected value for one or both firms. For example, for a driver in the Profit Stability/Growth category the partnership team might establish profitability metrics related to the partnership. As part of the partnership maintenance cycle, the relationship managers would review overall profitability and the effects of the partnership on their profitability and compare it to projected profitability. It is critical to find metrics that give clear feedback as to whether or not the driver is being realized. If the metrics are not being achieved, then management would take action to identify the root causes of the problem and implement corrective actions as appropriate.

Step 2: Gap Analysis. The relationship teams evaluate the outcomes related to each initiative and the overall relationship and identify gaps. Depending on which results are not achieved, areas for improvement can be identified. The relationship teams identify changes that need to be made to close performance gaps. The areas where the outcomes differ the most from the desired level of performance and are viewed as important or critical to the partnership represent the first gaps that the relationship teams will want to close. However, the relationship team members should understand which areas can be influenced immediately and which ones cannot. There may be some areas where improvements can be made with relatively little effort. The relationship teams should identify the resources that are required to improve the performance related to specific initiatives and estimate how the improvements will affect the overall relationship driver goals. The following is a five-step procedure that may be used to develop an action plan to address performance shortfalls:

The relationship teams identify changes that need to be made to close performance gaps.

- List all deviations from the desired level of performance and causes of the deviations.
- Rank by criticality.
- Rank by magnitude of deviation from desired level of performance.
- Rank by ease of implementation.
- Develop an action plan with timetable and responsibilities.

It is critical that an effort be made to determine the cause of deviation. If management does not understand why or what caused the deviation, chances are very good they will not come up with the best corrective action. It may be that when management looks at the cause they will conclude that the initiative could never be achieved because of some circumstances not present or apparent when it was initially established. In any event, the corrective action has to address the reason for the deviation if it is to produce a different result.

The relationship teams must decide if changes to the activities related to individual drivers are necessary. As input for this decision, it is critical to gather input from key members in each firm to identify problems. For example, if in the Marketing Advantage driver category a goal has been established related to the introduction of a jointly developed product within a certain time frame, current performance should be examined within the product development process of the customer to ensure the appropriate level of involvement exists to support achievement of this goal. If during the partnership session the customer identified and the supplier agreed to support the goal of a jointly developed product, the relationship team is responsible for making the changes necessary to achieve the appropriate engagement to support this goal. At this stage, the relationship team may decide if specific changes need to be implemented to help achieve this driver.

Consider the following example. Two firms in the frozen food processing industry had the goal to produce new variations of frozen foods. The ingredient supplier shared six new products they expected to be on line in the next quarter, but the frozen food manufacturer could not incorporate any of the new products into a new offering. Upon examination it was determined that the depth of knowledge about the advantages and applications of the new ingredients was not sufficient to help develop consumer products using documentation alone. The gap was closed by placing a member of the supplier R&D team in the customer's lab and inviting customer developers into the supplier's lab. This was appropriate given that the relationship was a Type III partnership and the joint goals were not being met.

Step 3: Implement Improvements. At the implement improvements step, the relationship teams translate the action plan that was established in the gap analysis into actual improvements for the partnership. For example, the relationship team decided that achievement of an Asset/Cost Efficiency driver related to inventory management required the implementation of Collaborative Planning, Forecasting and Replenishment (CPFR) with the partner. Therefore, the relationship team was responsible for developing a joint implementation plan as well as determining the details of this plan.

Implementation of improvements may require action by one side of the partnership or both sides of the partnership working together. The management components addressed in the partnership session provide the management methods for effectively pursuing improvements. For example, the planning and communication management components will be particularly important for the CPFR implementation previously mentioned. It is critical for the relationship team to monitor the level of implementation for the management components to ensure they are appropriate for achieving the desired improvements in the partnership. After improvements have been implemented, validation is the next stage in the cycle.

It is critical for the relationship team to monitor the level of implementation for the management components to ensure they are appropriate for achieving the desired improvements in the partnership.

Step 4: Validate Results. In the validate results step of the cycle, it is necessary to determine if the planned improvements have been successfully implemented. In order to decide whether an improvement has been implemented successfully, several measures of success are necessary. The specific measures are different from company to company and from situation to situation but generally an improvement is fully implemented when the identified performance gaps from Step 2 are closed. Implementing an improvement may require a significant investment in management time and resources.

An important aspect of a successful improvement implementation is whether the desired partnership benefits have been achieved. For example, if Vendor Managed Inventory was implemented in order to reduce inventory levels in support of an Asset/Cost Efficiency driver, the relationship team must determine if inventory was actually reduced and by how much in order to verify that the savings exceeded the costs of implementing the program. This information must be recorded in order to better quantify the success of similar drivers in the future. It should be remembered that both parties need to benefit. After this step has been completed, a new cycle begins with an assessment of performance.

Reexamination of a Partnership

Additional decisions must be made as part of partnership maintenance efforts. For example, should changes be made in terms of team membership, do the drivers need to be reevaluated, and have there been significant changes in the environment that affect the relationship? The relationship team should address each of these questions on a regular basis to ensure appropriate activities are occurring in the partnership.

Team Membership

The relationship team should evaluate continuously their membership roster. That is, the teams must ask if they have the right people involved. It may happen that members move into new positions or leave the company. Then, new managers must fill that void on the relationship team. When new managers join the firm, management might feel they should be involved in the partnership and ask them to join the relationship team. The right people are critical for successful partnership implementation and maintenance. Depending on the type of partnership targeted, the process of bringing the new members up to speed may be quite involved.

Also if a key player changes, especially either of the relationship sponsors, it will be important to hold a joint session to explain what has happened and how the partnership will be affected by the change. Both organizations need to know that the new person is aware of and understands what the partnership is all about and where that partnership fits on the priority list. Simply telling them about it is not adequate, the members involved with the relationship need to have a deep level of understanding in order to make commitments to the joint initiatives. Both sides need to know that the commitment is there.

In addition, it is important for the relationship team to ensure that the partnership initiatives are on the member's personal objectives/scorecard within their respective organizations. In large organizations which have a reward structure/evaluation process driven by the setting of and subsequent achievement of goals, the partnership initiatives must be integrated into the individuals goals or they will not get done no matter how much support there is from the executive level.

In large organizations which have a reward structure/evaluation process driven by the setting of and subsequent achievement of goals, the partnership initiatives must be integrated into the individuals goals or they will not get done no matter how much support there is from the executive level.

Drivers

Over time, successful partnerships will achieve most of the drivers that they identified in the initial partnership meeting. The relationship team should monitor closely the overall level of driver achievement in the partnership. At some point, another partnership meeting may be needed to establish a new comprehensive set of drivers. For example, management teams from Wendy's and Tyson were evaluating their partnership at a quarterly business review two years after their initial partnership meeting and it was jointly determined that they had been successful at achieving the drivers identified at the initial meeting. The teams decided that the time had come to hold another partnership meeting. Within three months this meeting was conducted and new drivers established. The second partnership meeting also provided an opportunity to review changes in facilitators between the two companies.

Environment

It is important for the relationship team to monitor the environment surrounding the relationship and identify significant changes when they occur. For example, this could take the form of a merger, a change in senior leadership, or a change in the financial condition of one of the partners. In one case, we saw a company's partnership affected by a change in oil prices. When oil prices reached $150 per barrel, a major resin supplier (who was a partner) reduced its focus on resins and moved efforts to other products. This shift in strategy by the supplier directly changed the nature of the relationship. When changes such as this occur, it is wise to recalibrate the relationship by conducting another partnership meeting. As part of their relationship maintenance, management was able to identify the resin availability problem early and implement appropriate changes to the partnership to deal with the issue.

Partnership Maintenance in Practice

In this section, we present three examples of the implementation of a partnership plan. The first example, based on The Coca-Cola Company, shows the importance of a consistent internal and external communication structure for the partnership. The second example, based on the Colgate-Palmolive Company, highlights the importance of trust-building activities for sustaining partnership. The third example is provided by Wendy's International and it demonstrates how the maintenance cycle can lead to another partnership session.

The Coca-Cola Company

In order to keep the partnership on track, the relationship teams must perform regular reporting and communication about the relationship and its progress both within each firm and across the organizations.

Management at The Coca-Cola Company has used the Partnership Model as part of the implementation of supplier relationship management (SRM). The SRM team segmented the company's suppliers. Those identified as strategic were candidates for partnership sessions using the partnership model discussed in this book. Management developed a partnership maintenance program for key relationships where partnership meetings were conducted. In order to keep the partnership on track, the relationship teams must perform regular reporting and communication about the relationship and its progress both within each firm and across the organizations. This reporting is done at joint team meetings, through internal newsletters, and managerial reports. For example, the Global SRM Program Manager prepares and distributes an SRM newsletter that keeps other employees aware of developments with key suppliers such as Cargill. It is through these mechanisms that the relationship teams ensure progress is being made towards the jointly developed goals for the partnership and that they identify and address any potential issues that might affect the relationship. It is important to broaden the awareness and appreciation of the benefits of specific partnerships so that a broad set of managers and employees understand why some behaviors may only help a partner while not clearly helping their own company. In the context of partnership, firms will look beyond short-term self-interest to gain advantages otherwise unavailable.

In order to act on opportunities identified during a partnership meeting, it is necessary to have a partnership governance framework. At Coca-Cola this framework includes roles and responsibilities and management routines to support the partnership (see Figure 5-2). In addition, the relationship managers create a joint business plan and a quarterly report to ensure the partnership activities are focused on the highest priorities and that results are measured for joint initiatives and the partnership overall.

The governance framework for partnerships at Coca-Cola includes clear roles

The governance framework for partnerships at Coca-Cola includes clear roles and responsibilities supported by management routines.

Figure 5-2
Partnership Governance Framework

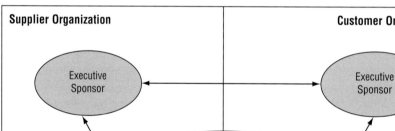

and responsibilities supported by management routines. Each partnership should have an executive sponsor and a relationship manager. The relationship manager coordinates interactions with the partner and takes on responsibility for overseeing and stewarding the success of the partnership. The partnership governance framework ensures that key customers and suppliers are managed in alignment with strategic objectives and reduces any potential conflict among corporate touch points. The result of these efforts is improved trust, leading to greater transparency and a willingness to make investments by both parties.

Colgate-Palmolive Company

Management of the Colgate-Palmolive Company used the Partnership Model as part of an initiative to increase the level of innovation with key suppliers. After conducting partnership meetings with the identified suppliers, they held quarterly business reviews to support maintenance of the relationships. Management reviewed the outcomes each quarter and assigned responsibility for results to individual managers/directors assigned to the relationships. As part of Colgate's transition to a centralized Global Procurement organization, they transferred relationship responsibility to the Global Category Team leader.

An example of the importance of having a structured partnership implementation plan was the relationship between Colgate and an abrasives supplier. Managers at both firms believed that they had established good alignment after the initial partnership meeting. However, when they met for their first quarterly business review, progress was very slow against the desired outcomes. The lesson learned was that they needed more frequent meetings particularly in the beginning of the partnership to keep focus on what they had agreed upon during the partnership session. In addition, they realized that they "bit off a bit more than they could chew and swallow" after the partnership meeting. The implementation plan allowed them to identify this issue and recalibrate their activities around a prioritized list of initiatives.

The lesson learned was that they needed more frequent meetings particularly in the beginning of the partnership to keep focus on what they had agreed upon during the partnership meeting.

Because of the sensitivity concerning the exchange of information within partnerships, the implementation plan must also consider trust issues. One relationship between Colgate and a supplier demonstrated trust issues during the partnership meeting around the need for of dedicated R&D and Sales personnel. The session did provide the opportunity for the companies to fix this issue by stipulating that Colgate would have a dedicated account representative and R&D personnel. However problems persisted in the relationship. During several of the quarterly business reviews, the supplier complained about Colgate not sharing information. Internal discussions among the members of Colgate's relationship team, which included the head of R&D, identified that many members of the Colgate side still did not trust the supplier. These issues were compounded by the fact that there was some evidence the supplier had developed an abrasive for a competitor and had not given Colgate the right of first refusal. The right of first refusal had been agreed upon during the partnership meeting. While the supplier denied that it had done this, it ultimately took a senior management face-to-face meeting between the partners to reiterate the expectations and trust requirements that had initially surfaced during the partnership meeting. After implementing this change, the relationship improved.

Wendy's International

Management at Wendy's International used the Partnership Model in December, 2003 to turn around a relationship with Tyson Foods a former poultry supplier. Both sides of the relationship had decided to no longer conduct business. Changes in Wendy's product mix strategy and the need to have another large supplier of poultry combined with Tyson's acquisition of IBP, a supplier of beef and a strong partner of Wendy's, provided a window of opportunity to use the partnership model. The session enabled management to see that they were not very far apart in their goals for the business which led to mutual understanding and commitment. After the partnership session, Wendy's increased purchases of Tyson products, the companies began to work more closely in the areas of R&D and marketing, and there was increased operational coordination. Both sides felt that the pace of improvement in their relationship was beyond what they could have reasonably expected at the end of the partnership session in December, 2003.

At a quarterly business review in the first quarter of 2006, management as part of their partnership maintenance cycle identified the need to conduct a new partnership meeting. The need for this new meeting was based on their joint appraisal that the drivers in 2003 had not only been met, they had been exceeded. For this reason, they believed that the time was right to conduct another one and one-half day partnership meeting to establish new goals for the relationship. In May, 2006, we facilitated the second partnership meeting between Wendy's and Tyson which resulted in a much more comprehensive range of new initiatives.

Conclusions

The ultimate success of partnerships depends on the implementation and maintenance of the action plan developed initially during the partnership meeting and updated as part of a regular monitoring process. Partnerships will be successful only if the implementation and maintenance efforts are effective. Institutionalizing a partnership requires rigor and discipline. Managers must be able to devote enough resources to the partnership, but they still must accomplish their day-to-day responsibilities and manage other relationships. Institutionalizing the partnership makes it sustainable and this chapter has provided a relationship maintenance framework that supports this goal.

The Partnership Model offers a systematic process for ensuring that partnerships are developed and managed in the most beneficial way for both firms. Users of the model have found that the most helpful aspect of the model is not the specific scores obtained, but rather that the process leads to a complete discussion of all important issues. However, the Partnership Model alone is not sufficient to guarantee effective relationship management. Business will continue "as usual" unless managers are provided with incentives and are rewarded for building and maintaining effective partnerships. Top management must not only embrace partnership ideals, they must also recognize and reward collaborative behavior.

The ultimate success of partnerships depends on the implementation and maintenance of the action plan developed initially during the partnership meeting and updated as part of a regular monitoring process.

Postscript: A Framework for Collaboration

The Collaboration Framework helped us refocus a relationship with a new supplier of a high potential new product where performance was not meeting the requirements of our key customers.

— Pete Koehn

Vice President, Global Operations, Imation

Overview

The Partnership Model should be used to structure relationships with key customers or suppliers where there is a history of working together and both sides view the relationship as having the potential for partnership. But, what should management do if these conditions are not met? To be successful, business-to-business relationships require that each side clarifies their expectations and mutually agree on goals for the relationship. In this chapter, we describe a framework that can be used to structure collaborative business relationships where the conditions for successfully using the partnership model have not been met. A new relationship with high potential or an important relationship to each side that is not a balanced relationship are examples where the framework for collaboration should be used.

A new relationship with high potential or an important relationship to each side that is not a balanced relationship are examples where the framework for collaboration should be used.

Introduction

The Partnership Model is a tool that can be used to structure an existing relationship between two organizations where management on both sides views the relationship as key. Because they have a history of working together, management is capable of scoring the drivers that can be addressed by the relationship. They are also able to jointly score the facilitators, that is, how well the two organizations will mesh. But this is not easily accomplished in a new business relationship where there is not a history of joint effort. Also, it may be difficult to bring the necessary levels of management together for a one and one-half day partnership meeting when one side does not view the relationship as important for corporate success as the other. However, all successful relationships require that the management team for each side clarify expectations for the relationship and then mutually set goals for the relationship. Once this has been accomplished, it is necessary to prioritize action items, assign responsibilities, establish timelines, and determine the metrics to define success. The next step is to document these action items and performance measures in a formal product and service agreement (PSA) so that the goals for the relationship are clear to all of those involved. The PSA specifies levels of performance, provides direction for joint improvement efforts and includes operational aspects of the relationships (the PSA is described in more detail in Chapter 2). Regular business reviews are required to ensure that the business goals for each side are being met. In this chapter, we describe a framework, developed based on our experience with the Partnership Model, that can be used to structure collaborative business relationships when a partnership meeting is not appropriate or feasible.

A Framework for Collaboration

Increasingly, customer relationship management (CRM) is being viewed as strategic, process-oriented, cross-functional, value-creating, and a means of achieving superior financial performance. The goal is to segment customers based on their value over time and increase customer loyalty by providing customized products and services. As part of the CRM process, customer teams tailor PSAs to meet the needs of key accounts and segments of other customers. In order for management of a company to be able to engage a customer in this manner, the customer, as part of its supplier relationship management process, needs to identify the company as a key supplier. Supplier relationship management (SRM) is the process that provides the structure for developing and maintaining relationships with suppliers.

Together, CRM and SRM provide the critical linkages throughout the supply chain. For each supplier in the supply chain, the ultimate measure of success for the CRM process is the change in profitability of an individual customer or segment of customers over time. For each customer, the most comprehensive measure of success for the SRM process is the impact that a supplier or supplier segment has on the firm's profitability. The goal is to increase the joint profitability through the co-production of value. The management team must determine which business relationships are candidates for a collaboration session.

The Collaboration Framework shown in Figure 6-1 provides a structure for developing and implementing PSAs with key customers and suppliers. The Collaboration Framework is comprised of six activities: assess drivers for each company, align expectations, develop action plans, develop product and service agreement, review performance, and periodically reexamine drivers. Assess drivers requires that each firm's representatives identify their business goals for the relationship. Align expectations involves mutually establishing goals for the relationship based on the drivers of both firms. Develop action plan includes prioritizing initiatives, assigning responsibilities, establishing time lines, and agreeing on the appropriate metrics. The product and service agreement is a written summary of the rules of engagement and the action plan. It is necessary to review performance to insure that each firm has achieved its drivers. Finally, the teams should periodically reexamine the drivers.

The Collaboration Framework is comprised of six activities: assess drivers for each company, align expectations, develop action plans, develop product and service agreement, review performance, and periodically reexamine drivers.

The Collaboration Meeting

The collaboration meeting is a one-day session in which expectations are set, action plans are developed, and responsibilities are assigned as shown in the shaded boxes in Figure 6-1. Specific details related to the meeting are described in the following sections: 1) preparation for the meeting; 2) introduction and expectation setting session; 3) drivers session; 4) alignment session; 5) action plan; and, 6) the wrap-up session. A general overview of the session is provided and where appropriate issues to consider are described.

Figure 6-1
The Collaboration Framework

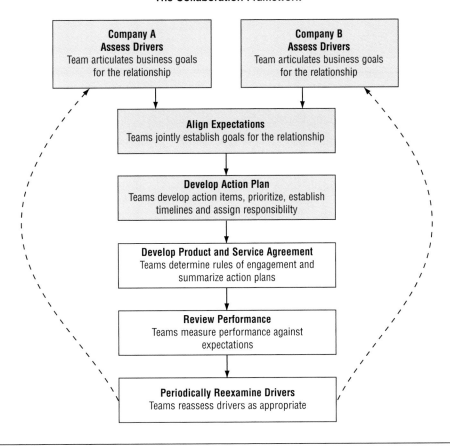

Preparation for Meeting. All parties involved, including meeting facilitators and participants, have activities that should be completed prior to the meeting. These activities include participant selection, meeting scheduling, meeting planning issues and distribution of pre-read material (*A Framework for Collaboration* included in the Resources and Tools section of this book).

> *The meetings are enhanced by the presence of individuals from multiple levels within the organizations who represent diverse functional expertise.*

The meetings are enhanced by the presence of individuals from multiple levels within the organizations who represent diverse functional expertise. The make-up of the group sends a message to those in the other firm about the importance of the relationship. It is important to involve the highest-level executives possible. The more levels of management above the people in the meeting, the more difficult it may be to achieve the commitments made. If key executives are not present and significant resource commitments are being made, then these executives should be briefed as soon as possible and their commitment obtained. The need to have the involvement of multiple levels of employees (senior vice president, vice president, directors, managers, etc.) with diverse functional expertise (sales, marketing, purchasing, logistics, operations, R&D, QA, etc.) makes scheduling difficult. A high-level executive from each organization should state that the meeting is a priority and these executives should attend the meeting.

Additional considerations when preparing for the meeting include:
- Publish a detailed agenda in order to establish expectations and maintain focus.
- Schedule meetings for one full day.
- Review the article, *A Framework for Collaboration,* in advance (this article is included in the Resources and Tools section of this book and reading it is a must for all participants).
- Make sure that meeting facilitators are conversant in the business situation.
- Provide a neutral location, spacious rooms, and proper supplies for documenting and communicating the outcomes of the meeting.
- Provide participants with materials that include and agenda, a list of participants, and copies of forms used for the session.
- Identify two individuals from outside the relationship to facilitate the meeting. The individuals serve as the meeting pace setters and must be skilled in building consensus, probing for more information, assuring closure, and reinforcing agreements on the action plan.

Introduction and Expectation Setting Session. The collaboration meeting should begin with an introduction that reinforces each side's motivations for the meeting, a review of the framework, and a discussion about the expectations for the session. For example, in one meeting, the vice president of the supplier organization stated that the motivation for using the framework was to achieve a structured and consistent approach to developing a PSA with the customer.

The collaboration meeting should begin with: an introduction that reinforces each side's motivations for the meeting, a review of the framework, and a discussion about the expectations for the session.

Drivers Assessment Session. It is important in the drivers assessment session that managers feel comfortable to express their opinions whatever they might be. This comfort level would be difficult to achieve without unbiased meeting facilitators. The drivers fall into the same four categories as the partnership model: asset/cost efficiencies, customer service, marketing advantage, and profit stability/growth.

- **Asset/Cost Efficiencies** include the potential for better utilization of assets and/or for cost reductions that might occur in areas such as transportation costs, handling costs, packaging costs, information costs, product costs, or managerial efficiencies.
- **Customer Service** improvements can lead to increased sales when customers experience benefits such as reduced inventory, improved availability (which leads to sales increases), and more timely and accurate information.
- **Marketing Advantage** can be achieved by: 1) an enhancement of an organization's marketing mix through joint programs; 2) entry into new markets; and 3) better access to technology and innovation.
- **Profit Stability/Growth** is the potential for stabilizing profit. Strengthening a relationship often leads to long-term volume commitments, reduced variability in sales, joint use of assets, and other improvements that reduce variability of profits.

The meeting facilitators should use the forms shown in Table 6-1 to ensure that each of these categories is explicitly addressed. For example, under asset/cost efficiencies, a team might specify desired savings in product costs, distribution, packaging, or information handling. For each team, the participants should identify specific bullet-point descriptions for each driver category with goals (including metrics and targets) and priorities. The meeting facilitator must encourage each team to articulate measurable goals for each driver which may be

Table 6-1
Assessment of Drivers
Drivers are business reasons for expanding the resource commitment to the relationship.
For each item, develop specific goals and identify the priority.
Priority is: 1=Critical, 2=Very Important, 3=Important.

ASSET/COST EFFICIENCY

1. What are the initiative that will reduce cost or improve asset utilization?

Driver	Goal	Priority
• Product costs savings	2% per year	1
• Distribution costs savings, handling costs savings	7% during 1st year	1
• Packaging cost savings and green initiatives	Satisfy Walmart's requirements	3
• Reduce the cash-to-cash cycle time	By 10 days	2
• No management time devoted to conference calls with key customer explaining service failures due to supplier problems	Zero within 3 months	1
• Assets utilization (reduce plant overtime due to supplier problems)	No surprise orders by quarter-end	2
• Integrate planning across business and plants (visibility of capacity available across plants)	Within 12 months	3

CUSTOMER SERVICE

2. What are the initiatives will improve customer service as measured by the customer?

Driver	Goal	Priority
• Improved on-time delivery	98.5%	1
• Better tracking of movement	Full visibility	2
• Paperless order processing	100% EDI	2
• Order accuracy	0 picking errors	1
• Improved cycle times	From 14 to 7 days	1
• Improved fill rates	From 96% to 99%	1
• Customer survey results	#1 in industry survey	2
• Improved response to inquiries	2 hours	3

MARKETING ADVANTAGE

3. What are the initiatives that will lead to marketing advantages?

Driver	Goal	Priority
• Promotion (joint advertising, sales promotion)	3 promotions/year	1
• Evaluate co-branding opportunities	Within 6 months	3
• Share market research data	1 meeting/year	3
• Product (jointly developed product innovation, branding opportunities)	7 ideas, 3 ready/year	1
• Expanded geographic coverage (buy our products in markets outside the USA)	$10,000,000 in 1st year	2
• Sell our latest technology	Within 12 months	1
• Innovation potential	2 brainstorming sessions/year	2

PROFIT STABILITY/GROWTH

4. What are the initiatives that will result in profit growth or reduced variability in profit?

Driver	Goal	Priority
• Growth	10% volume increase	1
• Cyclical leveling	1/3/5 year plan	2
• Monthly demand leveling (Eliminate end-of-quarter load)	Over next 12 months	1
• Price stability	Annual Contract	2
• Reduce sales volume fluctuation	A consistent 40% of your spend	1
• Evaluate growing/starting up in every market where you are present	1 market/year	3
• Grow share of "value added" products	20% increase	2

the toughest part of the session. It is not enough for a team to say that the company is looking for "improved asset utilization" or "product cost savings." The goals must be specific, such as improving utilization from 80% to 98% or cutting product costs by 7% per year.

Each party should independently assess the strength of their specific drivers by using the blank forms shown in Table 6-2. Table 6-1 provides examples of specific drivers. These examples are not meant to be all inclusive, but rather should be used only as a starting point. The team should develop an exhaustive list that can be summarized in a few bullet points. The participants should seek consensus for the final drivers for each of the four driver categories. Talking about differences and coming to consensus is useful and facilitates implementation later. Issues come out in the defense of specific drivers that otherwise would not emerge. There must be buy-in from the participants if the drivers are to be achieved. Further, goals must be set for each descriptor and they must be stated in terms that are measurable. For instance, under the driver Marketing Advantage, the parties must decide whether a joint advertising goal should be established. It is important that the descriptors of each driver be specified in measurable terms, such as three advertising campaigns per year, and agreed upon because the success of the relationship will be measured based upon whether the desired improvements are actually achieved. Priorities ranging from critical (1) to important (3) must be established for each goal. Unlike the Partnership Model, there is no need to score the drivers because this session is not designed to determine a partnership type but rather to develop a PSA.

Representatives of the two firms should evaluate drivers separately and the evaluation must be from a selfish perspective. It can be challenging to get suppliers to think in terms of their own self-interest particularly if the buyer initiated the meeting. Since they respond to the customer in a customer-oriented way in most discussions, taking a selfish perspective is sometimes difficult. It is important that the meeting facilitators stress this point to the participants.

Evaluation of the customer service driver often poses a problem for sellers. They want to include as a driver, customer service improvements to the customer. While these are advantages to the customer, they do not represent drivers for the seller. In order for the evaluation to be selfish on the part of the seller, only customer service improvements that can be offered to other customers should be counted. If a firm can develop a customer service delivery approach that can be offered to other accounts, then it represents a driver.

A marketing advantage that is harder to quantify in dollars is the identification of at least four new product ideas over a two-year period, one of which would reach commercialization. Only those potential drivers of profit that do not overlap with the others or do not focus on any one of the others should be included in profit stability and growth. If a customer service improvement by the seller yields lower inventories for the buyer, this is asset/cost efficiency for the buyer. If it yields better customer service to the buyer's customers, then it should be counted as a customer service improvement by the buyer. If a joint effort can level volumes, then it should be recorded in profit stability and growth.

After the group develops drivers specific to their situation, the meeting facilitator should challenge them to define measurable goals and establish priorities. There is no expectation that the drivers will be the same for each firm. Each side must identify drivers that meet its firm's needs.

Representatives of the two firms should evaluate drivers separately and the evaluation must be from a selfish perspective.

Table 6-2
Assessment of Drivers
Drivers are business reasons for expanding the resource commitment to the relationship.
For each item, develop specific goals and identify the priority.
Priority is: 1=Critical, 2=Very Important, 3=Important.

ASSET/COST EFFICIENCY

1. What are the initiative that will reduce cost or improve asset utilization?

Driver	Goal	Priority
•		
•		
•		
•		
•		
•		
•		

CUSTOMER SERVICE

2. What are the initiatives will improve customer service as measured by the customer?

Driver	Goal	Priority
•		
•		
•		
•		
•		
•		
•		
•		

MARKETING ADVANTAGE

3. What are the initiatives that will lead to marketing advantages?

Driver	Goal	Priority
•		
•		
•		
•		
•		
•		
•		
•		

PROFIT STABILITY/GROWTH

4. What are the initiatives that will result in profit growth or reduced variability in profit?

Driver	Goal	Priority
•		
•		
•		
•		
•		
•		
•		
•		

Align Expectations Session. Once each side has scored their drivers, the next step is to come together and present their drivers to each other. It is important to explain why the drivers were selected. This represents an expectations-setting session that is critical for success. One of the reasons that business relationships often yield disappointing results is unstated or unrealistic expectations on the part of one or both of the parties. The thinking behind the drivers needs to be understood by both sides of the relationship. If the representatives of the other firm indicate that they cannot or will not help achieve a particular driver, the driver should be reevaluated. If no one in the session objects to the other side's drivers, then management is obligated to help the other firm achieve its drivers.

Once each side has scored their drivers, the next step is to come together and present these drivers.

Drivers for the supplier and the buyer will rarely match by category. It is not important that the drivers match, just that both sides have compelling reasons to commit the necessary resources to achieve the drivers. If the drivers are quantified during the drivers' assessment, the evaluation of the performance over time is made much easier. An example for asset/cost efficiency is the goal of reducing product costs by 7% per year over the next three years. By knowing the exact expectation, there is more realistic buy-in and better tracking of progress.

Develop Action Plan Session. In the final session of the collaboration meeting, the mutually agreed upon drivers are prioritized and translated into an action plan. Action items should include a brief description (what), the individuals from each organization who will be responsible for achieving the driver (who) and a timeline for implementation (when) as shown in Table 6-3. For example, if the driver is to improve forecasting accuracy, the first step could be defined as "assess what the actual forecasting procedures are for each company and determine their impact on forecast accuracy."

When developing the action plan, management needs to balance workload and separate short-term opportunities from those that are longer-term. Management should avoid assigning too may items to the same people. Usually, there are action items that can be identified as quick-hits, those that can be materialized in one to three months. Other action items could be longer-term. For example, sharing actual

Table 6-3
Developing the Action Plan
From the drivers for each side of the relationship an action plan needs to be developed. Action items should include a brief description (what), who from each side are responsible for the item (who), and for when the next action is planned (when).

What	Who	When
1.		
2.		
3.		
4.		
5.		
6.		
7.		
8.		

performance measures could be a quick-hit; while the action item "Implement Collaborative, Planning, Forecasting, and Replenishment" might require some project management activities and several months to implement.

During the collaboration meeting, the following parts of the Collaboration Framework were addressed: drivers assessment, expectation alignment and action plan development. The final three parts of the framework are implemented after the meeting and they are described next.

Develop Product and Service Agreement

The PSA is a document that matches the requirements of the customer with the capabilities of the supplier. The PSA specifies levels of performance and provides direction for joint improvement efforts. The PSA documents business goals of the customer and supplier so that the expectations of each organization are realistic and understood by both sides.

It is necessary to take the action plan, responsibilities, and timelines developed during the collaboration meeting and include them in the PSA. In addition, the PSA should contain: information on key contacts for the relationship, order acceptance guidelines, credit terms, planning activities, returned products acceptance guidelines and credit rules. Also, the PSA should specify details related to achieving the agreed upon drivers such as market development funds, product introductions and asset utilization. It is also important to describe how communications will take place, for example monthly performance reviews, quarterly business reviews with the entire team and annual senior management reviews.

Review Performance

Improved service and reduced costs are potential outcomes from structuring a collaborative business relationship. While global performance outcomes such as profit enhancement and reducing the variability in profits over time, and competitive advantage outcomes such as market position, market share and knowledge gained are harder to measure, these measures should not be ignored.

Regular business reviews should be conducted so that management can determine if satisfactory progress is being made toward the goals established in the action plan and to measure the degree to which the commitments made in the product and service agreement are being fulfilled.

Regular business reviews should be conducted so that management can determine if satisfactory progress is being made toward the goals established in the action plan and to measure the degree to which the commitments made in the product and service agreement are being fulfilled. The team should review the action plan on a regular basis to determine if the action plan and PSA are adequately resourced and remain relevant.

Periodically Reexamine Drivers

It is necessary to periodically reexamine the drivers for three reasons. First, the PSAs should be updated annually which requires a new session. Second, changes in the business environment may require a reassessment of the drivers on a shorter cycle. Third, a performance review may reveal that the drivers have been achieved and it is time for another session.

Implementing the Collaboration Framework

It is appropriate to use the Collaboration Framework when either one of two conditions are met. First, the relationship is new and individuals in the two organizations do not have enough information about each other and/or their joint business opportunities to score the drivers and facilitators in a full partnership meeting, but significant potential from collaboration exists. Second, collaboration meetings are appropriate when the two organizations have significant joint business at stake but management in one or both firms do not view the relationship as strategic (top right hand quadrant of the segmentation analysis described in Chapter 2). The key points and challenges associated with the facilitation of a collaboration meeting are summarized in Table 6-4.

While use of this Collaboration Framework is appropriate for the situations described above, the framework should not be viewed as a replacement for the partnership model. As described in Chapters 3 and 4, consideration of the facilitators is important to ensure a smooth working relationship. Similarly, the evaluation of the components in the Partnership Model offers advantages with respect to using all of the available managerial tools for relationship building. Setting components at the appropriate level ensures optimal use of scarce managerial and other resources. The Partnership Model supports a depth of relationship that offers potentially greater rewards if the conditions of partnership are met. In particular, if symmetry is present and the knowledge of the joint environment is adequate, the Partnership Model is more appropriate.

Table 6-4
Implementing the Collaboration Framework – Key Points and Challenges

Stage	Key Points	Challenges
Preparation for Meeting	- read "A Collaboration Framework" prior to meeting - invite participants from multiple levels and functions	- scheduling difficulties
Introduction and Expectation Setting Session	- communicate that the business is not at risk - establish expectations of the session	- ensuring candid discussion
Assess Drivers Session	- communicate the need to be selfish when establishing drivers - ensure confidentiality of session - be prepared to present ideas to the other party	- establishing solid driver metrics - explaining the customer service driver to the supplier - learning how to score the drivers
Align Expectations Session	- explain format for session - gain agreement on drivers and set priorities	- ensuring candid discussion
Develop Action Plan Session	- connect to drivers - formulate action plan that address drivers	- connecting action plans to drivers - prioritizing action items - incorporating driver metrics
Develop Product and Service Agreement	- document action plan, responsibilities and timelines - include rules of engagement for the relationship and levels of performance - specify business goals	- producing a document - communicating PSA to all involved - updating the PSA
Review Performance	- establish appropriate follow-up schedule - establish appropriate assessment	- maintaining momentum - ensuring the allocation of managerial resources in order to execute action plans
Periodically Reexamine Drivers	- reexamine drivers annually or more frequently if the environment is volatile or if the drivers are achieved ahead of schedule	- being vigilant in terms of environmental scanning and monitoring performance

An Example of a Collaboration Meeting Using the Framework

The Collaboration Framework was used in a meeting with a company (ABC Corporation) that is based in the USA and a Chinese supplier (XYZ Company). While the organizations had a history of working together, a very successful new product line had increased the volume of business dramatically and the management of ABC Corporation believed that the potential for even greater growth was high. A primary reason for demand for ABC's new product significantly exceeding forecast was a large volume of purchases from ABC's largest customer who was becoming increasingly upset at ABC's inability to ship on time and in full. XYZ was caught by the unexpected increase in demand at a time when the economic crisis was causing its suppliers in China to not manufacture until orders were received which was increasing lead times for the components they were purchasing. Management of XYZ wanted to provide the volume now required by ABC but needed its customer's help in order to be successful.

Table 6-5 shows the top eight of 20 action items that were identified in the one-day meeting along with the person from each company who would take the lead on each action item and when the work would be completed. In the session, the XYZ Company was represented by the CEO, the Treasurer, the Business Manager responsible for the ABC business, the Director of Purchasing, the Operations Manager and the Senior Program Manager. ABC Corporation was represented by the Vice President of Operations, the Executive Director of Operations, the Lean Technologies and Supply Manager, the Director of Process Engineering & Lean Technologies, the Business Development Manager, the Director of Research and Development, and the Director of Quality. Because the key people from each organization participated in the collaboration meeting, it was possible to vent frustrations and move on to develop the plan to move the relationship forward.

Table 6-5
Action Plan for ABC Corporation and XYZ Company

From the drivers for each side of the relationship an action plan needs to be developed. Action items should include a brief description (what), who from each side are responsible for the item (who), and for when the next action is planned (when).

What	Who	When
1. ABC will look at remaining 2009 forecast and make a buy proposal for the finished products that it purchases from XYZ	Lean Technologies and Supply Manager (ABC)	6/15
2. ABC will look at remaining 2009 forecast and make a buy proposal for the two key components for those products	Lean Technologies and Supply Manager (ABC)	6/15
3. XYZ responds to 1 and 2 above	Business Manager (XYZ) responsible for the ABC business	6/22
4. XYZ determines what is needed for finished goods inventory build up	Business Development Manager (XYZ) and Director of Process Engineering & Lean Technologies (ABC)	6/8
5. ABC communicates to largest customer to confirm process acceptance	Business Development Manager (ABC)	6/15
6. Assess XYZ materials requirements planning and inventory management systems reliability. Pick randomly some items	Director of Purchasing (XYZ) and Director of Process Engineering & Lean Technologies (ABC)	6/8
7. XYZ will procure safety stock for the 64 critical items. Agree on the parameters and develop a plan for every unreliable supplier	Director of Purchasing (XYZ) and Director of Process Engineering & Lean Technologies (ABC)	6/8
8. Identify the one voice and propose a process to communicate and verify design and spec changes	Director of Research and Development (ABC)	6/15

Conclusions

The Partnership Model should be used to structure relationships with key customers or suppliers where there is a history of working together and both sides view the relationship as having the potential for partnership. The Collaboration Framework described in this chapter can be used when these conditions are not met. During the one-day collaboration meeting, managers from each organization involved in a business-to-business relationship clarify their expectations and mutually agree on goals for the relationship. In this chapter, we presented a framework that can be used to structure collaborative business relationships where the conditions for successfully using the Partnership Model have not been met: a new relationship with high potential or an important relationship to each side that is not a balanced relationship.

During the one-day collaboration meeting, managers from each organization involved in a business-to-business relationship clarify their expectations and mutually agree on goals for the relationship.

Tools and Resources

Appendix A: Partnership Model Toolkit

- Partnership Meeting Pre-read:
  "We're in this Together" – *Harvard Business Review*
- Two-page Executive Summary
- Sample Invitation E-mail
- Sample Agenda
- Partnership Meeting Overview Presentation
- Drivers Session
- Drivers Review Session
- Facilitators Session
- Targeting the Relationship Session
- Management Components Session
- Developing Action Plan
- Sustaining the Relationship

Appendix B: Collaboration Framework Toolkit

- Collaboration Meeting Pre-read:
  "A Framework for Collaboration"
- Two-page Executive Summary
- Sample Invitation E-mail
- Sample Agenda
- Collaboration Meeting Overview Presentation
- Drivers Session
- Align Expectations Session
- Action Plan Session
- Sustaining the Relationship

APPENDIX A: **Partnership Model Toolkit**

In this section of the book, we provide you with the tools and resources needed to initiate and conduct a partnership meeting in your organization. The Partnership Model Toolkit includes resources to help "sell" the benefits of the partnership meeting both within your company and to a potential partner, materials to help participants prepare for the meeting and all of the slides and handouts required to conduct a session. The first document is a reprint of the *Harvard Business Review* article "We're in This Together", which should be read by all participants prior to the meeting. Additional copies of the article can be purchased from *Harvard Business Review* (http://hbp.harvardbusiness.org/store/). This article provides a useful overview of the partnership building process. In addition, we have included a two-page summary of the Partnership Model. The third document is a sample e-mail that can be used to invite participants to the meeting. Next, we provide a sample agenda for the meeting. The final six sets of documents are slides and their associated notes to facilitate a meeting. The notes reflect our experiences from facilitation of over 80 meetings with world-class companies. These resources are available in an electronic format by completing your registration card included with the book. For more information, please visit our website at www.thepartnershipmodel.com.

Partnership Model Toolkit

Harvard Business Review

www.hbr.org

December 2004

Feeding
the Fire
...page 60

If your latest so-called supply chain partnership failed to live up to expectations, as so many do, it's probably because you never stated your expectations in the first place.

by Douglas M. Lambert and A. Michael Knemeyer

We're in This
Together

When managers from **Wendy's International** and Tyson Foods sat down together in December 2003 to craft a supply chain partnership, each side arrived at the table with misgivings. There were those on the Wendy's side who remembered all too well the disagreements they'd had with Tyson in the past. In fact, just a few years earlier, Wendy's had made a formal decision not to buy from Tyson again. On the Tyson side, some people were wary of a customer whose demands had prevented the business from meeting its profit goals.

A few things had changed in the meantime, or the companies wouldn't have been at the table at all. First, the menu at Wendy's had shifted with consumer tastes – chicken had become just as important as beef. The restaurant chain had a large-volume chicken supplier, but it wanted to find yet another. Second, Tyson had acquired leading beef supplier IBP, with which Wendy's had a strong relationship. IBP's president and COO, Richard Bond, now held the positions of president and COO of the combined organization, so Wendy's felt it had someone it could work with at Tyson.

One other thing had changed, too. The companies had a new tool, called the partnership model, to help start the relationship off on the right foot. Developed under the auspices of Ohio State University's Global Supply Chain Forum, the model incorporated lessons learned from the best partnering experiences of that group's 15 member companies. It offered a process for aligning expectations and determining the level of cooperation that would be most productive.

With this article, we put that tool in your hands. We'll explain how, over the course of a day and a half, it illuminates the drivers behind each company's desire for partnership, allows managers to examine the conditions that facilitate or

DECEMBER 2004

hamper cooperation, and specifies which activities managers in the two companies must perform, and at what level, to implement the partnership. The model – proven at Wendy's and in dozens of other partnership efforts – rapidly establishes the mutual understanding and commitment required for success and provides a structure for measuring outcomes.

No Partnership for Its Own Sake

Why do so many partnerships fail to deliver value? Often it's because they shouldn't have existed in the first place. Partnerships are costly to implement – they require extra communication, coordination, and risk sharing. They are justified only if they stand to yield substantially better results than the firms could achieve without partnering.

This point was driven home for us early in our research with the Global Supply Chain Forum when its members identified successful partnerships for study. One was an arrangement between a package delivery company and a manufacturer. The delivery company got the revenue it had been promised, and the manufacturer got the cost and service levels that had been stipulated. But it wasn't a partnership; it was a single-source contract with volume guaranteed. The point is that it's often possible to get the results you want without a partnership. If that's the case, don't create one. Just write a good contract. You simply don't have enough human resources to form tight relationships with every supplier or customer.

At Wendy's, managers distinguish between high- and low-value partnership opportunities using a two-by-two matrix with axes labeled "complexity to Wendy's" and "volume of the buy." Supplies such as drinking straws might be purchased in huge volumes, but they present no complexities in terms of taste, texture, or safety. Only if both volume and complexity are high – as with key ingredients – does Wendy's seek a partnership. Colgate-Palmolive similarly plots suppliers on a matrix according to "potential for cost reductions" and "potential for innovation" and explores partnering opportunities with those that rank high in both.

Reserving partnerships for situations where they're justified is one way to ensure they deliver value. Even then, however, they can fail if partners enter into them with

Douglas M. Lambert (lambert.119@osu.edu) holds the Raymond E. Mason Chair in Transportation and Logistics at Ohio State University's Fisher College of Business in Columbus and directs the Global Supply Chain Forum there. A. Michael Knemeyer (knemeyer.4@osu.edu) is an assistant professor of logistics at Fisher College of Business.

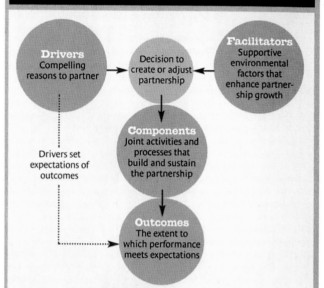

The Partnership Model

When the member companies of the Global Supply Chain Forum first convened in 1992, they agreed they needed insights on how to build effective partnerships. Research on their experiences formed the basis of a model that has been refined through dozens of partnership facilitation sessions. Managers state the drivers behind their desire to partner and examine the conditions that would facilitate cooperation. The model helps them decide on a partnership type and boost the needed managerial components. Later, if the partners aren't happy with the relationship, they determine whether drivers or facilitators have changed or components are at an appropriate level.

Diagram source: Douglas M. Lambert, Margaret A. Emmelhainz, and John T. Gardner, "So You Think You Want a Partner?" *Marketing Management,* Summer 1996.

mismatched expectations. Like the word "commitment" in a marriage, "partnership" can be interpreted quite differently by the parties involved – and both sides often are so certain that their interpretations are shared that their assumptions are never articulated or questioned.

What's needed, then, for supply chain partnerships to succeed is a way of targeting high-potential relationships and aligning expectations around them. This is what the partnership model is designed to do. It is not designed to be a supplier-selection tool. At Wendy's, for instance, the model was employed only after the company's senior vice president of supply chain management, Judy Hollis, had reduced the company's supplier base, consolidating to 225 suppliers. At that point, Wendy's could say: "Now the decision's been made. You're a supplier. Your business isn't at risk. What we're trying to do here is structure the relationship so we get the most out of it for the least amount of effort." That assurance helped people to speak more frankly about their hopes for the partnership–an absolute necessity for the partnership-building process to succeed.

A Forum for Frank Discussion

Under the model, key representatives of two potential partners come together for a day and a half to focus solely on the partnership. Little preparatory work is required of them, but the same can't be said for the meeting's organizers (usually staff people from the company that has initiated the process). The organizers face a number of important tasks before the session. First, they must find a suitable location, preferably off-site for both parties. Second, they must engage a session leader. It doesn't work to have someone who is associated with one of the companies, as we know from the experience of forum members. We recall one session in particular run by Don Jablonski of Masterfoods USA's purchasing operation. Don is an all-around good guy, is very able at running sessions, and was familiar with the model, but the supplier's people clammed up and the session went nowhere. They needed an outsider.

Third, the organizers must do some calendar juggling to ensure that the right people attend on both sides. Though there is no magic number of representatives, each team should include a broad mix of managers and individuals with functional expertise. The presence of high-level executives ensures that the work won't be second-guessed, and middle managers, operations people, and staff personnel from departments such as HR, finance, and marketing can provide valuable perspectives on the companies' expected day-to-day interactions.

Goals in the Cold Light of Day

After introductions and an overview, the morning of the first day is consumed by the "drivers session," in which each side's team considers a potential partnership in terms of "What's in it for us?" (See the sidebar "How to Commit in 28 Hours.")

The teams are separated in two rooms, and each is asked to discuss and then list the compelling reasons, from its point of view, for a partnership. It's vital that participants feel free to speak frankly about whether and how their own company could benefit from such a relationship.

What are the potential payoffs? For some teams, there aren't many. Other teams fill page after page of flip charts.

The partnership drivers fall into four categories–asset and cost efficiencies, customer service enhancements, marketing advantages, and profit growth or stability. The session leader and the provided forms ensure that each of these categories is explicitly addressed. For example, under asset and cost efficiencies, a team might specify desired savings in product costs, distribution, packaging, or information handling. The goal is for the participants to build specific bullet-point descriptions for each driver category with metrics and targets. For the session leader, whose job is to get the teams to articulate measurable goals, this may be the toughest part of the day. It isn't enough for a team to say that the company is looking for "improved asset utilization" or "product cost savings." The goals must be specific, such as improving utilization from 80% to 98% or cutting product costs by 7% per year.

Next, the teams use a five-point scale (1 being "no chance" and 5 being "certain") to rate the likelihood that the partnership will deliver the desired results in each of the four major categories. An extra point is awarded (raising the score to as high as 6) if the result would yield a sustainable competitive advantage by matching or exceeding the industry benchmark in that area. The scores are added (the highest possible score is 24) to produce a total driver score for each side.

This is the point at which the day gets interesting. The teams reassemble in one room and present their drivers and scores to each other. The rules of the game are made clear. If one side doesn't understand how the other's goals would be met, it must push for clarification. Failure to challenge a driver implies agreement and obligates the partners to cooperate on it. The drivers listed by a Wendy's supplier, for instance, included the prospect of doing more business with the Canadian subsidiary of Wendy's, Tim Hortons. The Wendy's team rejected the driver, explaining that the subsidiary's management made decisions autonomously. This is just the sort of expectation that is left unstated in most partnerships and later becomes a source of disappointment.

But expectations are adjusted upward as often as they are lowered. On several occasions, managers reacting to a drivers presentation have been pleasantly surprised to discover a shared goal that hadn't been raised earlier because both sides had assumed it wouldn't fly with the other.

The drivers session is invaluable in getting everyone's motivations onto the table and calibrating the two sides' expectations. It also offers a legitimate forum for discussing contentious issues or clearing the air on past grievances. During one Wendy's session, the discussion veered off on a very useful tangent about why the company's specifications were costly to meet. In another memorable session, we heard a manager on the buying side of a relationship say, "I feel like this is a marriage that's reached the point where you don't think I'm as beautiful as I used to be." His counterpart snapped: "Well, maybe you're not the woman I married anymore." The candor of the subsequent discussion allowed the two sides to refocus on what they could gain by working together. As Judy Hollis told us about the Wendy's-Tyson session, "What they presented to us during the sharing of drivers confirmed that we could have a deeper relationship with them. If we had seen things that were there just to please us, we wouldn't have been willing to go forward with a deeper relationship."

The Search for Compatibility

Once the two sides have reached agreement on the business results they hope to achieve, the focus shifts to the organizational environment in which the partnership would function. In a new session, the two sides jointly consider the extent to which they believe certain key factors that we call "facilitators" are in place to support the venture. The four most important are compatibility of corporate cultures, compatibility of management philosophy and techniques, a strong sense of mutuality, and symmetry between the two parties. The group, as a whole, is asked to score – again, on a five-point scale – the facilitators' perceived strengths. (This implies, of course, that the participants have a history of interaction on which to draw. If the relationship is new, managers will need to spend some time working on joint projects before they can attempt this assessment.)

For culture and for management philosophy and techniques, the point is not to look for sameness. Partners needn't have identical cultures or management approaches; some differences are benign. Instead, participants are asked to consider differences that are bound to create problems. Does one company's management push decision making down into the organization while the other's executives issue orders from on high? Is one side committed to continuous improvement and the other

How to Commit in 28 Hours

Before the Meeting
A cross-functional, multilevel team from each company is identified and commits to a meeting time. A location is found, preferably off-site for both parties.

Day One
Morning
Introductions and an Overview. The session leader explains the rationale for using the model.

Articulation of Drivers. The two teams meet separately to discuss why they are seeking a partnership and to list specific, selfish reasons in four categories: asset and cost efficiencies, customer service improvements, marketing advantages, and profit growth or stability. A score is assigned to each category, indicating the likelihood that the partnership would serve those goals.

Afternoon
Presentation of Drivers. The groups present their drivers to each other. Each team must challenge every driver it considers unsupportable or unacceptable. Failure to challenge a goal implies agreement and obligates the organization to help the potential partner achieve the aim. The teams also compare driver scores. The lower of the two becomes the driver score for the pro-

not? Are people compensated in conflicting ways? The session leader must counter the groups' natural tendency to paint too rosy a picture of how well the organizations would mesh. He or she can accomplish this by asking for an example to illustrate any cultural or management similarity participants may cite. Once the example is on the table, someone in the room will often counter it by saying, "Yeah, but they also do *this*…"

A sense of mutuality – of shared purpose and perspective – is vital. It helps the organizations move beyond a zero-sum mentality and respect the spirit of partnership, even if the earnings of one partner are under pressure. It

are present, they deepen the connection. Think of the extra closeness it must have given the McDonald's and Coke partnership in the 1990s that both companies loved to hate Pepsi (which at the time owned Kentucky Fried Chicken, Taco Bell, and Pizza Hut franchises, giving it more locations than McDonald's). Physical proximity certainly adds a dimension to the partnership Wendy's has with sauce supplier T. Marzetti. With both headquarters in Columbus, Ohio, the two companies' R&D staffs can collaborate easily. We saw the benefits of proximity, too, in 3M and Target's partnership. Twin Cities–based managers accustomed to interacting through local charities,

> Like the word "commitment" in a marriage, "partnership" can be interpreted quite differently by the parties involved.

may extend to a willingness to integrate systems or share certain financial information. Symmetry often means comparable scale, industry position, or brand image. But even if two companies are quite dissimilar in these respects, they might assign themselves a high score on symmetry if they hold equal power over each other's marketplace success – perhaps because the smaller company supplies a component that is unique, in scarce supply, or critical to the larger company's competitive advantage.

Beyond these four major facilitators, five others remain to be assessed: shared competitors, physical proximity, potential for exclusivity, prior relationship experience, and shared end users. Each can add one point to the total, for a maximum facilitator score of 25. These factors won't cripple a partnership if they are absent, but where they

arts organizations, and community-building efforts found it easy to collaborate in their work.

Assessing these issues carefully and accurately is worth the sometimes considerable effort, because the scores on facilitators and on drivers in the first session yield a prescription for partnering. The exhibit "The Propensity-to-Partner Matrix" shows how the scores indicate which type of association would be best – a Type I, II, or III partnership or simply an arm's-length relationship. The types entail varying levels of managerial complexity and resource use. In Type I, the organizations recognize each other as partners and coordinate activities and planning on a limited basis. In Type II, the companies integrate activities involving multiple divisions and functions. In Type III, they share a significant level of integration, with each viewing the

posed partnership (that's because the less motivated team is the relationship's limiting factor).
Evaluation of Facilitators. The teams jointly examine the features of the shared organizational environment that would help or hinder cooperation. Scores are assigned to four basic and five additional factors.
Prescription of Partnership Level. The group consults the propensity-to-

partner matrix, which yields a prescription based on the scores. The ideal relationship looks like a Type I, II, or III partnership or simply an arm's-length association.

Day Two
Morning
Examination of Components. The group examines the management components required for the level of

partnership prescribed by the matrix and considers to what extent those components currently exist on both sides. A plan is made for developing needed components. The plans include specific actions, responsible parties, and due dates.
Review. The drivers articulated on day one are reviewed to ensure that each has been targeted with specific action plans.

other as an extension of itself. Type III partnerships are equivalent, in alliance terminology, to strategic alliances, but we are careful to avoid such value-laden language because there should be no implication that more integration is better than less integration.

To put this in perspective, recall that Wendy's began by consolidating its buying to 225 suppliers. Of these, only the top 40 are being taken through the partnership-model process. And it appears that only a few of the partnerships will end up being Type III. Perhaps 12 or 15 will be Type II, and about 20 will be Type I. This feels like an appropriate distribution. We don't want participants aspiring to Type III partnerships. We simply want them to fit the type of relationship to the business situation and the organizational environment.

Naturally, the managers in the room do not have to simply accept the prescription. If the outcome surprises them in any way, it may well be time for a reality check. They should ask themselves: "Is it reasonable to commit the resources for this type of partnership, given what we know of our drivers and the facilitators?" If the answer is in doubt, the final session of the process, focusing on the managerial requirements of the partnership, will clarify matters.

Action Items and Time Frames

In the third session, the group reconvenes as a whole to focus on management components – the joint activities and processes required to launch and sustain the partnership. While drivers and facilitators determine which type of relationship would be best, management components are the building blocks of partnership. They include capabilities for planning, joint operating controls, communication, and risk/reward sharing. They are universal across firms and across business environments and, unlike drivers and facilitators, are under the direct control of the managers involved.

The two teams jointly develop action plans to put these components in place at a level that is appropriate for the partnership type. Participants are provided with a table of components, listed in order of importance (a portion of such a table is shown in the exhibit "Management Components for Partnerships"). The first task is for the teams to determine the degree to which the components are already in place. This is a quick process; the participants run through the components in the table, noting whether each type of activity is performed at a high, medium, or low level. Generally speaking, the components should be at a high level for Type III partnerships, a medium level for Type II, and a low level for Type I.

Under the heading of joint operating controls, for example, a Type III partnership would call for developing performance measures jointly and focusing those measures on the companies' combined performance. A Type II partnership, by contrast, would involve performance measures that focus on each company's individual performance, regardless of how well the partner performs. In a Type I partnership, the companies would not work together to develop mutually satisfactory performance measures, though they might share their results.

For each management component, the group must outline what, if anything, needs to be done to move from the

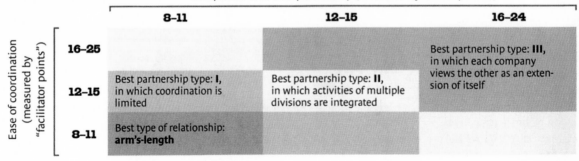

The Propensity-to-Partner Matrix

What type of partnership would be best? Once they have measured their desire to partner and determined how easily they could coordinate activities, companies considering working together can use this matrix to decide whether to form a partnership and, if so, at what level.

		Companies' desire for partnership (measured by "driver points")		
		8–11	**12–15**	**16–24**
Ease of coordination (measured by "facilitator points")	**16–25**			Best partnership type: **III**, in which each company views the other as an extension of itself
	12–15	Best partnership type: **I**, in which coordination is limited	Best partnership type: **II**, in which activities of multiple divisions are integrated	
	8–11	Best type of relationship: **arm's-length**		

Management Components for Partnerships*

Partnership Component	Low	Medium	High
Planning: > Style	> on ad hoc basis	> regularly scheduled	> systematic: both scheduled and ad hoc
> Level	> focus is on projects or tasks	> focus is on process	> focus is on relationship
> Content	> sharing of existing plans	> performed jointly, eliminating conflicts in strategies	> performed jointly and at multiple levels, including top management; each party participates in other's business planning
Joint Operating Controls: > Measurement	> performance measures are developed independently, but results might be shared	> measures are jointly developed and shared; focus is on individual firms' performance	> measures are jointly developed and shared; focus is on relationship and joint performance
> Ability to make changes	> parties may suggest changes to other's system	> parties may make changes to other's system after getting approval	> parties may make changes to other's system without getting approval
Communication: NONROUTINE	> very limited, usually just critical issues at the task or project level	> conducted more regularly, done at multiple levels; generally open and honest	> planned as part of the relationship; occurs at all levels; sharing of praise and criticism; parties "speak the same language"
DAY-TO-DAY > Organization	> conducted on ad hoc basis, between individuals	> limited number of scheduled communications; some routinization	> systematized method of communication; communication systems are linked
> Balance	> primarily one-way	> two-way but unbalanced	> balanced two-way communication flow
> Electronic	> use of individual systems	> joint modification of individual systems	> joint development of customized electronic communications
Risk/ Reward Sharing: > Loss tolerance	> very low tolerance for loss	> some tolerance for short-term loss	> high tolerance for short-term loss
> Gain commitment	> limited willingness to help the other gain	> willingness to help the other gain	> desire to help other party gain
> Commitment to fairness	> fairness is evaluated by transaction	> fairness is tracked year to year	> fairness is measured over life of relationship

*In general, Type III partnerships require high levels of most of these components, Type II partnerships require medium levels, and Type I relationships require low levels. (This is just a partial list of managerial components.)

current state to the capability level required by the partnership. Here, it is helpful to refocus on the drivers agreed to in session one and start developing action plans around each of them. It is in these action plans that the deficiencies of the current management components become apparent. It may be, for instance, that achieving a particular goal depends on systematic joint planning, but the group has just said planning is being performed at a low level. Clearly, planning must be ratcheted up.

One of the needs that became clear in the Tyson-Wendy's session was for increased communication at the upper levels. People at the operational level in the two companies were communicating regularly and effectively, but there was no parallel for that at the top. Joe Gordon, a commodity manager at Wendy's, explained why this was

and how our plants are audited [by Wendy's], rather than having [those processes] dictated to us."

The two companies' R&D and marketing groups have begun to explore new products that would allow Wendy's to expand its menu, with Tyson as a key supplier. In a recent interview, we asked the director of supply chain management for Wendy's, Tony Scherer, to recall the tense conversations of the December 2003 partnership session, and we wondered whether that history still colored the relationship. "No," he said. "I really do feel like we've dropped it now, and we can move on."

For other companies, the partnership model has paid off in different ways. Colgate-Palmolive used it to help achieve stretch financial goals with key suppliers of innovative products. TaylorMade-adidas Golf Company used

> **Expectations that are left unstated in partnerships can later become sources of disappointment.**

a problem: "All of us worker bees sometimes come to a point where we have obstacles in our day-to-day relationship, and in the past we might have given up on trying to overcome them." After an action plan was outlined for getting the top management teams together to talk, those problems became easier to address.

When the participants leave, they leave with action items, time frames for carrying them out, and a designation of responsible parties. The fact that so much is accomplished in such a brief period is a source of continued motivation. Donnie King, who heads Tyson's poultry operations, admitted that he had been skeptical going into the meeting. "You tend to believe it is going to be a process where you sit around the campfire and hold hands and sing 'Kumbaya' and nothing changes," he said. But when he left the meeting, he knew there would be change indeed.

A Versatile Tool

The current quality of interaction and cooperation between Tyson Foods and Wendy's International suggests that the partnership model is effective not only in designing new relationships but also in turning around troubled ones. Today, Wendy's buys heavily from Tyson and believes the partnership produces value similar to that of the other Wendy's key-ingredient partnerships. Richard Bond of Tyson told us: "There is a greater level of trust between the two companies. We have had a higher level of involvement in QA regulations

it to structure supplier relationships in China. At International Paper, the model helped to align expectations between two divisions that supply each other and have distinct P&Ls. And it served Cargill well when the company wanted several of its divisions, all dealing separately with Masterfoods USA, to present a more unified face to the customer. The session was unwieldy, with seven Cargill groups interacting with three Masterfoods divisions, but the give-and-take yielded a wide range of benefits, from better utilization of a Cargill cocoa plant in Brazil to more effective hedging of commodity price risk at Masterfoods.

But to focus only on these success stories is to miss much of the point of the model. Just as valuable, we would argue, are the sessions in which participants discover that their vision of partnership is not justified by the benefits it can reasonably be expected to yield. In matters of the heart, it may be better to have loved and lost, but in business relationships, it's far better to have avoided the resource sink and lingering resentments of a failed partnership. Study the relationships that have ended up as disappointments to one party or both, and you will find a common theme: mismatched and unrealistic expectations. Executives in each firm were using the same word, "partnership," but envisioning different relationships. The partnership model ensures that both parties see the opportunity wholly and only for what it is. ▽

Reprint R0412H
To order, see www.hbr.org

The Partnership Model

Douglas M. Lambert, A. Michael Knemeyer and John T. Gardner

A partnership is a <u>tailored</u> business relationship based on mutual trust, openness, shared risk and shared rewards that results in business performance greater than would be achieved by the two firms working together in the absence of partnership.

Partnerships can take multiple forms and the degree of partnership achieved can reflect tight integration across the firm boundaries, or only limited integration across the boundaries. Since partnership implementation requires potentially large managerial time commitments and often other resource commitments, the goal in building partnership is to fit the type of partnership with the business situation and the organizational environment. The types of partnership are Type I, Type II and Type III. These are called types not levels because there should be no implication that higher levels are better than lower levels. The goal should be to have the correct amount of partnering in the relationship.

Types of Relationships

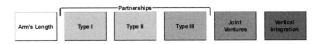

Lambert, Douglas M., Margaret A. Emmelhainz and John T. Gardner, "Building Successful Logistics Partnerships," *Journal of Business Logistics*, Vol. 20, No. 1 (1999), pp. 165-181.

The model separates the drivers of partnership, the facilitators of partnership and the components of partnership into three major areas for attention. Drivers are the compelling reasons to partner, and must be examined first when approaching a potential partner. Facilitators are characteristics of the two firms that will help or hinder the partnership development process. Components are the managerially controllable elements that can be implemented at various levels depending on the amount of partnership present. There are forms for assessing drivers and facilitators and a table of component descriptions for various levels of implementation.

Drivers

Why add managerial complexity and commit resources to a business relationship if a good, long-term contract that is well specified will do? To the degree that business as usual will not get the advantages needed, partnership may be indicated. By looking for compelling reasons to partner, the drivers of partnership, management in the two firms may find

that they both have an interest in tailoring the relationship. The model separates the drivers into four categories: asset/cost efficiencies, customer service improvements, marketing advantage, and profit stability and growth. All businesses are concerned with these four issues, and the four can capture the goals of managers for their relationships.

The Partnership Model

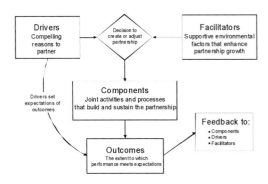

Lambert, Douglas M., Margaret A. Emmelhainz and John T. Gardner, "Building Successful Logistics Partnerships," *Journal of Business Logistics*, Vol. 20, No. 1 (1999), pp. 165-181.

Facilitators

The nature of the two firms involved in partnership implementation will determine how easy or hard it will be to tailor the relationship. If the two firms mesh easily, the managerial effort and resources devoted to putting the correct relationship in place will be lower for the same results. The elements that make partnership implementation easy or hard are called facilitators. They represent the internal environment of the partnership, those aspects of the two firms that will help or hinder partnership activities.

Management Components

While drivers and facilitators determine the potential for partnership, the management components are the building blocks of partnership. They are universal across firms and across business environments and unlike drivers and facilitators, are under the direct control of the managers involved. In other words, they are the activities that managers in the two firms actually perform to implement the partnership. There are eight components of partnership, each of which represents a managerial decision or decisions as to what and how to implement.

The Partnership Building Session Overview

The original partnership model was based on 18 relationships identified to be good partnerships by the members of The Global Supply Chain Forum. The method was case based with an interview guide to ensure uniformity. Over 60 interviews were analyzed and case studies prepared in order to build and authenticate the model. Over 80 partnership facilitations in a variety of contexts have been completed in order to improve the model and develop a clearer understanding of how to use it to facilitate the formation of partnerships. The implementation process for the model involves a number of steps:

- The correct team from each firm must be identified and committed to a meeting time. These teams should include top managers, middle managers, operations personnel and staff personnel. A broad mix both in terms of management level and functional expertise is required. As a result, scheduling can be a difficult process.

- A suitable site should be found, preferably off-site for both parties. There needs to be two meeting rooms for the first few hours since evaluating drivers should be done independently and confidentially by both buyer and seller organizations.

- At the one and one-half day meeting, there are a number of distinct sessions. The first session is for introductions and an overview of the model. Managers should share their motivation for using the model at the outset. If everyone has read a good description of the model beforehand, the overview would be brief.

- The next session is the driver evaluation session and the two teams meet separately to develop specific drivers of partnership. These sessions begin with open sharing of ideas on how the firm can benefit from more closely tailoring the business relationship. The goal is to build specific bullet point descriptions for each driver category with metrics and targets that would underlie each driver. It is important to be specific, for example, we are looking for seven percent product cost reductions per year. The focus should be "what is in it for us?" At the end of this session drivers are recorded and scored, and a means of sharing is prepared (a transparency, flip chart or PowerPoint presentation). It should be noted that in order to ensure openness and rigorous discussion during this session, there is a need for a disinterested party to facilitate the potential partner's breakout session.

- In the next session, each group presents its drivers to the other side. This represents a reality check. If either side sees a driver bullet that it feels it cannot support or requires an action that would not be possible, they must challenge that driver. Failure to challenge any of the other firm's drivers implies concurrence and carries with it the obligation of helping the potential partner achieve their drivers. This is the point at which expectations become clearer and commitment more explicit. One of the primary reasons for partnership failure is unrealistic expectations on the part of one or both parties. The driver session is all about setting realistic expectations for both firms.

- The evaluation of the facilitators comes next. This session jointly examines the shared organizational environment. The managers should have some history of operational experience on which to draw. When dealing with a new relationship, it would be best to operate for a period working on some joint projects in order to get a feel for the working environment before using the model. Facilitators are jointly scored in this session.

- Next, the propensity to partnership matrix is consulted and the prescription is shared. This serves as another reality check. Is it reasonable to commit the resources for the given type of partnership given the drivers and the facilitators? A review of the component table is appropriate here in order to clarify the managerial requirements for the various partnership types.

- The final session is the component setting process. The components are examined in two passes. First, the current levels of implementation are assessed. Second, the desired goal for each component is specified, keeping in mind the specifics of the drivers. In this process each row in the component table is examined in detail in order to translate the bullet points of the desired target component level into plans with specific actions, teams, responsible parties and delivery dates. The more specific the better. At the end of this session all of the drivers are reviewed to ensure that each is accounted for in some kind of action plan. It is critical that both firms feel that specific steps are being taken towards achieving their drivers.

Conclusions

The success of the partnership building process depends on the openness and creativity brought to the session by the participants. The process is not about whether to have a business relationship; it is about the style of the relationship. The partnership building session is only a first step in a challenging but rewarding long-term effort to tailor your business for enhanced results.

Sample Invitation E-mail

[*Insert Participant Name*],

The Partnership Model being used in our upcoming meeting is described in detail in the attached article – "We're in This Together". Please read the article carefully prior to the scheduled meeting. This pre-read is important because:

- It will provide an overview of the structure for our meeting.
- It will make the meeting much more productive.
- It will allow time for your questions about the approach to crystallize.
- It should only take about an hour.
- There is too much at stake in this relationship not to get the degree of partnership right.

As you will understand after reading the article, the goal of the upcoming meeting is not to build the strongest partnership possible but the right amount of partnership. Building excess partnership into a relationship would squander the considerable managerial resources of both firms. Rather, the goal is to build the appropriate amount of partnership into the relationship to achieve the desired results for both firms with the least amount of resources. The amount of tailoring of the relationship should match the rewards each side will reap from building a unique business relationship. Thanks again for your active participation in this important activity. Please contact me if you have any questions prior to the meeting.

Best regards,

[*Insert Meeting Sponsor Name*]

PARTNERSHIP MEETING

AGENDA

Location of Meeting

Date:
Host:

Time	Topic	Responsibility
7:45 – 8:15	Continental Breakfast	
8:15 – 9:00	Welcome, Introductions, Company Overviews & Expected Outcomes	Company Reps
9:00 – 9:45	Overview of the Model	Meeting Facilitators
9:45 – BREAK – 10:00		
10:00 – 12:30	Breakout Groups – Drivers Sessions (Each company meets separately)	ALL
12:30 – LUNCH/PHONES – 13:30		
13:30 – 15:00	Drivers Review Session	ALL
15:00 – BREAK – 15:15		
15:15 – 16:45	Facilitators Session	ALL
16:45 – 17:00	Targeting the Type of Partnership	ALL
17:00	WRAP-UP – DAY 1	Meeting Facilitators

PARTNERSHIP MEETING

AGENDA

Date:		
Host:		
Time	**Topic**	**Responsibility**
8:00 – 9:30	Management Components Session	ALL
9:30 – BREAK – 9:45		
9:45 – 11:00	Developing Action Plan	ALL
11: 00 – 11:30	Sustaining the Relationship	ALL
11:30 – 12:00	Final Meeting Wrap-Up & Forward Actions	ALL
12:00 END OF MEETING		

Building High Performance Business Relationships

Introductions

[Add name(s) of Presenters]

This session is designed to introduce the participants from both firms to one another, articulate each firm's motivation for conducting the meeting, stress the need for openness and active participation, and communicate the agenda for the session.

You may want to add presenter names and/or firm logos to the first slide in each section.

Often senior managers from each firm will provide a brief overview of their firm or unit and reassert the need to openly and actively participate in the sessions.

Review Agenda

- Meeting Facilitator(s) Introduction
- Agenda
- Electronic Device Reminder
- Pre-read

Start with an introduction of the meeting facilitator(s). This introduction should briefly highlight the facilitator's role in the process and ensure the confidentiality of all discussions during the session.

The agenda can be reviewed here.

A reminder is appropriate that commitment to the relationship may be measured by the disciplined non-use of electronic communication devices during the meeting. If managers are constantly leaving the room to make calls or check e-mail then the other party will assume that the relationship is relatively unimportant. The same comment can be made for those using electronic devices during the meeting.

An early read of how well the participants are prepared enables the facilitator to adjust his/her opening presentation as appropriate. A good place to start is by asking the group whether they have read the *Harvard Business Review* article – "We're in This Together" (included in the Resources and Tools section of the book) that describes the Partnership Model and its use by Wendy's International and Tyson Foods.

Firm A (replace with firm name) Introduction

- Who is participating in the meeting from our company
- About our company
- Explain how this meeting fits with our strategic focus

While there is no set presentation order, the firm that initiated the meeting typically presents first.

For each firm a number of introductory items are appropriate to cover:

- The names and roles of the participants should be shared. A good reinforcement is to collect a set of business cards for copying and distribution to the entire group. Also, participants may want to articulate their degree of experience with the relationship.

- The bullets provided are suggestions for the potential material to include in a brief (15 minutes) company presentation. It may or may not be appropriate to share overall strategic focus and how it fits with the relationship.

- If the relationship is a new relationship general coverage of the relevant history, structure and other demographics may be appropriate here.

Firm B (replace with firm name) Introduction

- Who is participating in the meeting from our company
- About our company
- Explain how this meeting fits with our strategic focus

While there is no set presentation order, the firm that initiated the meeting typically presents first.

For each firm a number of introductory items are appropriate to cover:

- The names and roles of the participants should be shared. A good reinforcement is to collect a set of business cards for copying and distribution to the entire group. Also, participants may want to articulate their degree of experience with the relationship.

- The bullets provided are suggestions for the potential material to include in a brief (15 minutes) company presentation. It may or may not be appropriate to share overall strategic focus and how it fits with the relationship.

- If the relationship is a new relationship general coverage of the relevant history, structure and other demographics may be appropriate here.

Building High Performance Business Relationships

Introduction to the Model

[Add name(s) of Presenters]

This session offers a complete overview of the Partnership Model. Each major portion of the model is reviewed further in subsequent sessions. It is important to verify that both teams' understand the complete model and confirm that all those involved in the session are using terms in the same way.

The session is designed to get all of the participants on the same page with respect to what partnership means and how it should be managed. While the article – "We're in This Together" was assigned as a pre-read for the meeting, it is important to ensure that all participants are familiar with the model and understand the steps in the model.

Partnership may go by other names in one or both firms, but "partnership" is the most common term used for these relationships.

In addition, this session provides information on the development and validation of the model.

Partnership - Definition

A partnership is a *tailored* business relationship based on mutual trust, openness, shared risk and shared rewards that results in business performance greater than would be achieved by two firms working together in the absence of partnership.

The Global Supply Chain Forum

Increasingly, executives in major corporations believe that partnerships are necessary for corporate success. Unfortunately, the term "partnership" while commonly used, is often misused. This definition of partnership was developed by members of The Global Supply Chain Forum. Key points in the definition are:

- It is a tailored relationship. If a firm would provide the same offering to anyone that provides it with this volume and type of business, then it is not a partnership.

- The benefits that are gained by each party must be greater than those that could be gained in the relationship without a partnership. There must be incremental benefits from the incremental closeness.

- It does not involve vertical integration or legal ownership such as a joint venture.

Types of Relationships

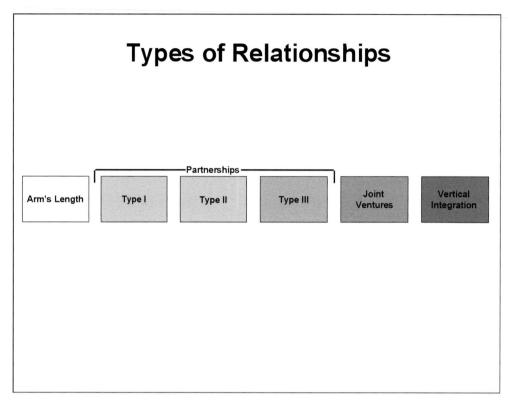

The range of possible relationships varies from arm's length to vertical integration. An arm's-length relationship is the most common type in terms of numbers. It is often characterized by a detailed contract where both parties operate according to the terms of a contract. At the other extreme is vertical integration, where one party purchases the other. Joint ventures, where the two parties' jointly own assets, are often mistakenly referred to as partnerships, but joint ownership of a business is not what most executives are referring to when they talk about a partnership. Relationships that qualify as partnerships fall between arm's length and joint ventures.

It is important to recognize that all partnerships are not the same. They can vary in the degree to which the two parties plan, communicate, measure performance, align activities, share risks and share rewards. There are three types of partnerships reflecting increased integration between the parties. More partnership is not necessarily better, implementing the right type of partnership is better.

The key is to try to obtain the type of relationship which is most appropriate given the situation. The Partnership Model helps management determine if a partnership is warranted and if so, the appropriate type of partnership.

Why Partner?

- To gain advantages of vertical integration while still maintaining organizational independence

- To take advantage of "best in class" expertise

- To achieve service improvements

- To gain operational efficiencies

- To respond to competition

One reason to partner is to gain the advantages of vertical integration without assuming the risks of ownership. For instance, Pepsi, by purchasing KFC, Pizza Hut and Taco Bell, assured distribution of its fountain drinks at these outlets. The Coca-Cola Company achieved similar results by establishing a Type III partnership with McDonald's. The decision by Pepsi to divest the restaurant chains because they diverted the attention of management away from the core business (snacks and beverages) and were a drain on profitability seems to support the strategy of Coca-Cola management to use partnership instead.

Coca-Cola chose to partner with Cargill to take advantage of Cargill's "best in class" sweetener development expertise. Rather than attempt to develop such expertise in-house, which would have required a substantial investment, Coca-Cola chose to gain access to this expertise through a partnership.

Partnerships can result in better service. Partnerships also make it possible to gain operational efficiencies as a result of process improvements made possible by the trust and information sharing that results from partnership.

Partnership Strategy

- Partnerships are costly to implement

- Not all relationships should be partnerships

- Partnership strategy should be driven by overall corporate strategy

- The Partnership Model developed by The Global Supply Chain Forum is a tool for developing and managing partnerships

While partnerships are generally viewed as a positive thing, they are costly in terms of the management time involved and for this reason, not every relationship should be a partnership.

Developing and maintaining a partnership requires time, effort, and resources from both parties. There are not enough management resources to have a partnership with every customer or supplier. Most relationships should be managed as arm's-length relationships. Only those relationships where the benefits of forming a closer relationship exceed the costs of doing so should be developed into a partnership.

Corporate strategy should drive partnership strategy. For example, it is far more important for Wendy's to have a partnership relationship with the supplier of a key raw material such as beef or chicken than it is to have a partnership with the supplier of straws or napkins.

The Partnership Model helps managers to determine which relationships should be partnerships and for each partnership, the appropriate amount of integration needed to achieve high performance.

Development of the Model

- Case approach
- Focused on members of The Global Supply Chain Forum
- Wide range of channel relationships
  - Retailer-Manufacturer
  - Service Provider-Manufacturer
  - Supplier-Customer
  - Carrier-Shipper

The Partnership Model is based on a study of 18 relationships identified by members of The Global Supply Chain Forum as good partnerships from which we could learn. The goal was to understand what made these relationships successful so that the member firms could use this information to develop more successful partnerships. Members indicated that most relationships that their firms entered into that were called partnerships, were ultimately disappointments to one or both parties involved.

Relationship Cases

- **AT&T Network Systems and Panalpina** for freight forwarding services of telecommunications equipment in the South American market.

- **UPS and a manufacturer** for national distribution of industrial products.

- **McDonald's and Martin-Brower** for the distribution of products and supplies to franchisees and company stores.

- **McDonald's and OSI** for the supply of hamburger patties to distributors.

- **McDonald's and Coca-Cola** for the supply of beverages to McDonald's restaurants.

- **Xerox and Ryder** for the delivery, installation, and removal of copiers.

- **Xerox and Ryder** for inbound transportation services to Xerox's manufacturing locations.

- **Whirlpool and ERX** for the warehousing and distribution of Whirlpool appliances in six of eight Quality Express locations.

- **Whirlpool and KP Logistics** for the warehousing and distribution of Whirlpool appliances in one of eight Quality Express locations.

- **Whirlpool and TRMTI (Leaseway)** for the warehousing and distribution of Whirlpool appliances to dealers in one of eight Quality Express locations.

- **3M and Yellow Freight** for LTL outbound transportation services.

- **Target and 3M**- seven distinct relationships involving the two corporations, and six 3M divisions that sell to six Target departments.

- **Goodyear and Yellow Freight** for the shipment of tires.

- **Goodyear and Sea-Land Services** for ocean carriage.

- **Texas Instruments and Photronics** for the supply of a critical component.

- **CSX and Allied Signal** for logistics services.

These are the business relationships that served as the basis for developing the model. All of these relationships were identified as good "partnerships". The cases represent a wide variety of settings. Some were new relationships, some were long-term relationships. In-depth study revealed that some were not partnerships and those that were partnerships were not the same. The cases developed for each relationship and the literature led to the development of the Partnership Model. The model has been validated in more than 80 partnership meetings with world-class organizations.

The Partnership Model

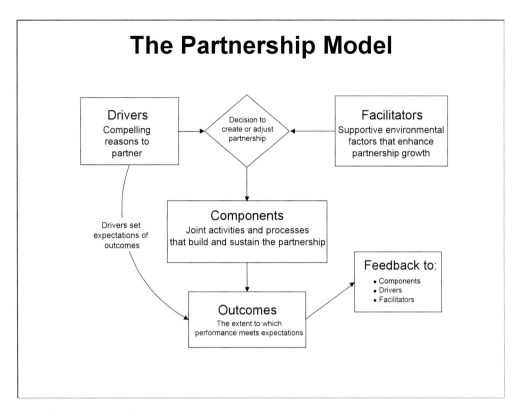

The Partnership Model should be used only after a decision has been made to do business with the potential partner. The purpose of this model is <u>not</u> to determine if you are going to do business with someone, but rather <u>how</u> you will do business together.

The main elements of the model are drivers, facilitators, components and outcomes.

- Drivers are the potential benefits which management in both of the firms expect to achieve by strengthening the relationship. Management in each organization must anticipate significant benefits in order to invest the time and effort needed to make a partnership work.

- Facilitators are the internal and external environmental conditions which can enhance the development and growth of the partnership.

- Drivers and facilitators are used to identify the potential for partnership.

- Components are the activities that individuals in the two firms do to implement the partnership.

- Outcomes reflect the results achieved by each of the firms and the extent to which each has achieved its drivers.

- The drivers and facilitators should be reassessed whenever a major change occurs at either firm or in the business environment.

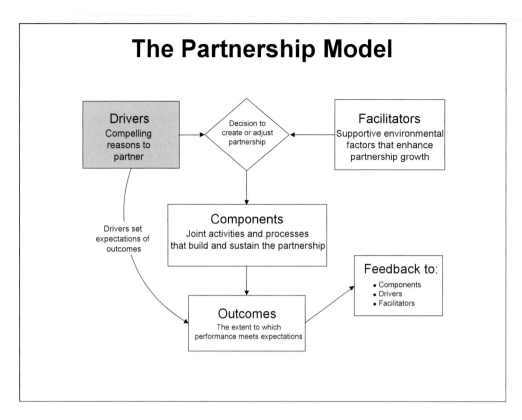

The Partnership Model

Drivers
Compelling reasons to partner

Decision to create or adjust partnership

Facilitators
Supportive environmental factors that enhance partnership growth

Drivers set expectations of outcomes

Components
Joint activities and processes that build and sustain the partnership

Feedback to:
• Components
• Drivers
• Facilitators

Outcomes
The extent to which performance meets expectations

Over the course of this meeting, each box of the Partnership Model will be covered in detail. Drivers and facilitators combine to determine whether to partner and if so, how much partnership to build into a relationship.

This session deals with the drivers of partnership and how to assess them.

Drivers must be analyzed separately by each firm since the benefits are company specific.

There are slides in this toolkit to address each of the boxes in the model, including those activities that take place after the partnership meeting. It is important to clearly set expectations as to what will be covered in the meeting and what will be done after the meeting.

Partnership Drivers

- Compelling reasons to partner

- Expected benefits from expanding a relationship
  - Improvement in asset/cost efficiencies
  - Improved customer service
  - Enhanced marketing advantage
  - Profit growth/stability

- The stronger the drivers, the more chance of a successful partnership

Drivers are the compelling reasons why management would enter into a partnership. Each party must reasonably expect to gain significant benefits from developing a closer relationship with the potential partner.

Drivers fall into one of four categories:
- Improvements in costs or asset utilization - For instance Wendy's, developed a partnership with an international forwarder to reduce its cost of entry into new Latin America markets.

- Improved customer service - By developing a partnership with a third-party logistics provider, Whirlpool was able to gain substantial improvements in customer service, raising its on-time performance from about 85% to 99%.

- Enhanced marketing advantage - McDonald's and Coca-Cola, through their partnership, jointly developed promotions and products (such as Happy Meal promotions), which provided an advantage to each company.

- Profit growth/stability – Through a partnership with Tyson, Wendy's was able to reduce the volatility of chicken prices thereby reducing variability in their profitability.

In general, the more and the stronger the drivers for both parties, the more likely a partnership will succeed.

Assessment of Drivers

Drivers are strategic factors which result in a competitive advantage and which help to determine the appropriate level of a business relationship. For each driver, circle the boxed number which reflects the probability of your organization **realistically** achieving a benefit **through forming a tighter relationship.**

			Probability		
	No Chance				Certain
ASSET/COST EFFICIENCY	0%	25%	50%	75%	100%
1. What is the probability that this relationship will substantially reduce channel costs or improve asset utilization?	1	2	3	4	5

-product costs savings
-distribution costs savings, handling costs savings
-packaging costs savings, information handling costs savings
-managerial efficiencies
-assets to the relationship

If you rated efficiencies in the shaded area and if the advantage is either a sustainable competitive advantage or it allows your firm to match benchmark standards in your industry, circle the 1 to the right.   [1]

Example: Wendy's lowered channel costs by partnering with a distributor

The first driver category is Asset/Cost Efficiencies. Independently, managers in each of the organizations should rate the probability that a partnership will provide their firm with an improvement in asset/cost efficiencies. Examples of these improvements include such things as product cost savings as a result of sharing forecasts, improved plant utilization as a result of improved communications, or reduced R&D expenses as a result of joint innovation efforts.

The bullet points in the slide are simply given as examples and must be replaced with company specific drivers which will ultimately be scored. The managers must identify the categories as well as quantifiable measures of performance. It is very important that the measures used be as specific as possible because these measures will be used to establish metrics for the measurement of outcomes. (For instance, a 5% reduction in product costs attributable to shared information).

The potential for competitive advantage is then determined to obtain the total score for this driver.

Assessment of Drivers

Drivers are strategic factors which result in a competitive advantage and which help to determine the appropriate level of a business relationship. For each driver, circle the boxed number which reflects the probability of your organization **realistically** achieving a benefit **through forming a tighter relationship.**

	Probability				
	No Chance				Certain
ASSET/COST EFFICIENCY	0%	25%	50%	75%	100%
1. What is the probability that this relationship will substantially reduce channel costs or improve asset utilization?	1	2	3	4	5

- _____
- _____
- _____
- _____
- _____
- _____
- _____

If you rated efficiencies in the shaded area and if the advantage is either a sustainable competitive advantage or it allows your firm to match benchmark standards in your industry, circle the 1 to the right.

	1

The meeting facilitators must work with each group to brainstorm the individual driver bullet points and then prioritize the items for inclusion on the blank driver forms provided to the participants.

Assessment of Drivers

Drivers are strategic factors which result in a competitive advantage and which help to determine the appropriate level of a business relationship. For each driver, circle the boxed number which reflects the probability of your organization **realistically** achieving a benefit **through forming a tighter relationship**.

	Probability				
CUSTOMER SERVICE	No Chance 0%	25%	50%	75%	Certain 100%
2. What is the probability that this relationship will substantially improve the customer service level as measured by the customer?	1	2	3	4	5

-improved on-time delivery
-better tracking of movement
-paperless order processing
-accurate order deliveries
-improved cycle times
-improved fill rates
-customer survey results
-process improvements

If you rated customer service in the shaded area and if the advantage is either a sustainable competitive advantage or if it allows your firm to match benchmark standards in your industry, circle the 1 to the right.   1

Example: Whirlpool created Quality Express, a Type III partnership, with a joint venture between a transportation company and a warehouse company to improve service.

Another driver category is Customer Service. For instance, when Whirlpool instituted its Quality Express program, it did so primarily to gain service improvements. Prior to the partnership, Whirlpool's service was considerably lower than that of competitors. The formation of a partnership with ERX raised Whirlpool's on-time delivery rate from less than 80% to over 99% in four months.

Ways in which a service improvement could be obtained through a partnership include better tracking of information and movement, improved cycle times and improved product availability.

Again, each party must specifically identify the type of service improvement expected and the level of service enhancement. (For instance, we expect a 10% improvement in delivery times). As with the other drivers, a determination must be made whether the service improvement will provide a competitive advantage.

It is unlikely that a seller would have an extensive list for this category, since improving this customer's customer service metrics is a benefit for the customer, not the seller. Managers for the seller organization may believe they can provide better customer service to other customers through a partnership with this customer by improving internal customer service delivery systems.

Assessment of Drivers

Drivers are strategic factors which result in a competitive advantage and which help to determine the appropriate level of a business relationship. For each driver, circle the boxed number which reflects the probability of your organization **realistically** achieving a benefit **through forming a tighter relationship.**

				Probability		
	No Chance					Certain
MARKETING ADVANTAGE	0%	25%	50%	75%		100%
3. What is the probability that this relationship will lead to substantial marketing advantages?	1	2	3	4		5

-new market entry
-promotion (joint advertising, sales promotion)
-price (reduced price advantage)
-product (jointly developed product innovation, branding opportunities)
-place (expanded geographic coverage, market saturation)
-access to technology
-innovation potential

If you rated marketing advantage in the shaded area and if the advantage is either a sustainable competitive advantage or if it allows your firm to match benchmark standards in your industry, circle the 1 to the right. |1|

Example: Target partnered with 3M to get special packaging and promotional support

Just as a reminder, it is unlikely that each partner will have the same drivers. The important thing is that both have substantial drivers.

The next driver category is Marketing Advantage. Improvements in marketing strategy and elements of the marketing mix may also result from a partnership. For instance, when Target partnered with 3M, they were able to obtain exclusive packaging and promotion arrangements.
Often one partner can aid the other with entry into a new market. For instance, Coca-Cola was of great help to McDonald's when it was starting up operations in the former Soviet Union.

McDonald's and Coca-Cola also use their partnership as a basis for developing joint promotions.

Each party must assess the potential for a marketing advantage, identify the specific benefit expected, and determine if it will provide a competitive advantage.

Assessment of Drivers

Drivers are strategic factors which result in a competitive advantage and which help to determine the appropriate level of a business relationship. For each driver, circle the boxed number which reflects the probability of your organization **realistically** achieving a benefit **through forming a tighter relationship.**

			Probability		
	No Chance				Certain
PROFIT STABILITY/GROWTH	0%	25%	50%	75%	100%
4. What is the probability that this relationship will result in profit growth or reduced variability in profit?	1	2	3	4	5

-growth
-cyclical leveling
-seasonal leveling
-market share stability
-sales volume
-assurance of supply

If you rated profit stability/growth in the shaded area and if the advantage is either a sustainable competitive advantage or if it allows your firm to match benchmark standards in your industry, circle the 1 to the right. [1]

Example: Long-term volume commitments are common in partnerships

The last driver category is Profit Stability/Growth. In many partnerships, a long-term volume commitment is common. While a volume commitment by itself does not indicate a partnership, having a partner who guarantees a certain level of volume can be a major benefit.

As with the other drivers, it is unlikely that both parties would identify this as a driver. Often it is the case that one party is looking for profit stability/growth while the other is looking for improved service and both are looking for marketing improvements and asset/cost efficiencies.

ASSESSMENT OF DRIVERS: SUMMARY SHEET

**Use totals from previous four pages of drivers score sheets
and transfer to this summary sheet.**

DRIVER	SCORE
1. Asset/Cost Efficiency	
2. Customer Service	
3. Marketing Advantage	
4. Profit Stability/Growth	
Total Driver Score	

Once each of the drivers have been scored, the summary sheet above should be completed in order to determine each firm's total driver scores. These scores will be used during the Targeting the Type of Partnership session.

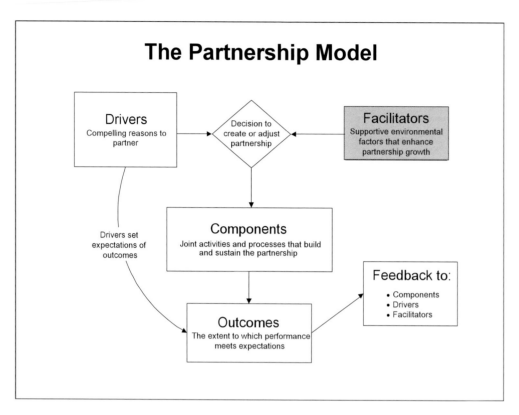

The Partnership Model

- Drivers
  Compelling reasons to partner
- Decision to create or adjust partnership
- Facilitators
  Supportive environmental factors that enhance partnership growth
- Drivers set expectations of outcomes
- Components
  Joint activities and processes that build and sustain the partnership
- Feedback to:
  - Components
  - Drivers
  - Facilitators
- Outcomes
  The extent to which performance meets expectations

After each organization has presented its drivers to the other side, the facilitators must be evaluated jointly. Facilitators combined with drivers determine if a partnership is appropriate and if so the most appropriate type of partnership. If the drivers are strong and the two organizations score facilitators high, then a strong Type III partnership would be appropriate.

Partnership Facilitators

- Factors which increase the likelihood of partnership success

- Favorable environmental conditions

- Facilitators possible in all relationships:

  - Corporate compatibility

  - Compatible management philosophy and techniques

  - A strong perspective of mutuality

  - Symmetry between the two parties

Drivers by themselves do not ensure partnership success. The business environment also must be supportive. Facilitators are the environmental factors which enhance the chance that the partnership will be a success.

There are four facilitators that apply to all relationships:

- Compatibility of corporate cultures. This includes basic values and beliefs. For instance, both Coca-Cola and McDonald's had a strong sense of community. It is not important that the cultures be exactly the same, but they should not clash.

- Similar management styles and philosophies are also important. For instance, a partnership would be more difficult between a firm with a military style command and control type of organization with many layers and a lean organization where lower level employees are empowered to make decisions.

- Mutuality refers to the ability to engage in two-sided thinking. Parties that can easily put themselves in "the other person's shoes" are more likely to be good partners than those that find it hard to do two-sided thinking.

- Symmetry. Partnerships seem to work the best where the two parties are similar in size, or market position. The goal is not to have a junior partner.

Assessment of Facilitators

Facilitators are factors which provide a supportive environment for the growth and maintenance of a partnership. For each facilitator, indicate the probability of it being a factor in this relationship, by circling one of the boxed numbers

	No Chance		Probability		Certain
	0%	25%	50%	75%	100%
CORPORATE COMPATIBILITY					
1. What is the probability that the two organizations will mesh smoothly in terms of:	1	2	3	4	5

(a) CULTURE?
   -Both firms place a value on keeping commitments
   -Constancy of purpose
   -Employees viewed as long - term assets
   -External stakeholders considered important
(b) BUSINESS?
   -Strategic plans and objectives consistent
   -Commitment to partnership ideas
   -Willingness to change

Example: Differences between the cultures and business objectives of a
public and private firm may affect partnership formation.

This is a sample facilitator worksheet that would be used during the session. Unlike the drivers session assessment, there is no need to rework the bullet points. Participants should use the bullet points provided as the basis for the discussion. In the case of corporate compatibility, the parties should jointly discuss their corporate cultures and business practices and agree on the probability that the firms will mesh smoothly.

It will be extremely difficult to evaluate the first three facilitators without some experience working together. Even then, examples should be elicited to support any claims made as the discussion unfolds.

Assessment of Facilitators

Facilitators are factors which provide a supportive environment for the growth and maintenance of a partnership. For each facilitator, indicate the probability of it being a factor in this relationship, by circling one of the boxed numbers

		Probability			
	No Chance				Certain
MANAGEMENT PHILOSOPHY AND TECHNIQUES	0%	25%	50%	75%	100%
2. What is the probability that the management philosophy and techniques of the two companies will match smoothly? -Organizational structure -Commitment to continuous improvement -Degree of top management support -Types of motivation used -Importance of teamwork -Attitudes toward "personnel churning" -Degree of employee empowerment	1	2	3	4	5

Example: McDonald's and Coca-Cola share similar operating methods and values

Managerial philosophy and techniques refer to business practices at the operational level. Even with similar cultures, it is possible that day-to-day management techniques and methods may vary significantly across firms.

Management in the two firms must analyze such things as the level of empowerment granted to employees and decision making techniques. For instance, it is unlikely that a firm which uses a consensus-based decision making process would feel comfortable partnering with a firm which uses a "top-down" approach to making decisions.

Another aspect of management philosophy is the use of continuous improvement. Is it used in both firms, and if so, is it applied in the same way in both firms?

If managers are frequently reassigned in an organization then a long-term partnership focus is more difficult.

As with corporate culture, the two firms must jointly agree on the probability that their management systems will mesh smoothly.

Assessment of Facilitators

Facilitators are factors which provide a supportive environment for the growth and maintenance of a partnership. For each facilitator, indicate the probability of it being a factor in this relationship, by circling one of the boxed numbers

	Probability				
	No Chance				Certain
MUTUALITY	0%	25%	50%	75%	100%
3. What is the probability both parties have the skills and predisposition needed for mutual relationship building?	1	2	3	4	5

Management skilled at:
   -two-sided thinking and action
   -taking the perspective of the other company
   -expressing goals and sharing expectations
   -taking a longer term view
   -mutual respect
Management willing to:
   -share financial information
   -integrate systems

Example: "Through the process it felt like there was a genuine desire to do something that was good for both of us."

Tyson representative

"A partnership must benefit both sides."

Wendy's representative

The third facilitator is mutuality, which is the ability to "put yourself in the other party's shoes". This is usually evidenced by the willingness to develop joint goals, to share sensitive information, and to try to see things from your partner's perspective.

A firm with managers who believe that it is generally "every one for themselves" is unlikely to be a good partner. On the other hand, a firm with managers who regularly search for a "win-win" solution to problems will most likely be an excellent partner.

In the partnership between Wendy's International and Tyson Foods, both sides were willing to look at things from the perspective of the other, and to take actions which helped the partner. This level of mutuality enhances the chances for partnership success.

Assessment of Facilitators

Facilitators are factors which provide a supportive environment for the growth and maintenance of a partnership. For each facilitator, indicate the probability of it being a factor in this relationship, by circling one of the boxed numbers

	Probability				
	No Chance				Certain
SYMMETRY	0%	25%	50%	75%	100%
4. What is the probability that the parties are similar on the following important factors that will affect the success of the relationship:	1	2	3	4	5

-Relative size in terms of sales
-Relative market share in their respective industries
-Financial strength
-Productivity
-Brand image/reputation
-Technological sophistication

Example: McDonald's and Coca-Cola are each the number one firm in their respective industries; McDonald's is Coca-Cola's largest customer and Coca-Cola is McDonald's largest supplier; both are franchise organizations with global operations. In short, there are many aspects of symmetry between McDonald's and Coca-Cola.

The last of the four primary facilitators is symmetry. This relates to how "demographically" similar the two parties are. Symmetry can be measured in a number of ways:

- Size - similar in sales volume and assets
- Market share - for instance, both are number one in their industries
- Brand image - both are internationally recognized
- Importance - each is critical in some way to the other's success

In a partnership between Texas Instruments and one of its suppliers, there was a significant difference in size of the two companies. However, Texas Instruments was the supplier's largest customer, and the supplier provided the vast majority of Texas Instruments supply of a critical raw material, resulting in a similar level of dependence.

McDonald's and Coca-Cola both have strong brand images, they are leaders in their industries, and McDonald's is the largest customer of Coca-Cola and Coca-Cola the largest supplier to McDonald's.

Partnership Facilitators

- Additional facilitators which may be present and which strengthen the likelihood of success:
    - Shared competitors
    - Physical proximity
    - Potential for exclusivity
    - Prior relationship experience
    - Shared end users
- The more facilitators, the better the chance of success

In addition to the facilitators which are potentially present in every relationship, there are five facilitators that, while not possible in every relationship, will strengthen the relationship when they are present. For instance, if the two firms share a competitor (as McDonald's and Coca-Cola did when PepsiCo owned KFC, Taco Bell and Pizza Hut) this makes it more likely that the partnership will succeed.

Likewise, if top decision makers, as well as day-to-day managers, are located close to each other, there are more opportunities for informal meetings and events which will strengthen the relationship. R&D personnel from Wendy's and Marzetti find it easy to closely work together because both firms are located in the Columbus, Ohio area.

A question often asked is, "does the relationship have to be monogamous?" The relationship is likely to be stronger if it is exclusive. While this is not practical in many business relationships, a willingness to develop exclusivity enhances the chance of partnership success.

Having had a successful relationship in the past and sharing important end users also enhance the potential for a partnership.

As with drivers, the more and the stronger the facilitators, the more likely it is that the partnership will succeed.

Assessment of Facilitators

ADDITIONAL FACTORS (BONUS POINTS)

	Yes	No
5. Do you have shared competitors which will tend to unite your efforts?	1	0
6. Are the key players in the two parties in close physical proximity to each other?	1	0
7. Is there a willingness to deal exclusively with your partner?	1	0
8. Do both parties have prior experience with successful partnerships?	1	0
9. Do both parties share a high value end user?	1	0

The first four facilitators, which have the potential of being present in every relationship, are scored on the basis of the probability that they will exist in the partnership under consideration. In addition there are five factors which are situation-specific. If these facilitators are not present, it will not necessarily hurt the relationship, but their presence will strengthen the relationship. Each of these facilitators is scored: yes or no.

- Shared competitors - While relatively rare, having the same competitor provides a strong foundation for a partnership. (For instance, McDonald's and Coca-Cola both viewed Pepsi as a competitor when Pepsi owned restaurants.)
- Close proximity - If key players from the two firms are physically close, this provides additional opportunities for joint activities.
- Exclusivity - If managers are willing to look for ways to establish an "exclusive" relationship, this will strengthen the partnership. This can be through a separate division (McDonald's/Coca-Cola) or through specialized promotions and packaging (Target/3M).
- Prior history - A firm with a history of successful partnership is generally more likely to succeed in future partnerships than one with a history of failure or no experience at all with integrated relationship.
- Shared end user - In a few cases, both parties serve the same end user. Having a common customer base strengthens the relationship.

ASSESSMENT OF FACILITATORS: SUMMARY SHEET

FACILITATOR	SCORE
Corporate Compatibility	
Management Philosophy and Techniques	
Mutuality	
Symmetry	
Bonus points (zero or one)	
Shared Competitors	
Close Proximity	
Exclusivity	
Prior Experience	
Share End User	
Total	

Once all of the facilitators have been jointly scored, the Assessment of Facilitators Summary Sheet should be completed.

Strength of Drivers and Facilitators Prescribe the Appropriate Type of Partnership

Propensity to Partner Matrix

		DRIVER POINTS		
		8-11 Points	12-15 Points	16-24 Points
FACILITATOR POINTS	8-11 Points	Arm's Length	Type I	Type II
	12-15 Points	Type I	Type II	Type III
	16-25 Points	Type II	Type III	Type III

Now that both drivers and facilitators have been analyzed, the firm's can determine the most appropriate type of relationship. High scores for facilitators and drivers indicate that a relationship should be highly integrated.

Notice on the chart that a low score on drivers can be offset by a higher score on facilitators and vice versa.

Using the matrix, the potential partners should locate the cell which matches the scores for drivers and the score for facilitators. The cell indicates the type of relationship which is appropriate. It is likely that the two firms will have different scores for drivers (however, the score for facilitators will be the same since that was jointly determined). If the scores for drivers are different and not in the same range, the lower score will determine the appropriate relationship. For instance, if one firm has a total driver score of 12, while the second firm has total driver score of 17, and the facilitator score is 13, the driver score of 12 should be used and the appropriate relationship is a Type II partnership.

Because the benefits of a Type III relationship are not present for the one firm (as indicated by its driver score of 12), it is not worthwhile for that firm to invest in resources necessary to develop a Type III relationship. And, like any relationship, the party that wants it the least or has the least to gain determines where it is going.

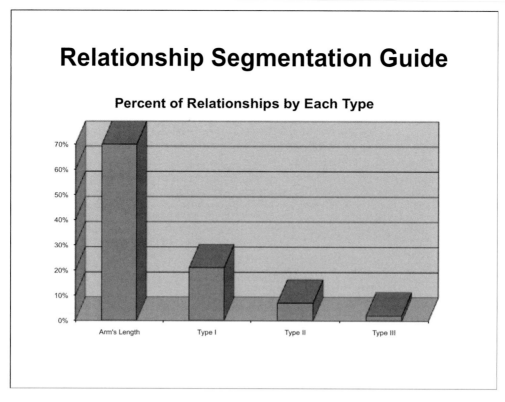

Relationship Segmentation Guide

Percent of Relationships by Each Type

This figure shows that if management was to examine 100 relationships, 70% of them would not be candidates for partnership. Of the 30 relationships that would be partnerships, 2 or 3 would be Type III, 5 or 6 would be Type II and the remainder (21-23) would be Type I. The majority of the 70 that are not candidates for partnership are typically easy to identify. The volume of business is not significant, there are alternatives and the products are low in criticality.

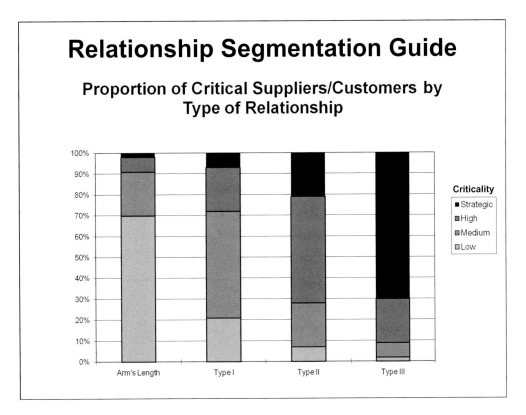

Relationship Segmentation Guide

Proportion of Critical Suppliers/Customers by Type of Relationship

This figure is designed to show that the majority of arm's length relationships involve items that are low in criticality. It is possible that the supplier of a critical item may be managed as an arm's length relationship because the supplier does not view the customer as a candidate for partnership when compared to other customers.

Similarly, the majority of Type III partnerships are going to involve products that are strategic. The supplier of products that are low in criticality may be in this group because of strategic products that it also provides.

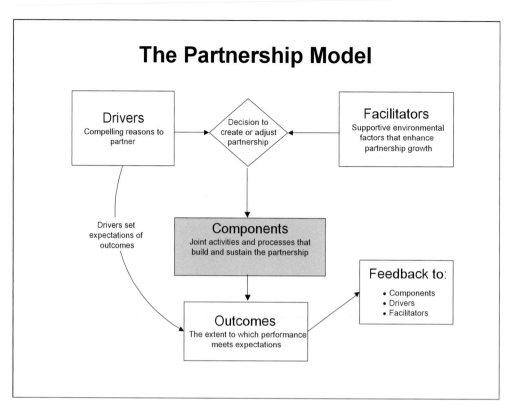

The Partnership Model

Drivers
Compelling reasons to partner

Decision to create or adjust partnership

Facilitators
Supportive environmental factors that enhance partnership growth

Drivers set expectations of outcomes

Components
Joint activities and processes that build and sustain the partnership

Feedback to:
- Components
- Drivers
- Facilitators

Outcomes
The extent to which performance meets expectations

While drivers and facilitators determine the potential for partnership and indicate what type of partnership (I, II, or III) the two firms should have, the components and how they are implemented determine the type of partnership that is actually achieved. Components are joint activities and management routines that build and sustain the partnership.

Management Components

- Managerial controllable elements of a partnership

- Partnerships normally include the following elements or components:
  - Planning
  - Joint operating controls
  - Communications
  - Risk/reward sharing
  - Trust and commitment
  - Contract style
  - Expanded scope
  - Financial investment

The components are the elements of a partnership which management from both firms can control. Management must decide how and to what degree each of these components will be jointly operated.

- Planning - the degree to which planning is done jointly.

- Joint operating controls - the degree to which managers in one firm can change the operation of the other firm.

- Communications - the type, the volume, and the level of communications.

- Risk/reward sharing - willingness of each party to "take a hit" for the other.

- Trust and commitment - how much confidence is placed in each partner by the other, trust building must be managed.

- Contract style - the length and language of the contract covering the partnership.

- Expanded scope - the number and importance of activities covered by the partnership.

- Financial investment - the degree to which the partners have invested in each other's equipment, facilities, etc.

Implementing Partnerships

- The combination of drivers and facilitators determine the level of partnering

- Three types of partnering exist:
    - Type I - components are present at a low level
    - Type II - components are present at a medium level
    - Type III- components are present at a high level

It is important to note that not all partnerships are the same and that components can be implemented and managed at different levels. The analysis of the drivers and facilitators indicates the type of partnership which is most appropriate. Based upon the type, the components must be implemented at the appropriate level. For instance, every partnership will have some degree of joint planning. In a Type I partnership, this may mean that the partners share their long-range plans. In a Type III partnership, the partners would actually jointly develop plans that focus on the business covered by the partnership.

The slides contained in this toolkit provide tables with descriptors for low, medium and high levels of component implementation.

The next four slides show all of the components (two per slide) and their major sub-components as well as descriptions of high, medium and low levels of each. The meeting facilitator should describe low to high levels using the wording provided in the tables.

Management Component Levels

	Management Component	Low	Medium	High
PLANNING	• Style • Level • Content	• On ad-hoc basis • Focus on projects or tasks • Sharing of existing plans	• Regularly scheduled • Focus on process • Performed jointly, eliminating conflicts in strategies	• Systematic: both scheduled and ad-hoc • Focus is on relationship • Performed jointly and at multiple levels, including top management; objective is to mesh strategies, each party participates in other's business planning
JOINT OPERATION CONTROLS	•Measurement •Ability to make changes	• Performance measures are developed independently and results are shared • Parties may suggest changes to other's system	• Measures are jointly developed and shared; focused on individual firm's performance • Parties may make changes to other's system after getting approval	• Measures are jointly developed and shared; focused on relationship and joint performance • Parties may make changes to other's system without getting approval

Planning can be tailored within a relationship at low, medium or high levels. Planning has three sub-components: style, level and content. For example, a low level of planning, which is typical for a Type I partnership, is ad-hoc, with a focus on projects or tasks and existing plans are shared. That is, if there is a damage problem, a task force is organized and when the problem is solved the task force is ended. There is a new product launch and a team is assembled. Once the launch is deemed successful, the team is no longer needed. Sharing existing plans avoids last minute surprises. For example, a customer informs a supplier that next year its purchases of a particular product (plastic bottles) will increase 50%. Because they are sharing plans, the supplier tells the customer that due to capacity constraints it will only be able to provide one-half of the increased volume. This allows the customer to identify another source of supply for the other one-half. If this was an arms-length relationship, the customer would not know about the supplier's capacity constraints.

In a Type II partnership, planning occurs on a regularly scheduled basis and the focus is on process improvement. Planning is performed jointly, eliminating conflicts in strategies. For example, in the previously described example of the customer and the packaging supplier, the supplier has enough trust in the customer's forecast that investments are made to increase capacity so the supplier can meet the customer's increased demand for plastic bottles.

In the case of a Type III partnership, planning is systematic, is focused on the relationship and is performed at multiple levels including top management.

Management Component Levels

	Management Component	Low	Medium	High
COMMUNICATIONS	**NON ROUTINE**	• Limited, usually just critical issues at the task or project level	• Conducted more regularly, done at multiple levels; open and honest	• Planned as a part of the relationship; occurs at all levels; sharing of both praise and criticism; parties "speak the same language"
	DAY-TO-DAY • Organization	• Conducted on ad-hoc basis, between individuals	• Limited number of scheduled communications; some routinization	• Systematized method of communication; may be manual or electronic; communication systems are linked
	• Balance	• Primarily one way	• Two-way but unbalanced	• Balanced two-way communications flow
	• Electronic	• Use of individual systems	• Joint modification of individual systems	• Joint development of customized electronic communications
RISK/ REWARD SHARING	• Loss tolerance • Gain commitment • Commitment to fairness	• Very low tolerance for loss • Limited willingness to help the other gain • Fairness is evaluated by transaction	• Some tolerance for short-term loss • Willingness to help the other gain • Fairness is tracked year to year	• High tolerance for short-term loss • Desire to help other party gain • Fairness is measured over life of relationship

In Type I partnerships, communications are usually implemented at a low level, that is, they are limited in nature, conducted on an ad-hoc basis between individuals, primarily one-way and the organizations use their own systems.

When communications are implemented at a high level, which is typical for a Type III partnership, they are planned as a part of the relationship, occur at all levels of the organization, involve sharing praise and criticism, etc. Also, there is a systematic method of communication, communications are balanced and two-way, and there is joint development of communications systems.

An example of strong risk and reward sharing is found in the Coca-Cola/McDonald's case. Coca-Cola held up a price increase for a year when McDonald's was in the midst of a price war with their competitors and their franchisees were being financially affected.

The meeting facilitator should describe low to high levels using the wording provided in the table.

Management Component Levels

	Management Component	Low	Medium	High
TRUST AND COMMITMENT	• Trust	• Trust is limited to belief that each partner will perform honestly and ethically	• Partner is given more trust than others, viewed as "most favored" supplier	• There is implicit, total trust; trust does not have to be earned
	• Commitment to each other's success	• Commitment of each party is to specific transaction or project; trust must be constantly "re-earned"	• Commitment is to a longer term relationship	• Commitment is to partner's long-term success; commitment prevails across functions and levels in both organizations
CONTRACT STYLE	• Timeframe	• Covers a short time frame	• Covers a longer time frame	• Contracts are very general in nature and are evergreen, or alternatively the entire relationship is on a handshake basis
	• Coverage	• Contracts are specific in nature	• Contracts are more general in nature	• Contract does not specify duties or responsibilities; rather, it only outlines the basic philosophy guiding the relationship

Trust is built over time when commitments are made, results are delivered and performance acknowledged. Trust and commitment targets vary based on the type of partnership. Trust is manageable in the sense that commitments can be made and the resulting performance can be communicated to the appropriate individuals in both organizations.

To the extent that a contract tries to specify each potential eventuality and enumerate penalties and rewards for every situation, the contract is not partnership friendly. A strong partnership would work best on a handshake, a two or three page general contract that outlines the spirit of the relationship or, alternatively an evergreen contract with each party having the ability to exit the relationship with a certain level of notice. However, this approach may be limited by corporate requirements. What is most important is how the contract is used in the relationship.

The meeting facilitator should describe low to high levels using the wording provided in the table.

Management Component Levels

	Management Component	Low	Medium	High
SCOPE	• Share	• Activity of partnership represents a small share of business for each partner	• Activity represents a modest share of business for at least one partner	• Activity covered by relationship represents significant business to both parties
	• Value-added	• Relationship covers only one or a few value-added steps (functions)	• Multiple functions, units are involved in the relationship	• Multiple functions, units are involved; partnership extends to all levels in both organizations
	• Critical activities	• Only activities which are relatively unimportant for partner's success	• Activities that are important for each partner's success are included	• Activities that are critical for each partner's success are included
INVESTMENT	•Financial	• There is low or no investment between the two parties	• May jointly own low-value assets	• High value assets may be jointly owned
	•Technology	• No joint development of products/technology	• There is some joint design effort and there may be some joint R&D planning	•There is significantly joint development; regular and significant joint R&D activity
	•People	• Limited personnel exchange	• Extensive exchange of personnel	• Participation on other party's board

A good example of adding scope to a relationship is asking a company to provide set-up and testing along with the delivery of their product. The addition of value-added steps enhances a partnership.

The overall joint investment will be much higher in a strong partnership. In the Whirlpool/ERX case, Whirlpool owned all of the equipment, demonstrating a strong financial commitment to the relationship and removing some risk for the much smaller partner. We have also seen cases where partners make joint investments in building dedicated production plants.

The meeting facilitator should describe low to high levels using the wording provided in the table.

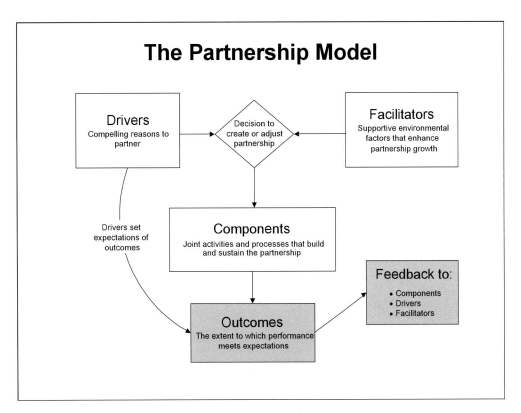

The Partnership Model

Drivers
Compelling reasons to partner

Decision to create or adjust partnership

Facilitators
Supportive environmental factors that enhance partnership growth

Drivers set expectations of outcomes

Components
Joint activities and processes that build and sustain the partnership

Feedback to:
• Components
• Drivers
• Facilitators

Outcomes
The extent to which performance meets expectations

As the managers in the two organizations interact and conduct business, overtime, in the type of relationship suggested by the model, it is important to ensure that both parties are achieving the desired benefits. This requires continual monitoring and evaluation of how well the partnership is performing in terms of achieving each organization's drivers.

When outcomes are not satisfactory, it is important to first revisit the components to determine if they have been properly implemented. If this does not explain the performance gaps, then the drivers and facilitators should be re-evaluated to determine if they have changed.

Partnership Outcomes

- Factors which reflect the performance of the partnership
- Generic outcomes include:
  - Global performance outcomes
    - Enhancement of profits
    - Leveling the flow of profits over time
  - Process outcomes
    - Improved service
    - Reduced costs
  - Competitive Advantage
    - Positioning
    - Share
    - Knowledge

The reason to build more closeness into a relationship is to gain incremental benefits from the increased integration. The drivers are the anticipated benefits. Outcomes are actual results. Specific outcomes achieved will depend upon the drivers and how the partnership is implemented. But in general, outcomes will fit into one of three categories:

- Global performance outcomes - overall enhancement of profits (for example, if margins increased due to product enhancements made possible through partnership) or leveling the flow of profits over time (for example, Wendy's management believed that a partnership would reduce the volatility of chicken prices.)

- Process outcomes - improvements in customer service (such as better on-time deliveries, higher fill rates, and lower damage rates) and reduced costs are an output of many partnerships. These measures are the most commonly used measures because they are the easiest to measure, but by themselves they are not adequate for measuring the total benefit of the relationship.

- Competitive advantage - improvements in market position, increased market share and better access to technology or information. For example, in the relationship between Wendy's and their Latin American distributor shared international experiences results with benefits for each firm.

Key Points

- Partnerships are *not* appropriate in all situations

- General guidelines exist to determine if a partnership is appropriate

- Different settings require different types of partnering

- The appropriate partnership can improve performance of both firms

In most cases a partnership is *not* the appropriate relationship. Trying to force a relationship that should be arm's length into a partnership will waste time and resources and is unlikely to benefit either party. But having the right type of relationship will improve the performance of each firm.

The main benefit of this model is that it provides a way to determine the most appropriate type of relationship - which may not always be a partnership.

Not all partnerships are the same and there are differing degrees of closeness that are appropriate depending upon the business potential that exists between partners. Partnership necessarily involves both firms realizing benefits from the tailoring process, it is not enough for only one side of the relationship to gain all the benefits.

Communicate to the participants that during the remaining sessions of the meeting, the drivers, facilitators and components will be described in more detail and they will be provided an opportunity to work through the determination of the most appropriate type of relationship.

Uses of the Partnership Model

- Evaluate a potential new partnership

- Analyze a portfolio of relationships

- Diagnose relationships

- Review of relationship management

The partnership model can be used to evaluate the potential of a new partnership, but it should not be used for a new relationship. Both parties must have sufficient experience working together to be able to evaluate the drivers and facilitators. For new relationships, you may want to consider the Collaboration Framework described in this book.

Management can use this model with key customers or suppliers to determine which relationships should be strengthened and which are best left at their current level of integration.

The model can be used to evaluate how well a current relationship is working. Both Wendy's and Coca-Cola have used this model to assess a current relationship with a supplier. In each case, the firms (along with their partners) assessed drivers and facilitators, determined what was the appropriate type of relationship, and then compared that to the existing relationship in place.

Finally, the model can be used to standardize how relationships are developed and managed throughout the firm. Wendy's, Coca-Cola and Colgate Palmolive are representative of the companies that have used this model as the guideline for relationship management. There is great value in everyone in the organization viewing partnership in the same way.

Things to Watch for in Working Through the Model

- People have a tendency to *want* a Type III relationship

- Marketing and sales representatives on the supplier side tend to rate things very positively

- In an on-going relationship, those involved in day-to-day operations tend to rate things lower than does management

As you use this model, there are some common pitfalls to avoid:

- Most managers will want to have a Type III partnership. Since this is the most integrated, many people automatically assume it must be better. In fact, the best relationship is the most appropriate one, and that may very well be arm's length. Only a very few, critical relationships warrant a Type III partnership.

- Those on the sales side will tend to be very positive in assessing drivers and facilitators, particularly if they believe that the business is still at risk. For this reason, the business should not be on the line. The partnership model should be used to determine the appropriate type of relationship only after it has been determined how much business is involved. It is critical that everyone involved be absolutely honest in their assessments.

- In general, we have found that operations-level personnel will score drivers and facilitators lower than top management. This may be because the operations personnel deal with problems and issues that are never seen by top management. Because of this, it is very important that individuals from different levels of the organization and different functions are part of the teams that assess the drivers and facilitators.

Session Summary

- Definition of partnership: tailored business relationship

- Drivers and facilitators determine the type of relationship

- Management components are the tools for building partnership

- Achieving the right type of partnership is key

We have seen that partnerships are tailored business relationships appropriate only when both sides gain enhanced business performance. Drivers and facilitators determine the potential for partnership. Components are the tools for building partnership. There are three types of partnership possible between arm's length and vertical integration and the goal should be to establish the appropriate type of partnering and not to achieve a Type III.

In this session each firm's team meets separately to brainstorm their selfish reasons to tailor the relationship.

The Partnership Model

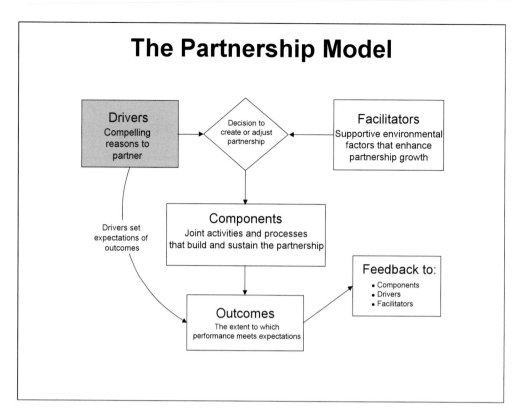

This is a visual representation of the Partnership Model. Over the course of the meeting, each box will be covered in detail. Drivers and facilitators combine to determine whether to partner and if so, how much partnership to build into a relationship.

This session deals with the drivers of partnership and how to evaluate them.

Drivers Working Session

- Break into groups by firm
- Consider each driver
- Capture "selfish goals" as they arise
- Identify the specific bullet points relevant to *this* partnership (Do not close the door too quickly on ideas)
- Score the set of drivers (One score for each driver category)

In this session we will each evaluate the partnership drivers from our own perspective. _____ (firm A) will meet in _____ (room) and _____ (firm B) will meet in _____ (room). The goal is to fill out each driver form and the Assessment of Drivers Summary Sheet.

To accomplish this, each bullet point for each driver should be considered. Specific advantages possible through tighter inter-firm coordination should be identified and when consensus is reached added as bullets to the attached forms.

There are a number of points to keep in mind. Do not be too quick to judge a potential benefit to be impossible. Brainstorming rules apply in this session. Also, thought should be given to the measurement of the outcomes related to each driver or bullet point. Target metrics should be recorded.

Two cautions apply. Don't double count. For example, if you put added sales in marketing advantage, don't put it in profit stability/growth. Don't count customer service gains your customer will offer to their customers as customer service. This category is meant for customer service gains that *you* offer *your* customers through adding partnership to the relationship.

Session Organization

- Need a recorder/presenter for each group
- Need a method to report your results to your potential partner
  - Flip chart sheets
  - PowerPoint presentation
- Need to establish success metrics for each driver element where possible

Each group identifies a recorder and a presenter. The ideas must be captured and reported to the other group in the next phase of the partnership meeting.

The findings concerning drivers for each group must be accurately and succinctly reported to the other group. Both flip charts and PowerPoint presentations have been used successfully in this regard.

Along with the description of the driver, target metrics are needed where possible. Examples might be good where measurement is difficult.

Drivers

- Expected benefits from integrating the relationship

- Four basic drivers, each scored on a 5 point scale

- Competitive advantage - if sustainable, adds 1 point to the driver

- Drivers should be scored separately by each firm

Both parties must realistically expect a significant reward in some form from the partnership. Unless such benefits are anticipated, it is not worth the time and effort to develop and maintain an integrated relationship. As mentioned earlier, there are four categories of drivers. Each party must assess each driver in detail and determine the likelihood of obtaining benefits from the partnership. Drivers are scored on a five point scale with five indicating that managers are 100% certain that a particular benefit will be achieved. In addition, if the benefit provides a firm with a competitive advantage (for instance moves it to a position that competitors are unlikely to be able to duplicate) or if the benefit will bring the firm up to current industry standards, an additional point is added to the score for that driver.

Drivers must be analyzed separately by each firm since the benefits are company specific. At this point, each group of managers should be evaluating the benefits of a closer relationship for their own company. Now we will take a detailed look at each driver.

Assessment of Drivers

Drivers are strategic factors which result in a competitive advantage and which help to determine the appropriate level of a business relationship. For each driver, circle the boxed number which reflects the probability of your organization **realistically** achieving a benefit **through forming a tighter relationship.**

	Probability				
ASSET/COST EFFICIENCY	**No Chance** 0%	25%	50%	75%	**Certain** 100%
1. What is the probability that this relationship will substantially reduce channel costs or improve asset utilization?	1	2	3	4	5

-product costs savings
-distribution costs savings, handling costs savings
-packaging costs savings, information handling costs savings
-managerial efficiencies
-assets to the relationship

If you rated efficiencies in the shaded area and if the advantage is either a sustainable competitive advantage or it allows your firm to match benchmark standards in your industry, circle the 1 to the right.

     1

Example: Wendy's lowered channel costs by partnering with a distributor

---

The first driver is asset/cost efficiencies. Each of the two potential partners should rate the probability that a partnership will provide that firm with an improvement in assets/cost efficiencies. Examples of these improvements include such things as savings on product development costs due to sharing of R&D, a lowering of distribution costs due to outsourcing that activity. The bullets shown above are simply given as examples. The sample bullets must be replaced with company specific advantages which will ultimately be scored. The managers must identify not only the specific categories, but also the specific level expected. It is very important that this determination be as specific as possible, rather than general in nature. (For instance, a 10% reduction in production costs due to shared R&D). The more specific the drivers, the easier it will be to evaluate the outcomes.

The potential for competitive advantage is then determined to obtain the total score for this driver.

Assessment of Drivers

Drivers are strategic factors which result in a competitive advantage and which help to determine the appropriate level of a business relationship. For each driver, circle the boxed number which reflects the probability of your organization **realistically** achieving a benefit **through forming a tighter relationship.**

	Probability				
	No Chance				Certain
ASSET/COST EFFICIENCY	0%	25%	50%	75%	100%
1. What is the probability that this relationship will substantially reduce channel costs or improve asset utilization?	1	2	3	4	5

- _____
- _____
- _____
- _____
- _____
- _____
- _____

If you rated efficiencies in the shaded area and if the advantage is either a sustainable competitive advantage or it allows your firm to match benchmark standards in your industry, circle the 1 to the right.   1

The drivers are assessed using a blank form that requires specific bullets be developed by the firm's team for this relationship. The blank spaces should contain the bullet name and, if at all possible, an associated metric.

An example for asset/cost efficiency could be:

- Reduce packaging costs by 6% per year by jointly reformulating the materials specifications

Assessment of Drivers

Drivers are strategic factors which result in a competitive advantage and which help to determine the appropriate level of a business relationship. For each driver, circle the boxed number which reflects the probability of your organization **realistically** achieving a benefit **through forming a tighter relationship.**

	Probability				
	No Chance				Certain
CUSTOMER SERVICE	0%	25%	50%	75%	100%
2. What is the probability that this relationship will substantially improve the customer service level as measured by the customer?	1	2	3	4	5

-improved on-time delivery
-better tracking of movement
-paperless order processing
-accurate order deliveries
-improved cycle times
-improved fill rates
-customer survey results
-process improvements

If you rated customer service in the shaded area and if the advantage is either a sustainable competitive advantage or if it allows your firm to match benchmark standards in your industry, circle the 1 to the right. | 1 |

Example: Whirlpool created Quality Express, a Type III partnership, with a joint venture between a transportation company and a warehouse company to improve service.

Another potential driver is customer service. For instance when Whirlpool instituted its Quality Express program, it did so primarily to gain service improvements. Prior to the partnership, Whirlpool's service was considerably lower than that of competitors. The partnership with ERX raised Whirlpool's on-time delivery rate from less than 80% to over 99% in four months.

Ways in which a service improvement could be obtained through a partnership include better tracking of information and movement, improved cycle times and improved product availability.

Again, each party must specifically identify the type of service improvement expected and the level of service enhancement. (For instance, we expect a 10% improvement in delivery times). As with the other drivers, a determination must be made whether the service improvement will provide a competitive advantage.

Assessment of Drivers

Drivers are strategic factors which result in a competitive advantage and which help to determine the appropriate level of a business relationship. For each driver, circle the boxed number which reflects the probability of your organization **realistically** achieving a benefit **through forming a tighter relationship.**

	Probability				
	No Chance				Certain
CUSTOMER SERVICE	0%	25%	50%	75%	100%
2. What is the probability that this relationship will substantially improve the customer service level as measured by the customer?	1	2	3	4	5

• _____

• _____

• _____

• _____

• _____

• _____

• _____

If you rated customer service in the shaded area and if the advantage is either a sustainable competitive advantage or if it allows your firm to match benchmark standards in your industry, circle the 1 to the right. | 1 |

The drivers are assessed using a form that requires specific bullets developed by the firm's team for this relationship. The blank spaces should contain the bullet name and, if at all possible, an associated metric.

An example for customer service might be:

• Improve on-time delivery of raw material. Metric – reduce safety stock by 50%

• This may be possible only through sharing production planning system access with attendant systems integration difficulties.

Assessment of Drivers

Drivers are strategic factors which result in a competitive advantage and which help to determine the appropriate level of a business relationship. For each driver, circle the boxed number which reflects the probability of your organization **realistically** achieving a benefit **through forming a tighter relationship.**

	Probability				
MARKETING ADVANTAGE	**No Chance** 0%	25%	50%	75%	**Certain** 100%
3. What is the probability that this relationship will lead to substantial marketing advantages?	1	2	3	4	5

  -new market entry
  -promotion (joint advertising, sales promotion)
  -price (reduced price advantage)
  -product (jointly developed product innovation, branding opportunities)
  -place (expanded geographic coverage, market saturation)
  -access to technology
  -innovation potential

If you rated marketing advantage in the shaded area and if the advantage is either a sustainable competitive advantage or if it allows your firm to match benchmark standards in your industry, circle the 1 to the right.　　　　　　　　　　　　　　　　　　　　　　　1

Example: Target partnered with 3M to get special packaging and promotional support

Just as a reminder, it is unlikely that each partner will have the same drivers. The important thing is that both have substantial drivers.

Improvements in marketing strategy and elements of the marketing mix may also result from a partnership. For instance, when Target partnered with 3M, they were able to obtain exclusive packaging and promotion arrangements. Often one partner can aid the other with entry into a new market. For instance, Coca-Cola was of great help to McDonald's when it was starting up operations in the former Soviet Union.

McDonald's and Coca-Cola also use their partnership as a basis for developing joint promotions.

Each party must assess the potential for a marketing advantage, identify the specific benefit expected, and determine if it will provide a competitive advantage.

Assessment of Drivers

	Probability				
MARKETING ADVANTAGE	No Chance 0%	25%	50%	75%	Certain 100%
3. What is the probability that this relationship will lead to substantial marketing advantages?	1	2	3	4	5

- _____
- _____
- _____
- _____
- _____
- _____
- _____

If you rated marketing advantage in the shaded area and if the advantage is either a sustainable competitive advantage or it allows your firm to match benchmark standards in your industry, circle 1 to the right.   1

The drivers are assessed using a form that requires specific bullets developed by the firm's team for this relationship. The blank spaces should contain the bullet name and, if at all possible, an associated metric.

An example for marketing advantage might be:

- Initiate joint promotions using point-of-purchase information on quality of components. Metric: positive consumer feedback on field trial.
- This would be analogous to the Intel-inside promotions by computer manufacturers. It is a driver if it would require joint planning and execution made possible through partnership.

Assessment of Drivers

Drivers are strategic factors which result in a competitive advantage and which help to determine the appropriate level of a business relationship. For each driver, circle the boxed number which reflects the probability of your organization **realistically** achieving a benefit **through forming a tighter relationship.**

	Probability				
	No Chance				Certain
PROFIT STABILITY/GROWTH	0%	25%	50%	75%	100%
4. What is the probability that this relationship will result in profit growth or reduced variability in profit?	1	2	3	4	5

-growth
-cyclical leveling
-seasonal leveling
-market share stability
-sales volume
-assurance of supply

If you rated profit stability/growth in the shaded area and if the advantage is either a sustainable competitive advantage or if it allows your firm to match benchmark standards in your industry, circle the 1 to the right. | 1 |

Example: Long-term volume commitments are common in partnerships

The last driver is profit stability/growth. In many partnerships, a long-term volume commitment is common. While a volume commitment by itself does not indicate a partnership, having a partner who guarantees a certain level of volume can be a major benefit.

As with the other drivers, it is unlikely that both parties would identify this as a driver. Often it is the case that one party is looking for profit stability/growth while the other is looking for improved service and both are looking for marketing improvements.

Assessment of Drivers

		No Chance		Probability		Certain
		0%	25%	50%	75%	100%
PROFIT STABILITY/GROWTH						
4. What is the probability that this relationship will result in profit growth or reduced variability in profit?		[1]	[2]	[3]	[4]	[5]

- _____
- _____
- _____
- _____
- _____
- _____
- _____

If you rated profit stability/growth in the shaded area and if the advantage is either a sustainable competitive advantage or it allows your firm to match benchmark standards in your industry, circle 1 to the right.   [1]

The drivers are assessed using a form that requires specific bullets developed by the firm's team for this relationship. The blank spaces should contain the bullet name and, if at all possible, an associated metric.

An example for profit stability and growth might be:

- Limit the margin squeeze during economic tight times. The metric may be maintain margins at 80% of the norm

- This may be appropriate if by working collaboratively with the customer a long-term price floor and price ceiling could be agreed upon. The agreement may require more openness than the firm is comfortable with in the absence of partnership.

ASSESSMENT OF DRIVERS: SUMMARY SHEET

Use totals from previous four pages of drivers score sheets
and transfer to this summary sheet.

DRIVER	SCORE
1. Asset/Cost Efficiency	
2. Customer Service	
3. Marketing Advantage	
4. Profit Stability/Growth	
Total Driver Score	

The driver scores for each of the four drivers are recorded and summed. This should be done in a manner that will allow for easy sharing of the scores in the next session.

Scoring Drivers

- The two key words for scoring are probability and substantial

- Customer service improvements must be to customers other than the potential partner

- The scores for individuals should not be averaged

- The scores relate to the specific bullets and metrics developed for <u>this</u> relationship

Scoring must be based on the presence of substantial potential advantages and strong probabilities of gaining the advantages. The advantages should be only those that come from working jointly with the opposite party, not those that flow from business as usual.

Customer service advantages are hard to score. Only those advantages that go to other customers should be scored for sellers.

It is important not to average the viewpoints in the room, consensus should be sought. This forces managers to defend their scores with examples and insights that may sway the group.

The score represents the team's assessment of the potential for the full set of bullets they have identified, and represent their assessment of the potential for tailoring the relationship with this partner.

Scoring Drivers (continued)

- Scores are summed up for each firm

- If no partnership is indicated then the two parties may choose to focus the remaining meeting time on the contract terms if needed

- Be sure to consider all perspectives prior to scoring

Once scores are determined for each driver they need to be recorded and summed. If the score is below 8 points then there is no prospect for partnership. This is due to the fact that the lowest score wins when using the propensity to partner matrix. In this case it may be useful consider using the Collaboration Framework (as presented in Chapter 6).

In the scoring process it is important to hear from all of the participants and consider their views. Often observations of a single participant at a lower level reveal a good insight with respect to potential shared gains or relationship obstacles.

The scores for each driver should be recorded in a manner that works well for sharing with the other team in the next session.

Building High Performance Business Relationships

Drivers Review Session

In the driver review session the two parties come back together and share their agreed upon drivers and the resulting scores. This session is very important in aligning expectations across the relationship. Again, the drivers do not have to match up, they just need to be sufficient to compel efforts and set expectations.

Drivers Review Session

- Members from each firm present their drivers to the other team
- Teams assess the feasibility of achieving both firms' drivers
- Use the lowest score for assessment of the partnership potential
- Internalize the drivers of the opposite party (their goals were not our goals, but the combination of their goals and our goals become joint goals)

Each team will present the drivers that they independently identified. Both teams must assess all of the drivers to determine if they are likely to be achieved. If the totals of the driver scores for each company do not fall in the same range (8-11, 12-15, 16-24) use the lowest total drivers score for the type of partnership choice.

One of the major reasons for partnership failures is unrealistic expectations on the part of one or both of the involved parties. This session is all about setting joint expectations. If you accept the drivers of the other firm without challenge, then you are obligated to help them achieve these drivers.

Shared understanding of opposite party's drivers is a key outcome of this session as well as a key to partnership success.

Typical Approach

- Each side presents its entire set of drivers
- If the opposite party cannot help achieve a driver, the drivers may have to be re-scored
- Metrics for each driver are very important to share
- The session should end with a quick review of commitments to drivers

In the driver review session each side needs to present their drivers to the opposite team. If agreement is reached that the driver can become a joint goal of the two parties, then the score stands. If the opposite party indicates that they cannot help attain that driver due to internal or external constraints, then the driver score should potentially be revised. The sharing is done bullet by bullet to include target metrics.

In the end it is important to have a clear understanding as to the benefits which both parties will accrue are reasonably balanced and that the goals the drivers encompass are substantial.

During this session the teams agree on a joint set of drivers including the related metrics. The rules of the session are that if a team accepts the drivers of the other firm without challenge, then they are obligated to help them achieve these drivers.

Building High Performance Business Relationships

Facilitators Session

In the facilitator session the two teams will jointly evaluate the environmental factors that will either make partnership easier to execute or more difficult. Taken together with the driver scores, the facilitator scores will determine the recommended type of partnership .

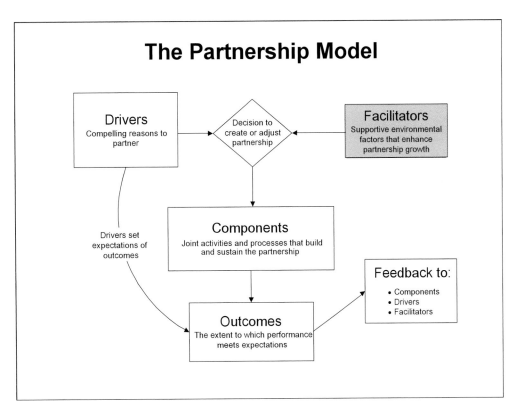

The Partnership Model

Drivers
Compelling reasons to partner

Decision to create or adjust partnership

Facilitators
Supportive environmental factors that enhance partnership growth

Drivers set expectations of outcomes

Components
Joint activities and processes that build and sustain the partnership

Feedback to:
- Components
- Drivers
- Facilitators

Outcomes
The extent to which performance meets expectations

Facilitators combine with drivers to determine the most appropriate type of relationship between two firms. If there are many good motives for close relationship and if the two firms can get close without excessive friction and miscommunication, then a strong partnership might be the best choice.

Facilitators Session

- Each facilitator is considered by the entire group, point by point
- Each facilitator is scored on overall probability (bullet points are considered, but the score is for the overall attribute, e.g. corporate culture across the two firms)
- The session is particularly useful for getting issues which might otherwise be overlooked onto the table

In this session the two firms' representatives will jointly evaluate whether their shared environment is conducive to partnership building.

The scores for each item should be consensus scores, not average scores.

Facilitators

- Measure the supportiveness of the environment

- Four basic facilitators scored on a five point scale

- Five additional facilitators scored as Yes (1 point) or No (0 points)

- Facilitators should be scored jointly by the two firms

- Managers should offer specific examples that support their assertions

Once both parties have individually determined that anticipated benefits are substantial enough to potentially warrant pursuing a partnership, the parties must jointly assess the environment in which the partnership will operate. Facilitators are those factors which enhance the chance of partnership success. Because the facilitators reflect the *combined or joint environment*, they must be assessed jointly by the two potential partners. Facilitators indicate how well the two firms will mesh.

There are four basic facilitators (corporate compatibility, management philosophy and techniques, mutuality, and symmetry) that have the potential to be present in every partnership. These are scored on a five point scale similar to the one used for drivers, with a five indicating certainty that the facilitator exists. There are five situation-specific facilitators which may exist but cannot be expected in every relationship. These are scored using a one indicating the facilitator is present, or a zero indicating it is not.

Assessment of Facilitators

Facilitators are factors which provide a supportive environment for the growth and maintenance of a partnership. For each facilitator, indicate the probability of it being a factor in this relationship, by circling one of the boxed numbers

		Probability		
	No Chance			Certain
CORPORATE COMPATIBILITY	0%	25%	50%	75%	100%
1. What is the probability that the two organizations will mesh smoothly in terms of:	1	2	3	4	5

(a) CULTURE?
  -Both firms place a value on keeping commitments
  -Constancy of purpose
  -Employees viewed as long - term assets
  -External stakeholders considered important
(b) BUSINESS?
  -Strategic plans and objectives consistent
  -Commitment to partnership ideas
  -Willingness to change

Example: Culture and business objectives must mesh.

For an integrated relationship to succeed, the culture and business objectives of the two firms must mesh smoothly. It is not necessary that the cultures be identical, but they can not clash. For instance, a firm that views employees as key, long-term assets is likely to have trouble partnering with a firm in which employees are viewed as expendable resources.

The more similar the culture and objectives, the more comfortable the partners are likely to feel and the better the chance of partnership success.

In assessing this facilitator, the parties should jointly discuss their corporate cultures and business practices and agree on the probability that the firms will mesh smoothly.

Unlike the evaluation of drivers where the bullet points must be replaced by company-specific items, the bullet points describing facilitators can be used in their current form to structure the discussion and evaluation.

Assessment of Facilitators

Facilitators are factors which provide a supportive environment for the growth and maintenance of a partnership. For each facilitator, indicate the probability of it being a factor in this relationship, by circling one of the boxed numbers

	Probability				
	No Chance				Certain
MANAGEMENT PHILOSOPHY AND TECHNIQUES	0%	25%	50%	75%	100%
2. What is the probability that the management philosophy and techniques of the two companies will match smoothly?	1	2	3	4	5

-Organizational structure
-Commitment to continuous improvement
-Degree of top management support
-Types of motivation used
-Importance of teamwork
-Attitudes toward "personnel churning"
-Degree of employee empowerment

Example: McDonald's and Coca-Cola share similar operating methods and values

Managerial philosophy and techniques refer to business practices at the operational level. Even with similar cultures, it is possible that day-to-day management techniques and methods may vary significantly across firms.

The two firms must analyze such things as the level of empowerment granted to employees and decision making techniques. For instance, it is unlikely that a firm which uses a consensus-based decision making process would feel comfortable partnering with a firm which uses a "top-down" approach to making decisions.

Another aspect of management philosophy is the use of continuous improvement. Is it used in both firms, and if so, is it applied in the same way in both firms?

If a firm frequently reassigns managers or other key employees, a long-term partnership focus is difficult.

As with corporate culture, the two firms must jointly agree on the probability that their management systems will mesh smoothly.

Assessment of Facilitators

Facilitators are factors which provide a supportive environment for the growth and maintenance of a partnership. For each facilitator, indicate the probability of it being a factor in this relationship, by circling one of the boxed numbers

	Probability				
	No Chance				Certain
MUTUALITY	0%	25%	50%	75%	100%
3. What is the probability both parties have the skills and predisposition needed for mutual relationship building?	1	2	3	4	5

Management skilled at:
-two-sided thinking and action
-taking the perspective of the other company
-expressing goals and sharing expectations
-taking a longer term view
-mutual respect
Management willing to:
-share financial information
-integrate systems

Example: "You have to be willing to give up your own identity."
ERX representative

"A partnership must benefit both sides."
Whirlpool representative

The third facilitator is mutuality, which is the ability to "put yourself in the other party's shoes". This is usually evidenced by the willingness to develop joint goals, to share sensitive information, and to try to see things from your partner's perspective.

A firm with managers who believe that it is generally "every one for themselves" is unlikely to be a good partner. On the other hand, a firm with managers who regularly search for a "win-win" solution to problems will most likely be an excellent partner.

In the Whirlpool/ERX partnership both sides were willing to look at things from the perspective of the other and to take actions which helped the partner. This level of mutuality enhances the chance of partnership success.

Assessment of Facilitators

Facilitators are factors which provide a supportive environment for the growth and maintenance of a partnership. For each facilitator, indicate the probability of it being a factor in this relationship, by circling one of the boxed numbers

			Probability			
		No Chance				Certain
SYMMETRY		0%	25%	50%	75%	100%
4. *What is the probability that the parties are similar on the following important factors that will affect the success of the relationship:*		1	2	3	4	5

-Relative size in terms of sales
-Relative market share in their respective industries
-Financial strength
-Productivity
-Brand image/reputation
-Technological sophistication

Example: McDonald's and Coca-Cola are each the number one firm in their respective industries; McDonald's is Coca-Cola's largest customer and Coca-Cola is McDonald's largest supplier; both are franchise organizations with global operations. In short, there are many aspects of symmetry between McDonald's and Coca-Cola.

The last of the four basic facilitators is symmetry. This relates to how "demographically" similar the two parties are. Symmetry can be measured in a number of ways:

- Size - similar in sales volume and assets.
- Market share - for instance, both are number one in their industries.
- Brand image - both are internationally recognized.
- Importance - each is critical in some way to the other's success.

In a partnership between Texas Instruments and one of its suppliers, there was a significant difference in size of the two companies. However, Texas Instruments was the supplier's largest customer, and the supplier provided the vast majority of Texas Instruments supply of a critical raw material, resulting in a similar level of importance.

McDonald's and Coca-Cola both have strong brand images, they are leaders in their industries, and McDonald's is the largest customer of Coca-Cola and Coca-Cola the largest supplier to McDonald's.

Assessment of Facilitators

ADDITIONAL FACTORS (BONUS POINTS)

	Yes	No
5. Do you have shared competitors which will tend to unite your efforts?	1	0
6. Are the key players in the two parties in close physical proximity to each other?	1	0
7. Is there a willingness to deal exclusively with your partner?	1	0
8. Do both parties have prior experience with successful partnerships?	1	0
9. Do both parties share a high value end user?	1	0

The first four facilitators, which have the potential of being present in every relationship, are scored on the basis of the probability that they will exist in the partnership under consideration. In addition there are five factors which are situation-specific. If these facilitators are not present, it will not necessarily hurt the relationship, but their presence will strengthen the relationship. Each of these facilitators is scored: yes or no.

- Shared competitors - While relatively rare, having the same competitor provides a strong foundation for a partnership. (For instance, McDonald's and Coca-Cola both viewed Pepsi as a competitor when Pepsi owned restaurants.)
- Close proximity - If key players from the two firms are physically close, this provides additional opportunities for joint activities.
- Exclusivity - If managers are willing to look for ways to establish an "exclusive" relationship, this will strengthen the partnership. This can be through a separate division (McDonald's/Coca-Cola) or through specialized promotions and packaging (Target/3M).
- Prior history - A firm with a history of successful partnership is generally more likely to succeed in future partnerships than one with a history of failure or no experience at all with an integrated relationship.
- Shared end user - In a few cases, both parties serve the same end user. Having a common customer base strengthens the relationship.

ASSESSMENT OF FACILITATORS: SUMMARY SHEET

Facilitator	Score
Corporate Compatibility	[ ]
Management Philosophy and Techniques	[ ]
Mutuality	[ ]
Symmetry	[ ]
Bonus points (zero or one)	
Shared Competitors	[ ]
Close Proximity	[ ]
Exclusivity	[ ]
Prior Experience	[ ]
Share End User	[ ]
Total	[ ]

The facilitators must be recorded and summed in order to move on to the next session. This summary sheet is provided to come up with a grand total facilitators score that will be used with the Propensity to Partner Matrix.

Building High Performance Business Relationships

Target Type of Partnership

At this point in the meeting, it is time to assess if a partnership is appropriate and is it a Type I, Type II or Type III.

Strength of Drivers and Facilitators Prescribe the Appropriate Type of Partnership

Propensity to Partner Matrix

	DRIVER POINTS		
	8-11 Points	12-15 Points	16-24 Points
8-11 Points	Arm's Length	Type I	Type II
12-15 Points	Type I	Type II	Type III
16-25 Points	Type II	Type III	Type III

FACILITATOR POINTS

Now that both drivers and facilitators have been analyzed, you can determine the most appropriate type of relationship. High scores for facilitators and drivers indicate that a relationship should be highly integrated.

Notice on the chart that a low score on drivers can be offset by a higher score on facilitators and vice versa.

Using the matrix, each potential partner should locate the cell which matches the score for drivers and the score for facilitators. The cell indicates the type of relationship which is appropriate.

It is likely that the two firms will have different scores for drivers (however, the score for facilitators will be the same since that was jointly determined). If the scores for drivers are different and not in the same range, the lower score will determine the appropriate relationship. For instance, if one firm has a total driver score of 12, while the second firm has total driver score of 17, and the facilitator score is 13, the appropriate relationship is a Type II partnership.

Because the benefits of a Type III relationship are not present for the one firm (as indicated by its driver score of 12), it is not worthwhile for that firm to invest in resources necessary to develop a Type III relationship.

Implementing the Partnership

- Type is determined based upon drivers and facilitators.

- Decision is made on level of implementation of each component.

Arm's Length	Type I Partnership	Type II Partnership	Type III Partnership
Components of partnership are absent	Predominance of low level partnership components	Predominance of medium level partnership components	Predominance of high level partnership components

- Components are implemented in connection with action plans.

- Action plans include goals, time-tables, ownership, reporting specifics, and metrics from the related drivers.

Once the appropriate type of relationship is determined, you must actually put the partnership in place. This is done through the implementation and management of the components. There are eight components that will be present in every partnership, and the degree to which they are implemented will vary depending upon the type of partnership.

In general, with a Type I partnership, the eight components are implemented at a low level (as defined on the following charts). For a Type II relationship the predominance of the components are at a medium level, and for Type III they are typically at a high level of implementation. This does not mean that in a Type I relationship all of the components must be implemented at a low level. Rather, it means that most of them will be at a low level of implementation.

Therefore, management from the two firms must decide (jointly) how the components are to be implemented and at what level. Since it is likely that all components can not be implemented at the same time, the order in which they will be implemented should be established. In addition, a timetable for implementation and an understanding of the resources needed for implementation should be established.

This process helps each partner clearly understand the expectations and the requirements of the partnership.

Building High Performance Business Relationships

Management Components Session

No meeting is complete or worthwhile if it does not culminate with an action plan, specific assignments and timetables for change. With the large investment in human resources, travel and other expenses, this partnership session clearly must include an action plan with significant work on assignments and timetables.

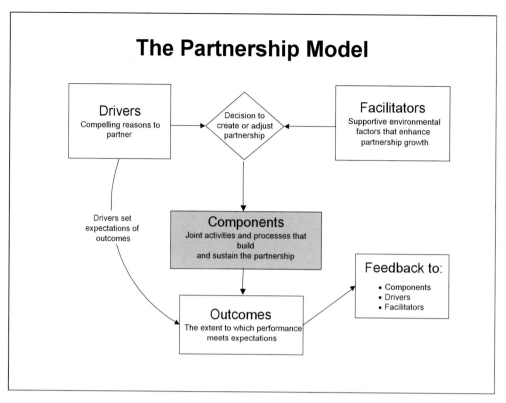

The Partnership Model

- Drivers
  Compelling reasons to partner
- Decision to create or adjust partnership
- Facilitators
  Supportive environmental factors that enhance partnership growth
- Drivers set expectations of outcomes
- Components
  Joint activities and processes that build and sustain the partnership
- Feedback to:
  • Components
  • Drivers
  • Facilitators
- Outcomes
  The extent to which performance meets expectations

While drivers and facilitators reveal the potential for partnership, the components determine the type of partnership that is actually achieved. Components are joint activities and processes that build and sustain the partnership.

The toolkit provides descriptions of the components and their major sub-components as well as descriptions of high, medium and low levels of each.

Each component will be examined in subsequent slides.

Current State Assessment

- For each component, jointly determine the current status
- Use the descriptors for high, medium and low in the tables as a guide
- Look at each element independently within a component, e.g., style, level and content within the planning component

The management components are evaluated before and after the action plan is developed. Before hand the goal is to determine whether the relationship is generally operating at the prescribed partnership type in general. This is the current state assessment. The process is to go through each of the components and determine whether the managers from the two firms feel the level at the current time is at a high, medium or low status. For planning, there will be a short discussion as to whether the bullets in each column are most descriptive of the current state. Share, value-added and critical activities are each done separately. The printed table with all of the components on a single page makes a good recording device.

If most of the components are marked as being in the high, medium or low column, then a Type III, Type II or a Type I partnership is the current status of the relationship. After the action plan is complete a quick additional review of the components is done to see if there is clear stated or implied movement in the components. This review will make explicit any implied changes, will identify any components that might need attention, or will confirm that tackling the action plan will move the relationship toward the desired type.

Both the current state assessment and the final review of the components are not intended to be time-consuming, detailed analyses. A quick assessment is all that is required. For the final review, only items that may have been overlooked should entail much discussion and/or revisions to the action plan. The final review of components is recommended.

Management Component Levels

	Management Component	Low	Medium	High
PLANNING	• Style • Level • Content	• On ad-hoc basis • Focus on projects or tasks • Sharing of existing plans	• Regularly scheduled • Focus on process • Performed jointly, eliminating conflicts in strategies	• Systematic: both scheduled and ad-hoc • Focus is on relationship • Performed jointly and at multiple levels, including top management; objective is to mesh strategies, each party participates in other's business planning
JOINT OPERATION CONTROLS	•Measurement •Ability to make changes	• Performance measures are developed independently and results are shared • Parties may suggest changes to other's system	• Measures are jointly developed and shared; focused on individual firm's performance • Parties may make changes to other's system after getting approval	• Measures are jointly developed and shared; focused on relationship and joint performance • Parties may make changes to other's system without getting approval

Planning can be tailored within a relationship at low, medium or high levels. Planning has three sub-components style, level and content. For example, a low level of planning, which is typical for a Type I partnership, is ad-hoc, with a focus on projects or tasks and existing plans are shared. That is, if there is a damage problem, a task force is organized and when the problem is solved the task force is ended. There is a new product launch and a team is assembled. Once the launch is deemed successful, the team is no longer needed. Sharing existing plans avoids last minute surprises. For example, a customer informs a supplier that next year its purchases of a particular product (plastic bottles) will increase 50%. Because they are sharing plans, the supplier tells the customer that due to capacity constraints it will only be able to provide one-half of the increased volume. This allows the customer to identify another source of supply for the other one-half. If this was an arms-length relationship, the customer would not know about the supplier's capacity constraints.

In a Type II partnership, planning occurs on a regularly scheduled basis and the focus is on process improvement. Planning is performed jointly, eliminating conflicts in strategies. For example, in the previously described example of the customer and the packaging supplier, the supplier has enough trust in the customer's forecast that investments are made to increase capacity so the supplier can meet the customer's increased demand for plastic bottles.

In the case of a Type III partnership, planning is systematic, is focused on the relationship and is performed at multiple levels including top management.

Management Component Levels

	Management Component	Low	Medium	High
COMMUNICATIONS	**NON ROUTINE**	• Limited, usually just critical issues at the task or project level	• Conducted more regularly, done at multiple levels; open and honest	• Planned as a part of the relationship; occurs at all levels; sharing of both praise and criticism; parties "speak the same language"
	DAY-TO-DAY • Organization	• Conducted on ad-hoc basis, between individuals	• Limited number of scheduled communications; some routinization	• Systematized method of communication; may be manual or electronic; communication systems are linked
	• Balance	• Primarily one way	• Two-way but unbalanced	• Balanced two-way communications flow
	• Electronic	• Use of individual systems	• Joint modification of individual systems	• Joint development of customized electronic communications
RISK/ REWARD SHARING	• Loss tolerance • Gain commitment • Commitment to fairness	• Very low tolerance for loss • Limited willingness to help the other gain • Fairness is evaluated by transaction	• Some tolerance for short-term loss • Willingness to help the other gain • Fairness is tracked year to year	• High tolerance for short-term loss • Desire to help other party gain • Fairness is measured over life of relationship

In Type I partnerships, communications are usually implemented at a low level, that is, they are limited in nature, conducted on an ad-hoc basis between individuals, primarily one-way and the organizations use their own systems.

When communications are implemented at a high level, which is typical for a Type III partnership, they are planned as a part of the relationship, occur at all levels of the organization, involve sharing praise and criticism, etc. Also, there is a systematic method of communication, communications are balanced and two-way, and there is joint development of communications systems.

An example of strong risk and reward sharing is found in the Coca-Cola/McDonald's case. Coca-Cola held up a price increase for a year when McDonald's was in the midst of a price war with their competitors and their franchisees were being financially affected.

The meeting facilitator should describe low to high levels using the wording provided in the table.

Management Component Levels

	Management Component	Low	Medium	High
TRUST AND COMMITMENT	• Trust	• Trust is limited to belief that each partner will perform honestly and ethically	• Partner is given more trust than others, viewed as "most favored" supplier	• There is implicit, total trust; trust does not have to be earned
	• Commitment to each other's success	• Commitment of each party is to specific transaction or project; trust must be constantly "re-earned"	• Commitment is to a longer term relationship	• Commitment is to partner's long-term success; commitment prevails across functions and levels in both organizations
CONTRACT STYLE	• Timeframe	• Covers a short time frame	• Covers a longer time frame	• Contracts are very general in nature and are evergreen, or alternatively the entire relationship is on a handshake basis
	• Coverage	• Contracts are specific in nature	• Contracts are more general in nature	• Contract does not specify duties or responsibilities; rather, it only outlines the basic philosophy guiding the relationship

Trust is built over time when commitments are made, results are delivered and performance acknowledged. Trust and commitment targets vary based on the type of partnership. Trust is manageable in the sense that commitments can be made and the resulting performance can be communicated to the appropriate individuals in both organizations.

To the extent that a contract tries to specify each potential eventuality and enumerate penalties and rewards for every situation, the contract is not partnership friendly. A strong partnership would work best on a handshake, a two or three page general contract that outlines the spirit of the relationship, or alternatively an evergreen contract with each party having the ability to exit the relationship with a certain level of notice. However, this approach may be limited by corporate requirements. What is most important is how the contract is used in the relationship.

The meeting facilitator should describe low to high levels using the wording provided in the table.

Management Component Levels

	Management Component	Low	Medium	High
SCOPE	• Share	• Activity of partnership represents a small share of business for each partner	• Activity represents a modest share of business for at least one partner	• Activity covered by relationship represents significant business to both parties
	• Value-added	• Relationship covers only one or a few value-added steps (functions)	• Multiple functions, units are involved in the relationship	• Multiple functions, units are involved; partnership extends to all levels in both organizations
	• Critical activities	• Only activities which are relatively unimportant for partner's success	• Activities that are important for each partner's success are included	• Activities that are critical for each partner's success are included
INVESTMENT	•Financial	• There is low or no investment between the two parties	• May jointly own low-value assets	• High value assets may be jointly owned
	•Technology	• No joint development of products/technology	• There is some joint design effort and there may be some joint R&D planning	•There is significantly joint development; regular and significant joint R&D activity
	•People	• Limited personnel exchange	• Extensive exchange of personnel	• Participation on other party's board

A good example of adding scope to a relationship is asking a company to provide set-up and testing along with the delivery of their product. The addition of value-added steps enhances a partnership.

The overall joint investment will be much higher in a strong partnership. In the Whirlpool/ERX case, Whirlpool owned all of the equipment, demonstrating a strong financial commitment to the relationship and removing some risk for the much smaller partner. We have also seen cases where partners make joint investments in building dedicated production plants.

The meeting facilitator should describe low to high levels using the wording provided in the table.

Building High Performance Business Relationships

Developing Action Plan

In this session an action plan is developed from the agreed upon drivers.

Action Planning Process

- Action plan is developed: 3-5 targeted actions to improve/initiate the partnership
- Review the drivers to assure coverage in the action plans
- Review to determine the type of partnership intended
- Must have owners in each firm, clear outcomes, due dates and resource commitments

In this session, the two firms' representatives jointly develop an action plan.

The role of the components of partnership is considered while developing the plan. While most of the components should be implemented at a specific level (low, median or high) for the type of partnership selected (I, II or III, respectively), there can be some degree of variation in the implementation of the components if a clear advantage is indicated.

The action plan is based on the two firms' drivers. The action plan is often designed to meet the needs of both parties, but not always.

It is important to choose initiatives that can be achieved and supported by the resources of the two firms.

For each action item it is important to record the who, what and when. See the next slide for an example.

Action Plan Example

Driver	Objective	Initiative	Timeline	Team Leaders	Goal
Asset/Cost Efficiencies *Buyer* **Profit Stability and Growth** *Seller*	**Cost reduction while maintaining supplier margins**	Specification simplification	New functional specifications by Q2	Smith and Jones	5%/year product spend reduction
		Quality assurance alignment	New single, joint quality process by Q4	Roberts and Carlson	
		Joint forecasting	Shared forecasting by Q3	Hines and West	
Customer Service *Buyer* **Asset /Cost Efficiencies** *Seller*	**Maintain continuity of supply**	Advanced notice/early commitment by buyer	Beginning of next fiscal year	Owens and Lee	100% in stock when within 20% of forecast
		Joint forecasting	See above	Owens and Lee	
Marketing Advantage *Buyer/Seller*	**Reduction of new product development timeline**	Digital printing of packaging	Testing – by Q2, Implementation by Q4	Joyce and Meyer	Changeover for LTO (limited time offers) to three weeks
		Shared graphic systems	Six weeks to testing, Q2 to changeover	Lance and Miller	
Profit Stability and Growth *Buyer/Seller*	**Profit Reducing variability**	Joint price ceiling and floor multi-year agreement	Outline by next quarter, approval by Q2	Wells and Pryor	Limit price shocks to each party by percent TBD

This slide provides an example of the action plan that should result from the partnership meeting. It is important that the meeting facilitator communicate the importance of capturing who is responsible on each side of the relationship and to set dates for completion or milestones. An action plan can be more or less detailed based on practices typical in the individual firms, but the plan must capture the most important items to record in order to maintain the momentum from the meeting.

Action Plan Template

From the drivers for each side of the relationship an action plan needs to be developed. Action items should include a brief description (what), who from each side are responsible for the item (who), and for when the next action is planned (when).

Driver	Objective	Initiative	Timeline	Team Leaders	Goal

This slide is used to record the action plan that results from the partnership meeting. Again, it is important to capture who is responsible on each side of the relationship and to set dates for completion or milestones.

Building High Performance Business Relationships

Sustaining the Relationship

This session focuses on verifying the rewards from the incremental investments made to tailor the relationship are being realized. Both parties should be achieving results that are substantially greater than they would achieve by doing business as usual.

If timing does not permit, this content may be covered after the meeting by a conference call or by other means. However, partnership maintenance and performance measurement is critical for the long-term success of the relationship.

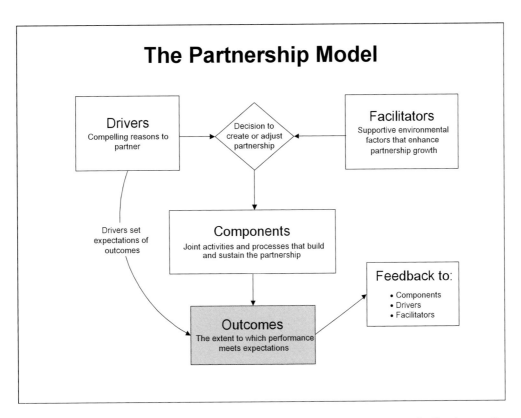

The Partnership Model

Drivers
Compelling reasons to partner

Decision to create or adjust partnership

Facilitators
Supportive environmental factors that enhance partnership growth

Drivers set expectations of outcomes

Components
Joint activities and processes that build and sustain the partnership

Feedback to:
- Components
- Drivers
- Facilitators

Outcomes
The extent to which performance meets expectations

As we interact and conduct business, overtime, with our partner, in the type of relationship suggested by the Partnership Model, it is important to ensure that both parties are achieving the desired benefits. This requires continual monitoring and evaluation of how well the partnership is working.

Partnership Outcomes

- Factors which reflect the performance of the partnership
- Generic outcomes include:
  - Global performance outcomes
    - Enhancement of profits
    - Leveling the flow of profits over time
  - Process outcomes
    - Improved service
    - Reduced costs
  - Competitive Advantage
    - Positioning
    - Share
    - Knowledge

The reason to enter into a partnership is to gain benefits from a more integrated relationship. The drivers are the anticipated benefits. Outcomes are actual results. The specific outcomes achieved will depend upon the drivers and how the partnership is implemented.

In general, outcomes will fit into one of three categories:

- Global performance - Overall enhancement of profits.

- Process outcomes - Improvements in customer service such as better on-time deliveries, higher fill rates and lower damage rates, or reduced costs.

- Competitive advantage - Improvement in market position, access to better technology or knowledge for future growth.

Partnership Development and Maintenance

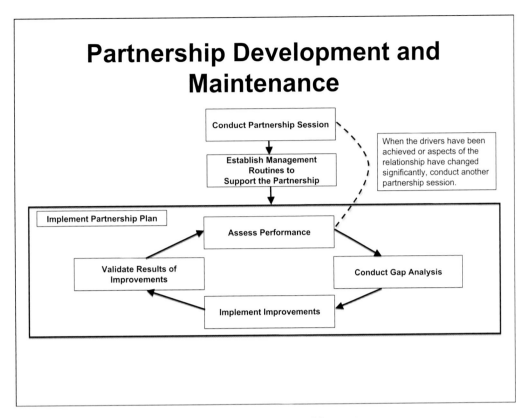

A partnership maintenance cycle is made up of four steps:

Step 1: Assess Performance. To ensure sustained commitment to the partnership, it is important to track progress on the initiatives that have been jointly established. In this step, management uses various control methods to ensure the desired goals are being met.

Step 2: Gap Analysis. The relationship teams evaluate the outcomes related to each initiative and the overall relationship and identify gaps. Depending on which results are not achieved, areas for improvement can be identified.

Step 3: Implement Improvements. At the implement improvements step, the relationship teams translate the action plan that was established in the gap analysis into actual improvements for the partnership.

Step 4: Validate Results. In the validate step of the cycle, it is necessary to determine if the planned improvements have been successfully implemented. In order to decide whether an improvement has been implemented successfully, several measures of success are necessary.

Depending on the type of partnership that has been formed, the cycle may vary in timing. Periodically the team should consider if changes should be made in team membership, if drivers need to be reevaluated, and if there have been significant changes in the environment that affect the relationship. If any of these situations exist, the partners may want to consider holding another partnership meeting.

Long-term Responsibilities

- A top level manager in each company must be responsible for the relationship
- Responsibilities must be institutionalized
  - Incorporate responsibilities into job descriptions
  - Include the relationship in strategic plans
- Cross-firm teams must be institutionalized

In every discussion of partnership building the support and commitment of top executives is stressed. Thus, it is important to assign the ownership of the relationship to the highest level possible.

Partnerships must survive an individual's departure from the firm. Therefore, it is important to include partnership responsibilities in job descriptions and include partnership roles in strategic plans.

If appropriate, formalization of cross-firm, cross-functional teams is a good idea at this point. In this session, a beginning on these points should be attempted.

APPENDIX B: Collaboration Framework Toolkit

In this section of the book, we provide you with the tools and resources needed to initiate and conduct a collaboration meeting in your organization. The Collaboration Framework Toolkit includes resources to help "sell" the benefits of the collaboration session both within your company and to a potential collaborator, materials to help participants prepare for the meeting and all of the slides and handouts required to conduct a meeting. The first document is the article "A Framework for Collaboration", which should be read by all participants prior to the meeting. This article provides a useful overview of the Collaboration Framework. In addition, we have included a two-page summary of the framework. The third document is a sample e-mail that can be used to invite participants to the meeting. Next, we provide a sample agenda for the meeting. The final five sets of documents are slides and their associated notes to facilitate a meeting. The notes reflect our experiences from facilitation of collaboration meetings. These resources are available in an electronic format by completing your registration card included with the book. For more information, please visit our website at www.thecollaborationframework.com.

Collaboration Framework Toolkit

> The Collaboration Framework helped us refocus a relationship with a new supplier of a high potential new product where performance was not meeting the requirements of our key customers.
>
> — Pete Koehn
>
> Vice President, Global Operations, Imation

A Framework for Collaboration

by Douglas M. Lambert and Sebastián J. García-Dastugue

Increasingly, customer relationship management (CRM) is being viewed as strategic, process-oriented, cross-functional, value-creating, and a means of achieving superior financial performance. The goal is to segment customers based on their value over time and increase customer loyalty by providing customized products and services. As part of the CRM process, customer teams tailor product and service agreements (PSAs) to meet the needs of key accounts and segments of other customers. In order to engage a customer in this manner, the customer, as part of its supplier relationship management process, needs to identify the company as a key supplier. Supplier relationship management (SRM) is the process that provides the structure for developing and maintaining relationships with suppliers.

Together, CRM and SRM provide the critical linkages throughout the supply chain. For each supplier in the supply chain, the ultimate measure of success for the CRM process is the change in profitability of an individual customer or segment of customers over time. For each customer, the most comprehensive measure of success for the SRM process is the impact that a supplier or supplier segment has on the firm's profitability. The goal is to increase the joint profitability through the co-production of value. The management team must determine which business relationships are candidates for a collaboration meeting.

The Collaboration Framework, shown in Figure 1, provides a structure for developing and implementing PSAs with key customers and suppliers. The collaboration framework is comprised of six activities: assess drivers for each company, align expectations, develop action plan, develop product and service agreement, review performance, and periodically reexamine drivers. Assess drivers requires that each firm's representatives identify their business goals for the relationship. Align expectations involves mutually establishing goals based on the drivers of

> *The Collaboration Framework is comprised of six activities: assess drivers for each company, align expectations, develop action plans, develop product and service agreement, review performance, and periodically reexamine drivers.*

Figure 1
Framework for Collaboration

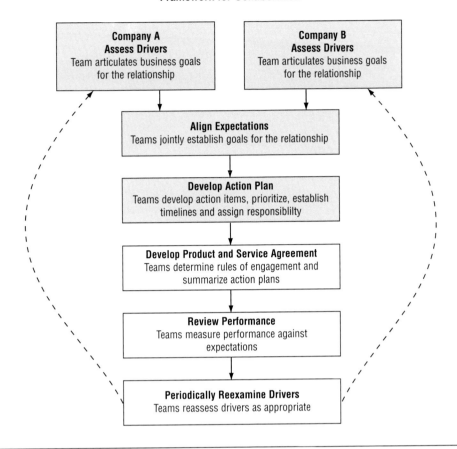

both firms. Develop action plan includes prioritizing initiatives, assigning responsibilities, establishing timelines, and agreeing on the appropriate metrics. The product and service agreement is a written summary of the rules of engagement and action plans. It is necessary to review performance to insure that each firm has achieved its drivers. Finally, the teams should periodically reexamine the drivers.

The Collaboration Meeting

The collaboration meeting is a one-day session in which expectations are set, an action plan is developed, and responsibilities are assigned as shown in the shaded boxes in Figure 1. Specific details related to the meeting are described in the following sections: 1) preparation for the meeting; 2) introduction and expectation setting session; 3) drivers session; 4) alignment session; 5) action plan; and, 6) the wrap-up session. A general overview of the session is provided and where appropriate issues to consider are described.

Preparation for Meeting

All parties involved, including meeting facilitators and participants, have activities that should be completed prior to the meeting. These activities include participant selection, meeting scheduling, meeting planning issues and distribution of pre-read article, *A Framework for Collaboration*.

The meetings are enhanced by the presence of individuals from multiple levels within the organizations who represent diverse functional expertise. The make-up of the group sends a message to those in the other firm about the importance of the relationship. It is important to involve the highest-level executives possible. The more levels of management above the people in the meeting, the more difficult it may be to achieve the commitments made. If key executives are not present and significant resource commitments are being made, then these executives should be briefed as soon as possible and their commitment obtained. The need to have the involvement of multiple levels of employees (senior vice president, vice president, directors, managers, etc.) with diverse functional expertise (sales, marketing, purchasing, logistics, operations, R&D, QA, etc.) makes scheduling difficult. A high-level executive from each organization should state that the meeting is a priority and these executives should attend the meeting.

Additional considerations when preparing for the meeting include:
- Publish a detailed agenda in order to establish expectations and maintain focus.
- Schedule sessions for one full day.
- Review the article, *A Framework for Collaboration,* in advance.
- Make sure that meeting facilitators are conversant in the business situation.
- Provide a neutral location, spacious rooms, and proper supplies for documenting and communicating the outcomes of the meeting.
- Provide participants with materials that include an agenda, a list of participants, and copies of forms used for the session.
- Identify two individuals from outside the relationship to facilitate the session. The individuals serve as the meeting pace setters and must be skilled in building consensus, probing for more

information, assuring closure, and reinforcing agreements on the action plan.

Introduction and Expectation Setting Session

The collaboration meeting should begin with an introduction that reinforces each side's motivations for the meeting, a review of the framework, and a discussion about the expectations for the session. For example, in one meeting, the vice president of the supplier organization stated that the motivation for using the framework was to achieve a structured and consistent approach to developing a PSA with the customer.

Drivers Assessment Session

It is important in the drivers assessment session that managers feel comfortable to express their opinions whatever they might be. This comfort level would be difficult to achieve without unbiased meeting facilitators. The drivers fall into four categories: asset/cost efficiencies, customer service, marketing advantage, and profit stability/growth.
- **Asset/Cost Efficiencies** include the potential for better utilization of assets and/or for cost reductions that might occur in areas such as transportation costs, handling costs, packaging costs, information costs, product costs, or managerial efficiencies.
- **Customer Service** improvements can lead to increased sales when customers experience benefits such as reduced inventory, improved availability (which leads to sales increases), and more timely and accurate information.
- **Marketing Advantage** can be achieved by: 1) an enhancement of an organization's marketing mix through joint programs; 2) entry into new markets; and 3) better access to technology and innovation.

The collaboration meeting should begin with: an introduction that reinforces each side's motivations for the meeting, a review of the framework, and a discussion about the expectations for the session.

• **Profit Stability/Growth** is the potential for stabilizing profit. Strengthening a relationship often leads to long-term volume commitments, reduced variability in sales, joint use of assets, and other improvements that reduce variability of profits.

The meeting facilitators should use the forms shown in Table 1 to ensure that each of these categories is addressed explicitly. For each team, the participants should identify specific bullet-point descriptions for each driver category with goals (including metrics and targets) and priorities. The meeting facilitator must encourage each team to articulate measurable goals for each driver which may be the toughest part of the session. It is not enough for a team to say that the company is looking for "improved asset utilization" or "product cost savings." The goals must be specific, such as improving utilization from 80% to 98% or cutting product costs by 7% per year.

Each party should independently assess the strength of their specific drivers by using the blank forms shown in Table 2. Table 1 provides examples of specific drivers. These examples are not meant to be all inclusive, but rather should be used only as a starting point. The team should develop an exhaustive list that can be summarized in a few bullet points. The participants should seek consensus for the final drivers for each of the four driver categories. Talking about differences and coming to consensus is useful and facilitates implementation later. Issues come out in the defense of specific drivers that otherwise would not emerge. There must be buy-in from the participants if the drivers are to be achieved.

Goals must be set for each descriptor and they must be stated in terms that are measurable. For instance, under the driver Marketing Advantage, the parties must decide whether a joint advertising goal should be established. It is important

that the descriptors of each driver be specified in measurable terms, such as three advertising campaigns per year, and agreed upon because the success of the relationship will be measured based upon whether the desired improvements are actually achieved. Priorities ranging from critical (1) to important (3) must be established for each goal to provide guidance to the teams when they develop the joint action plans.

Representatives of the two firms should evaluate drivers separately and the evaluation must be from a selfish perspective. It can be challenging to get suppliers to think in terms of their own self-interest particularly if the buyer initiated the meeting. Since they respond to the customer in a customer-oriented way in most discussions, taking a selfish perspective is sometimes difficult. It is important that the meeting facilitators stress this point to the participants.

Evaluation of the customer service driver often poses a problem for sellers. They want to include as a driver, customer service improvements to the customer. While these are advantages to the customer, they do not represent drivers for the seller. In order for the evaluation to be selfish on the part of the seller, only customer service improvements that can be offered to other customers should be counted. If a firm can develop a customer service delivery approach that can be offered to other accounts, then it represents a driver.

A marketing advantage that is harder to quantify in dollars is the identification of at least four new product ideas over a two-year period, one of which would reach commercialization. Only those potential drivers of profit that do not overlap with the others or do not focus on any one of the others should be included in profit stability and growth. If a customer service improvement by the seller yields lower inventories for the

Representatives of the two firms should evaluate drivers separately and the evaluation must be from a selfish perspective.

Table 1
Assessment of Drivers
Drivers are business reasons for expanding the resource commitment to the relationship.
For each item, develop specific goals and identify the priority.
Priority is: 1=Critical, 2=Very Important, 3=Important.

ASSET/COST EFFICIENCY

1. What are the initiative that will reduce cost or improve asset utilization?

Driver	Goal	Priority
• Product costs savings	2% per year	1
• Distribution costs savings, handling costs savings	7% during 1st year	1
• Packaging cost savings and green initiatives	Satisfy Walmart's requirements	3
• Reduce the cash-to-cash cycle time	By 10 days	2
• No management time devoted to conference calls with key customer explaining service failures due to supplier problems	Zero within 3 months	1
• Assets utilization (reduce plant overtime due to supplier problems)	No surprise orders by quarter-end	2
• Integrate planning across business and plants (visibility of capacity available across plants)	Within 12 months	3

CUSTOMER SERVICE

2. What are the initiatives will improve customer service as measured by the customer?

Driver	Goal	Priority
• Improved on-time delivery	98.5%	1
• Better tracking of movement	Full visibility	2
• Paperless order processing	100% EDI	2
• Order accuracy	0 picking errors	1
• Improved cycle times	From 14 to 7 days	1
• Improved fill rates	From 96% to 99%	1
• Customer survey results	#1 in industry survey	2
• Improved response to inquiries	2 hours	3

MARKETING ADVANTAGE

3. What are the initiatives that will lead to marketing advantages?

Driver	Goal	Priority
• Promotion (joint advertising, sales promotion)	3 promotions/year	1
• Evaluate co-branding opportunities	Within 6 months	3
• Share market research data	1 meeting/year	3
• Product (jointly developed product innovation, branding opportunities)	7 ideas, 3 ready/year	1
• Expanded geographic coverage (buy our products in markets outside the USA)	$10,000,000 in 1st year	2
• Sell our latest technology	Within 12 months	1
• Innovation potential	2 brainstorming sessions/year	2

PROFIT STABILITY/GROWTH

4. What are the initiatives that will result in profit growth or reduced variability in profit?

Driver	Goal	Priority
• Growth	10% volume increase	1
• Cyclical leveling	1/3/5 year plan	2
• Monthly demand leveling (Eliminate end-of-quarter load)	Over next 12 months	1
• Price stability	Annual Contract	2
• Reduce sales volume fluctuation	A consistent 40% of your spend	1
• Evaluate growing/starting up in every market where you are present	1 market/year	3
• Grow share of "value added" products	20% increase	2

Table 2
Assessment of Drivers
Drivers are business reasons for expanding the resource commitment to the relationship.
For each item, develop specific goals and identify the priority.
Priority is: 1=Critical, 2=Very Important, 3=Important.

ASSET/COST EFFICIENCY

1. What are the initiative that will reduce cost or improve asset utilization?

Driver	Goal	Priority
•		
•		
•		
•		
•		
•		
•		

CUSTOMER SERVICE

2. What are the initiatives will improve customer service as measured by the customer?

Driver	Goal	Priority
•		
•		
•		
•		
•		
•		
•		
•		

MARKETING ADVANTAGE

3. What are the initiatives that will lead to marketing advantages?

Driver	Goal	Priority
•		
•		
•		
•		
•		
•		
•		
•		

PROFIT STABILITY/GROWTH

4. What are the initiatives that will result in profit growth or reduced variability in profit?

Driver	Goal	Priority
•		
•		
•		
•		
•		
•		
•		
•		

buyer, this is asset/cost efficiency for the buyer. If it yields better customer service to the buyer's customers, then it should be counted as an improvement in customer service by the buyer. If a joint effort can level volumes, then it should be recorded in profit stability and growth.

After the group develops drivers specific to their situation, the meeting facilitator should challenge them to define measurable goals and establish priorities. There is no expectation that the drivers will be the same for each firm. Each side must determine the drivers that best satisfy their firm's needs.

Align Expectations Session

Once each side has scored their drivers, the next step is to come together and present their drivers to each other. It is important to explain why the drivers were selected. This represents an expectations setting session that is critical for success. One of the reasons that business relationships often yield disappointing results is unstated or unrealistic expectations on the part of one or both of the parties. The thinking behind the drivers needs to be understood by both sides of the relationship. If the representatives of the other firm indicate that they cannot or will not help achieve a particular driver, the driver should be reevaluated. If no one in the session objects to the other side's drivers, then management is obligated to help the other firm achieve its drivers.

Drivers for the supplier and the buyer will rarely match by category. It is not important that the drivers match, just that both sides have compelling reasons to commit the necessary resources to achieve the drivers. If the drivers are quantified during the drivers' assessment, the evaluation of the performance over time is made much easier. An example for asset/cost efficiency is the goal of reducing product costs by 7% per year

over the next three years. By knowing the exact expectation, there is more realistic buy-in and better tracking of progress in achieving the goal for the driver.

Develop Action Plan Session

In the final session of the collaboration meeting, the mutually agreed upon drivers are prioritized and translated into an action plan. Action items should include a brief description (what), the individuals from each organization who will be responsible for achieving the driver (who) and a timeline for implementation (when) as shown in Table 3. For example, if the driver is to improve forecasting accuracy, the first step could be defined as assess what the actual forecasting procedures are for each company and determine their impact on forecast accuracy.

When developing the action plan, management needs to balance workload and separate short-term opportunities from those that are longer-term. Management should avoid assigning too may items to the same people. Usually, there are action items that can be identified as quick-hits, those that can be materialized in one to three months. Other action items could be longer-term. For example, sharing actual performance measures could be a quick-hit; while implementing CPFR (Collaborative, Planning, Forecasting, and Replenishment) might require some project management activities and several months to implement.

During the collaboration meeting, the following parts of the Collaboration Framework were addressed: drivers assessment, expectation alignment and action plan development. The final three parts of the framework are implemented after the meeting and they are described next.

Once each side has scored their drivers, the next step is to come together and present these drivers.

Table 3
Developing the Action Plan

From the drivers for each side of the relationship an action plan needs to be developed. Action items should include a brief description (what), who from each side are responsible for the item (who), and for when the next action is planned (when).

What	Who	When
1.		
2.		
3.		
4.		
5.		
6.		
7.		
8.		

Develop Product and Service Agreement

The PSA is a document that matches the requirements of the customer with the capabilities of the supplier. The PSA specifies levels of performance and provides direction for joint improvement efforts. The PSA documents business goals of the customer and supplier so that the expectations of each organization are realistic and understood by both sides.

It is necessary to take the action plan, responsibilities, and timelines developed during the collaboration meeting and include them in the PSA. In addition, the PSA should contain: information on key contacts for the relationship, order acceptance guidelines, credit terms, planning activities, returned products acceptance guidelines and credit rules. Also, the PSA should specify details related to achieving the agreed upon drivers such as market development funds, product introductions and asset utilization. It is also important to describe how communications will take place, for example monthly performance reviews, quarterly business reviews with the entire team and annual senior management reviews.

Review Performance

Improved service and reduced costs are potential outcomes from structuring a collaborative business relationship. While global performance outcomes such as profit enhancement and reducing the variability in profits over time, and competitive advantage outcomes such as market position, market share and knowledge gained are harder to measure, these measures should not be ignored.

Regular business reviews should be conducted so that management can determine if satisfactory progress is being made toward the goals established in the action plan and to measure the degree to which the commitments made in the product and service agreement are being fulfilled. The team should review the action plan on a regular basis to determine if the action plan and PSA are adequately resourced and remain relevant.

Regular business reviews should be conducted so that management can determine if satisfactory progress is being made toward the goals established in the action plan and to measure the degree to which the commitments made in the product and service agreement are being fulfilled.

Periodically Reexamine Drivers

It is necessary to periodically reexamine the drivers for three reasons. First, the PSAs should be updated annually which requires a new session. Second, changes in the business environment may require a reassessment of the drivers on a shorter cycle. Third, a performance review may reveal that the drivers have been achieved and it is time for another session.

An Example of a Collaboration Session Using the Framework

The collaboration framework was used in a session with a company (ABC Corporation) that is based in the USA and a Chinese supplier (XYZ Company). While the organizations had a history of working together, a very successful new product line had increased the volume of business dramatically and the management of ABC Corporation believed that the potential for even greater growth was high. A primary reason for demand for ABC's new product significantly exceeding forecast was a large volume of purchases from ABC's largest customer who was becoming increasingly upset at ABC's inability to ship on time and in full. XYZ was caught by the unexpected increase in demand at a time when the economic crisis was causing its suppliers in China to not manufacture until orders were received which was increasing lead times for the components they were purchasing. Management of XYZ wanted to provide the volume now required by ABC but needed its customer's help in order to be successful.

Table 4 shows the top eight of 20 action items that were identified in the one-day session along with the person from each company who would take the lead on each action item and when the work would be completed. In the session, the XYZ Company was represented by the CEO, the Treasurer, the Business Manager responsible for the ABC business, the Director of Purchasing, the Operations Manager and the Senior Program Manager. ABC Corporation was represented by the Vice President of

---

Table 4
Action Plan for ABC Corporation and XYZ Company
From the drivers for each side of the relationship an action plan needs to be developed. Action items should include a brief description (what), who from each side are responsible for the item (who), and for when the next action is planned (when).

What	Who	When
1. ABC will look at remaining 2009 forecast and make a buy proposal for the finished products that it purchases from XYZ	Lean Technologies and Supply Manager (ABC)	6/15
2. ABC will look at remaining 2009 forecast and make a buy proposal for the two key components for those products	Lean Technologies and Supply Manager (ABC)	6/15
3. XYZ responds to 1 and 2 above	Business Manager (XYZ) responsible for the ABC business	6/22
4. XYZ determines what is needed for finished goods inventory build up	Business Development Manager (XYZ) and Director of Process Engineering & Lean Technologies (ABC)	6/8
5. ABC communicates to largest customer to confirm process acceptance	Business Development Manager (ABC)	6/15
6. Assess XYZ materials requirements planning and inventory management systems reliability. Pick randomly some items	Director of Purchasing (XYZ) and Director of Process Engineering & Lean Technologies (ABC)	6/8
7. XYZ will procure safety stock for the 64 critical items. Agree on the parameters and develop a plan for every unreliable supplier	Director of Purchasing (XYZ) and Director of Process Engineering & Lean Technologies (ABC)	6/8
8. Identify the one voice and propose a process to communicate and verify design and spec changes	Director of Research and Development (ABC)	6/15

Operations, the Executive Director of Operations, the Lean Technologies and Supply Manager, the Director of Process Engineering & Lean Technologies, the Business Development Manager, the Director of Research and Development, and the Director of Quality. Because the key people from each organization participated in the collaboration session, it was possible to vent frustrations and move on to develop the plan to move the relationship forward.

Conclusions

During the one-day collaboration meeting, managers from each organization involved in a business-to-business relationship clarify their expectations and mutually agree on goals for the relationship. In this article, we presented a framework that can be used to structure collaborative business relationships.

The collaboration meeting is only a first step in a challenging but rewarding long-term effort to tailor a business-to-business relationship for both parties involved. The benefits of building collaborative, win-win, business-to-business relationships are well documented. However, replicating successes and avoiding failures is difficult. Since companies do not compete in isolation but through the integration of operations with key customers and key suppliers, building high-performance business relationships becomes a competitive advantage difficult to replicate.

About the Authors

Douglas M. Lambert is the Raymond E. Mason Chair in the Department of Marketing and Logistics, and Director of The Global Supply Chain Forum at Fisher College of Business, The Ohio State University. He led the research that developed the Collaboration Framework and facilitates sessions using the model. Dr. Lambert has served as a faculty member for over 500 executive development programs in North and South America, Europe, Asia and Australia. He is the author or co-author of eight books and more than 100 articles. In 1986, Dr. Lambert received the CLM Distinguished Service Award. He holds an honors BA and MBA from the University of Western Ontario and a Ph.D. from The Ohio State University.

Sebastián J. García-Dastugue is Associate Professor at Universidad de San Andrés in Buenos Aires, Argentina. He is a member of the research team of the The Global Supply Chain Forum at The Ohio State University. His research deals with cross-functional integration and business-to-business relationships. He has more than 10 years of experience in industry. Dr. García-Dastugue received his Ph.D. from The Ohio State University, his MBA from IAE - Universidad Austral, and his BA in MIS from Universidad CAECE.

A Framework for Collaboration

Douglas M. Lambert and Sebastián García-Dastugue

One of the reasons that business relationships often yield disappointing results is unrealistic expectations on the part of one or both of the parties. To be successful, business-to-business relationships require that both sides clarify their expectations and mutually agree on goals for the relationship. Once this has been accomplished, it is necessary to prioritize action items, assign responsibilities, establish timelines, and determine the metrics that define success. The next step is to document these action items and performance measures in a formal product and service agreement (PSA) so that the goals for the relationship are clear to all of those involved. The PSA specifies levels of performance, provides direction for joint improvement efforts and includes operational aspects of the relationships. Regular business reviews are required to ensure that the business goals for each side are met.

The Collaboration Meeting Overview

The collaboration meeting is a one-day session in which expectations are set, action plans are developed, and responsibilities are assigned as shown in the shaded boxes in Figure 1. Specific details related to the meeting are described next: 1) introduction and expectation setting session; 2) drivers session; 3) alignment session; 4) action plans; and, 5) the wrap-up session.

Introduction and Expectation Setting Session

The collaboration meeting should begin with an introduction that reinforces each side's motivations for the meeting, a review of the framework, and a discussion about the expectations for the session. For example, in one meeting, the vice president of the supplier organization stated that the motivation for using the framework was to achieve a structured and consistent approach to developing a PSA with the customer.

Drivers Assessment Session

It is important in the drivers assessment session that managers feel comfortable to express their opinions whatever they might be. This comfort level would be difficult to achieve without unbiased meeting facilitators. The drivers fall into four categories:

- *Asset/Cost Efficiencies* include the potential for better utilization of assets and/or for cost reductions that might occur in areas such as transportation costs, handling costs, packaging costs, information costs, product costs, or managerial efficiencies.
- *Customer Service* improvements can lead to increased sales when customers experience benefits such as reduced inventory, improved availability (which leads to sales increases), and more timely and accurate information.
- *Marketing Advantages* can be achieved by: 1) an enhancement of an organization's marketing mix through joint programs; 2) entry into new markets; and 3) better access to technology and innovation.
- *Profit Stability/Growth* is the potential for stabilizing profit. Strengthening a relationship often leads to long-term volume

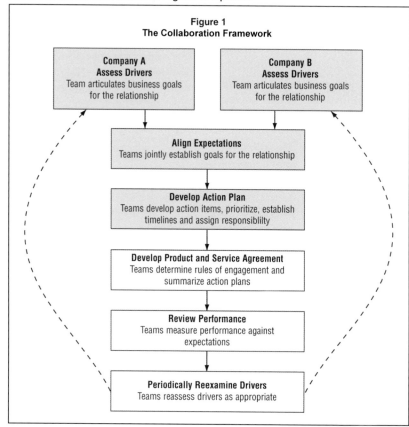

Figure 1
The Collaboration Framework

Company A
Assess Drivers
Team articulates business goals for the relationship

Company B
Assess Drivers
Team articulates business goals for the relationship

Align Expectations
Teams jointly establish goals for the relationship

Develop Action Plan
Teams develop action items, prioritize, establish timelines and assign responsibility

Develop Product and Service Agreement
Teams determine rules of engagement and summarize action plans

Review Performance
Teams measure performance against expectations

Periodically Reexamine Drivers
Teams reassess drivers as appropriate

commitments, reduced variability in sales, joint use of assets, and other improvements that reduce variability of profits.

For each team, the participants should identify specific bullet-point descriptions for each driver category with goals (including metrics and targets) and priorities. Representatives of the two firms should evaluate drivers separately and the evaluation must be from a selfish perspective.

Align Expectations Session

Once each side has scored their drivers, the next step is to come together and present their drivers to each other. It is important to explain why the drivers were selected. This represents an expectations-setting session that is critical for success. One of the reasons that business relationships often yield disappointing results is unrealistic expectations on the part of one or both of the parties. The thinking behind the drivers needs to be understood by both sides of the relationship. If the representatives of the other firm indicate that they cannot or will not help achieve a particular driver, the driver should be reevaluated. If no one in the session objects to the other side's drivers, then management is obligated to help the other firm achieve its drivers.

Develop Action Plan Session

In the final session, the mutually agreed upon drivers are prioritized and translated into an action plan. Action items should include a brief description (what), the individuals from each organization that will have responsibility for achieving the driver (who) and a timeline for implementation (when). When developing the action plan, management needs to balance workload and separate short-term opportunities from those that are longer-term.

Develop Product and Service Agreement

The PSA is a document that matches the requirements of the customer with the capabilities of the supplier. The PSA specifies levels of performance and provides direction for joint improvement efforts. The PSA documents business goals of the customer and supplier so that the expectations of each organization are realistic and understood by both sides. It is necessary to take the action plan, responsibilities, and timelines developed during the collaboration meeting and include them in the PSA.

Review Performance

Regular business reviews should be conducted so that management can determine if satisfactory progress is being made toward the goals established in the action plan and to measure the degree to which the commitments made in the

product and service agreement are being fulfilled. The team should review the action plan on a regular basis to determine if the action plan and PSA are adequately resourced and remain relevant.

Periodically Reexamine Drivers

It is necessary to periodically reexamine the drivers for a number of reasons. First, the PSAs should be updated annually which requires a new session. Second, changes in the business environment may require a reassessment of the drivers on a shorter cycle. Third, a performance review may reveal that the drivers have been achieved and it is time for another session.

An Example of a Collaboration Session Using the Framework

One example of the use of the Collaboration Framework is a US-based company (ABC Corporation) and a Chinese supplier (XYZ Company). While the organizations had a history of working together, a very successful new product line had increased the volume of business substantially and the management of ABC Corporation believed that the potential for even greater growth was high. A primary reason for demand for ABC's new product significantly exceeding forecast was a large volume of purchases from ABC's largest customer who was becoming increasingly upset at ABC's inability to ship on time and in full. XYZ was caught by the unexpected increase in demand at a time when the economic crisis was causing its suppliers in China to not manufacture until orders were received which was increasing lead times for the components they were purchasing. Management of XYZ wanted to provide the volume now required by ABC but needed its customer's help in order to be successful.

Conclusions

The collaboration meeting is only a first step in a challenging but rewarding long-term effort to tailor a business-to-business relationship so that both parties achieve enhanced results. The idea of building collaborative, win-win, business-to-business relationships is well received by most managers. However, replicating success and avoiding failures is difficult. Since companies do not compete in isolation but rather with some degree of integration with key customers and key suppliers, building high-performance business relationships becomes a competitive advantage difficult to replicate.

Sample Invitation E-mail

[*Insert Participant Name*],

The Collaboration Framework that is being used for our upcoming meeting is described in detail in the attached article – "*A Framework for Collaboration.*" Please read the article carefully prior to our scheduled meeting. This pre-read is important because:

- It will provide an overview of the structure for our meeting.
- It will make the meeting much more productive.
- It will allow time for your questions about the approach to crystallize.
- It should only take about an hour.

As you will understand after reading the article, one of the reasons that business relationships often yield disappointing results is the existence of unstated or unrealistic expectations on the part of one or both of the parties. To be successful, business-to-business relationships require that both sides clarify their expectations and mutually agree on goals for the relationship. This upcoming meeting is focused on clarifying these expectations and developing action items and performance measures so that the goals of the relationship are clear to all of those involved. Thanks again for your active participation in this important activity. Please contact me if you have any questions prior to the meeting.

Best regards,

[*Insert Meeting Sponsor Name*]

COLLABORATION MEETING

AGENDA

Location of Meeting

Time	Topic	Responsibility
Date:		
Host:		
7:45 – 8:15	Continental Breakfast	
8:15 – 8:45	Welcome, Introductions, Company Overviews & Expected Outcomes	Company Reps
8:45 – 9:15	Overview of the Framework	Meeting Facilitators
Each group breaks as needed during the next session		
9:15 – 12:00	Breakout Groups – Drivers Assessment Sessions (Each company meets separately)	ALL
12:00 – LUNCH/PHONES – 13:00		
13:00 – 14:30	Align Expectations Session (Organizations present drivers to each other)	ALL
14:30 – BREAK – 14:45		
14:45 – 16:15	Develop Action Plan Session	ALL
16:15 – 16:45	Sustaining the Relationship	ALL
16:45 – 17:00	Evaluations and Wrap-up	ALL

Structuring Collaborative Relationships

Introductions

[Add name(s) of Presenters]

This session is designed to introduce the participants from both firms to one another, articulate the motivation for holding the meeting, stress the need for openness and active participation, and communicate the agenda for the meeting.

You may want to add presenter names and/or firm logos to the first slide in each session.

Often the senior manager from each firm provides a brief overview of his/her business and reasserts the need to openly and actively participate in the sessions.

Review Agenda

- Meeting Facilitator(s) Introduction
- Agenda
- Electronic Device Reminder
- Pre-read

Start with an introduction of the meeting facilitator(s). This introduction should briefly highlight the facilitator's role in the process and ensure the confidentiality of all discussions during the session.

The agenda can be reviewed here.

A reminder is appropriate that commitment to the relationship may be measured by the disciplined non-use of electronic communication devices during the meeting. If managers are constantly leaving the room to make calls or check e-mail then the other party will assume that the relationship is relatively unimportant. The same comment can be made for those using electronic devices during the meeting.

An early read of how well the participants are prepared will enable the facilitator to adjust his/her opening presentation as appropriate. A good place to start is by asking the group whether they have read the article, "A Framework for Collaboration," (included in the Resources and Tools section of this book) that was assigned as a pre-read.

Firm A (replace with firm name) Introduction

- Who is participating in the meeting from our company
- About our company
- Explain how this meeting fits with our strategic focus

Both firms should introduce themselves. Typically, the firm that initiated the session presents first.

For each firm a number of introductory items are appropriate to cover:

- The names and roles of the participants should be shared. A good reinforcement is to collect a set of business cards for copying and distribution to the entire group. Also, participants may want to articulate their degree of experience with the relationship.

- The bullets provided are suggestions for the potential material to include in a brief (15 minutes) company presentation. It may or may not be appropriate to share overall strategic focus and how it fits with the relationship.

- If the relationship is a new relationship general coverage of the relevant history, structure and other demographics may be appropriate here.

Firm B (replace with firm name) Introduction

- Who is participating in the meeting from our company
- About our company
- Explain how this meeting fits with our strategic focus

For each firm a number of introductory items are appropriate to cover:

- The names and roles of the participants should be shared. A good reinforcement is to collect a set of business cards for copying and distribution to the entire group. Also, participants may want to articulate their degree of experience with the relationship.

- The bullets provided are suggestions for the potential material to include in a brief (15 minutes) company presentation. It may or may not be appropriate to share overall strategic focus and how it fits with the relationship.

- If the relationship is a new relationship general coverage of the relevant history, structure and other demographics may be appropriate here.

Structuring Collaborative Relationships

Overview of the Framework

[Add name(s) of Presenters]

While the article, "A Framework for Collaboration," was assigned as a pre-read for the meeting, it is important to ensure that all participants are familiar with the framework and understand the steps in the framework.

This session is designed to get all of the participants on the same page with respect to what the day's goals are and how things will proceed.

The Collaboration Framework

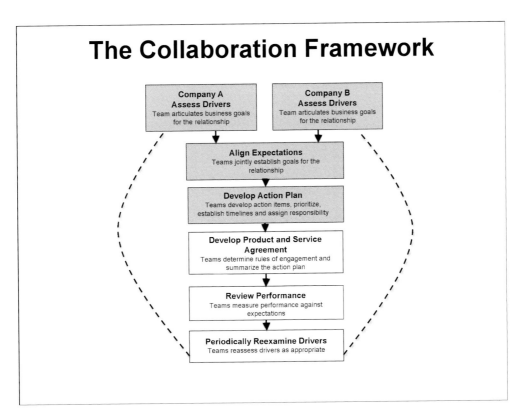

Over the course of the collaboration meeting, there are structured sessions addressing each of the shaded boxes.

While the responsibilities for overseeing the development of the product service agreement will be assigned as an action item, the actual development of the PSA, review of performance and periodic reassessment of drivers will take place after the meeting.

There are slides in this toolkit to address each of the boxes in this framework, including those activities that take place after the collaboration meeting. It is important to clearly set expectations as to what will be covered in the meeting and what will be done after the meeting.

Assess Drivers

- Identify drivers
- Prioritize drivers
- Share drivers
- Adjust expectations as necessary

A key outcome of this meeting is the identification of specific drivers and a shared understanding of the motivations for doing business from both firms' perspectives. For collaboration to be appropriate, there should be drivers that require a degree of cross-firm cooperation.

It is important to prioritize the drivers in order to focus efforts on achieving the most important benefits for each firm. In the align expectations session, the drivers and their priority are shared across the teams.

Align Expectations

- Each team presents their drivers
- Rationale for each driver given
- Agreement by both teams that the driver can become a joint goal
- Drivers will not necessarily match

In this session the two firms' representatives share their drivers, goals and metrics. It is in this session that agreement on joint goals and metrics takes place.

Gaining a deeper understanding of the drivers and goals of the other organization should enhance planning for the relationship moving forward.

It should not be expected that all drivers will be addressed. Similarly, do not expect that all goals will be accepted. However, experience indicates that each side may be surprised to see how often their drivers are consistent with the other side. That is, the other side of the relationship wants the same things but have never formally articulated these goals.

Develop Action Plan

- The teams jointly determine and prioritize initiatives
- The set of initiatives should be relatively small
- There should be a balance of short-term and long-term initiatives
- The action plan needs to include clear statements of what is to be done, who is responsible, and a timeline for results

In this session, the two firms' representatives jointly identify initiatives which advance the goals of one or both firms. The firms are committing to specific actions and joint efforts. The action items should be prioritized.

The set of initiatives should be relatively small. In addition, be careful when assigning responsibility for an item. It is easy to verbally commit parties not present in the meeting to tasks that are important to the relationship. Also, remember that it is much more difficult to get parties motivated and moving on multiple initiatives. It is important to set realistic goals and achieve them to help reinforce the value of the relationship.

It is important in most relationships to achieve early wins. A balance of short-term and long-term initiatives sustain collaboration better. Early gains reinforce the relationship, and reaching milestones in longer-term projects offers encouragement.

The action plan needs to include clear statements of what is to be done, who is responsible, and a timeline for results. The what, who and when are captured on the worksheet provided in this toolkit.

Develop Product and Service Agreement

- Specifies the levels of performance and provides for joint improvement efforts
- Documents business goals
- Additional items that may be documented in the PSA beyond those in the action plan include:
    - Key contacts or relationship owners
    - Order acceptance guidelines
    - Credit terms
    - Planning activities
    - Returned products
    - Driver-specific commitments
    - Performance review process

The product service agreement (PSA) is a document that guides the relationship for a defined time period. It matches the requirements of the customer with the capabilities of the supplier.

The responsibilities for overseeing the development of the product service agreement will be assigned in the develop action plan session. The actual development of the PSA will take place after the meeting.

After the meeting but before the enthusiasm for the collaboration efforts wane, the two firms' representatives need to jointly work on producing a detailed outline of their PSA. Be aware that PSA's can take many forms. The items above represent suggested items for inclusion beyond the specifics of the action plan that result from this meeting.

Review Performance

- Performance related to the plan must be monitored
- Timing of reviews must be determined
- Methods of reporting must be specified
- Metrics must be based on the action plan
- Hard-to-measure action items should not be ignored

Depending on the specifics surrounding the relationship, progress reviews may take a number of forms and be conducted within a variety of timeframes.

The reviews can be performed monthly, quarterly or biannually.

The parties should consider what form the reporting process will take and who needs to receive the information.

The reporting should include references to the action items and the metrics specified in the action plan.

The reviews also need to address those items that defy simple quantification.

Periodically Reexamine Drivers

- Typically an annual activity
- Timing depends on volatility of the environment
- With good continuity of participants this may not require meeting facilitators for subsequent years

The two firms' representatives will develop a plan for initiating the next collaboration session.

In a volatile situation, the drivers may need to be reassessed more often. In the rare case where the drivers are quickly and substantially met, it may be worthwhile to revisit the drivers.

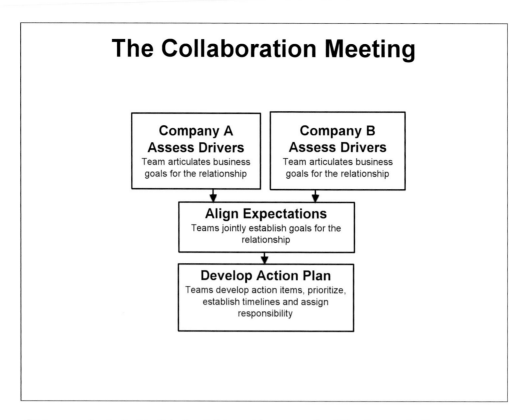

The Collaboration Meeting

Company A Assess Drivers
Team articulates business goals for the relationship

Company B Assess Drivers
Team articulates business goals for the relationship

Align Expectations
Teams jointly establish goals for the relationship

Develop Action Plan
Teams develop action items, prioritize, establish timelines and assign responsibility

Slides are included in this toolkit to address each of the boxes in the Collaboration Framework. It is important to clearly set expectations as to what parts of the framework are covered in the meeting and what parts occur after the meeting.

The assess drivers sessions regularly take between two to three hours. It is important not to short change this session. This may mean that a working lunch is required or the day is extended if the meeting facilitators determine that more time is needed to get the drivers right. The two parallel drivers sessions may not end simultaneously without meeting facilitator intervention. Be aware that busy executives have low tolerances for long waits, thus the meeting facilitators should be in regular contact regarding the progress of the other side.

Structuring Collaborative Relationships

Drivers Assessment Session

In this session the drivers are identified, goals set and priorities determined.

Assess Drivers Session

- Break into groups by firm
- Consider each driver
- Capture "selfish goals" as they arise
- Identify the specific bullet points relevant to *this* relationship (Do not close the door too quickly on ideas)

In this session participants evaluate the collaboration drivers from their own perspective. _____ (firm A) will meet in _____ (room) and _____ (firm B) will meet in _____ (room). The goal is to fill out each driver form and be ready to share with the other side.

To accomplish this, each bullet point for each driver should be considered. Specific advantages possible through inter-firm coordination should be identified and when consensus is reached added as bullets to the forms provided.

There are a number of points to keep in mind. Do not be too quick to judge a potential benefit to be impossible. Brainstorming rules apply in this session. Also, thought should be given to the measurement of the outcomes related to each driver or bullet point. Target metrics should be recorded.

.

Session Organization

- Need a recorder/reporter for each group
- Need a method to report your results to your potential partner
  - Flip chart sheets
  - PowerPoint presentation
- Need to establish success metrics for each driver element where possible

Each group identifies a recorder and a presenter. The ideas must be captured and reported to the other group in the next phase of the collaboration meeting.

The findings concerning drivers for each group must be accurately and succinctly reported to the other group. Flip charts, overhead projectors, and PowerPoint presentations have been used successfully in this regard.

Along with the description of the driver, target metrics are needed where possible. Examples might be good where measurement is difficult.

Prioritizing the drivers is important using the priority scale with 1=Critical, 2=Very Important and 3=Important.

Drivers

- Goals for the relationship

- Four basic drivers
  - Improvement in asset/cost efficiencies
  - Improved customer service
  - Enhanced marketing advantage
  - Profit growth/stability

- Capture the driver first, be specific

- Quantify the goal

- Prioritize the set of drivers

Each party must assess each driver in detail and determine quantifiable goals.

Drivers must be analyzed separately by each firm since the benefits are company specific. Now we will take a detailed look at each driver.

Assessment of Drivers

Drivers are business reasons for expanding the resource commitment to the relationship. For each item, develop specific goals and identify the priority. Priority is: 1=Critical, 2=Very Important, 3=Important.

ASSET/COST EFFICIENCY

1. What are the initiative that will reduce cost or improve asset utilization?

Driver	Goal	Priority
• Product costs savings	2% per year	1
• Distribution costs savings, handling costs savings	7% during 1st year	1
• Packaging costs savings and green initiatives	Satisfy Wal-Mart's requirements	3
• Reduce order-to-cash cycle time	By 10 days	2
• No management time devoted to conference call to key customers explaining service failures due to supplier problems	Zero within 3 months	1
• Assets utilization (reduce plant over-time due to surprise orders)	No surprise orders by quarter-end	2
• Integrate planning across business and plants (visibility of capacity available across plants)	Within 12 months	3

Here is an example for the Asset/Cost Efficiency driver category.

The company has a product cost reduction goal of 2% per year. The team believed that there were areas where these cost savings could be realized through collaboration. The first three bullets on the driver form represent these potential initiatives. Goals are set for each initiative and they are prioritized.

Reducing order-to-cash cycle time should improve asset utilization. While the goal is stated in days, it could have been stated in dollars freed up by the improvment in cycle time. These choices of metrics are important.

Assessment of Drivers

Drivers are business reasons for expanding the resource commitment to the relationship. For each item, develop specific goals and identify the priority. Priority is: 1=Critical, 2=Very Important, 3=Important.

ASSET/COST EFFICIENCY

1. What are the initiatives that will reduce cost or improve asset utilization?

Driver	Goal	Priority

This is the blank driver form that needs to be populated with your firm's specific driver bullets, goals and priorities.

Assessment of Drivers

Drivers are business reasons for expanding the resource commitment to the relationship. For each item, develop specific goals and identify the priority. Priority is: 1=Critical, 2=Very Important, 3=Important.

CUSTOMER SERVICE

2. What are the initiatives will improve customer service as measured by the customer?

Driver	Goal	Priority
• Improved on-time delivery	From 98.5% to 100%	1
• Better tracking of movement	Full visibility	2
• Paperless order processing	100% EDI	2
• Order accuracy	0 picking errors	1
• Improved cycle times	From 14 to 7 days	1
• Improved fill rates	From 96% to 99%	1
• Customer survey results	#1 in industry survey	2
• Improved response to inquires	2 hours	3

Here is an example for the Customer Service driver category.

This would represent the buyer's drivers. It is unlikely that the seller would have such an extensive list, since improving this customer's customer service metrics is a benefit for the customer, not the seller. Managers for the seller organization may believe they can provide better customer service to other customers through collaboration with this customer by improving customer service systems .

Assessment of Drivers

Drivers are business reasons for expanding the resource commitment to the relationship. For each item, develop specific goals and identify the priority. Priority is: 1=Critical, 2=Very Important, 3=Important.

CUSTOMER SERVICE

2. What are the initiatives will improve customer service as measured by the customer?

Driver	Goal	Priority

This is the blank driver form that needs to be populated with your firm's specific driver bullets, goals and priorities.

Assessment of Drivers

Drivers are business reasons for expanding the resource commitment to the relationship. For each item, develop specific goals and identify the priority. Priority is: 1=Critical, 2=Very Important, 3=Important.

MARKETING ADVANTAGE

3. What are the initiatives that will lead to marketing advantages?

Driver	Goal	Priority
• Promotion (joint advertising, sales promotion)	3 promotions/year	1
• Evaluate co-branding opportunities	Within 6 months	3
• Share market research data	1 meeting/year	3
• New product (jointly developed product innovation)	7 ideas, 3 ready per year	1
• Expand geographic coverage (buy our products in markets outside the USA)	$10,000,000 in 1st year	2
• Sell our latest technology	Within 12 months	1
• Innovation potential	2 brainstorming sessions/year	2

Here is an example for the Marketing Advantage driver category.

Joint promotions were a top priority for the firm. Management believed that through collaboration three successful joint promotions per year were possible.

Assessment of Drivers

Drivers are business reasons for expanding the resource commitment to the relationship. For each item, develop specific goals and identify the priority. Priority is: 1=Critical, 2=Very Important, 3=Important.

MARKETING ADVANTAGE

3. What are the initiatives that will lead to marketing advantages?

Driver	Goal	Priority

This is the blank driver form that needs to be populated with your firm's specific driver bullets, goals and priorities.

Assessment of Drivers

Drivers are business reasons for expanding the resource commitment to the relationship. For each item, develop specific goals and identify the priority. Priority is: 1=Critical, 2=Very Important, 3=Important.

PROFIT STABILITY/GROWTH

4. What are the initiatives that will result in profit growth or reduced variability in profit?

Driver	Goal	Priority
• Growth	10% volume increase	1
• Cyclical leveling	1/3/5 year plan	2
• Monthly demand leveling (eliminate end-of-quarter load)	Over next 12 months	1
• Price stability	Annual contract	2
• Reduce sales volume fluctuation	A consistent 40% of your spend	1
• Evaluate growing/starting up in every market you are present	1 market/year	3
• Grow share of "value added" products	20% increase	2

Here is an example for Profit Stability/Growth driver category.

Management wanted to reduce profit volatility through the leveling of sales across the quarter by eliminating the end-of-quarter load. They viewed this as a top priority to be completed over the next 12 months.

Assessment of Drivers

Drivers are business reasons for expanding the resource commitment to the relationship. For each item, develop specific goals and identify the priority. Priority is: 1=Critical, 2=Very Important, 3=Important.

PROFIT STABILITY/GROWTH

4. What are the initiatives that will result in profit growth or reduced variability in profit?

Driver	Goal	Priority

This is the blank driver form that needs to be populated with your firm's specific driver bullets, goals and priorities.

Structuring Collaborative Relationships

Align Expectations Session

In this session, the two firms jointly share their drivers, goals and priorities. This is an important session for clarifying expectations between the two firms. Managers should be reminded to have an open and honest dialog concerning the issues that emerge in the session.

Drivers Review and Expectations Alignment

- Members from each firm present their drivers to the other team
- Teams assess the feasibility of achieving both firms' drivers
- Teams agree a joint set of drivers
- Every effort should be made to insure that both organizations win

This session is all about setting joint expectations. Each team presents the drivers that they independently identified. Together the teams must assess each of the drivers to determine which are likely to be achieved.

The next step is for the teams to agree on a joint set of drivers including the related metrics. The rules of the session are that if a team accepts the drivers of the other firm without challenge, then they are obligated to help them achieve these drivers.

Shared understanding of opposite party's drivers is an important outcome of this session. The most important outcome is the agreement on the set of drivers that serve as the basis of the action plan developed in the next session.

It is useful to have the full set of agreed-upon drivers visible for the next session. This can be done by having them on a flip chart, having them printed and distributed to the group or by using a projector.

Structuring Collaborative Relationships

Action Plan Session

In this session the action plan and action items are derived from the agreed upon drivers .

Action Plan Session

- The goal of this session is to identify and specify an action plan to achieve the agreed-upon drivers
- Resources and capabilities must be considered
- The action plan should specify what, who and when

In this session, the two firms' representatives jointly develop an action plan. The action plan is typically built around one or more drivers. The action plan is often designed to meet the needs of both parties, but not always.

It is important to choose initiatives that can be achieved and supported by the resources of the two firms.

For each action item it is important to record the who, what and when. See the next slide for an example.

Action Plan for ABC Corporation and XYZ Company

From the drivers for each side of the relationship an action plan needs to be developed. Action items should include a brief description (what), who from each side are responsible for the item (who), and for when the next action is planned (when).

What	Who	When
1. ABC will look at remaining 2009 forecast and make a buy proposal for the finished products that it purchases from XYZ	Lean Technologies and Supply Manager (ABC)	6/15
2. ABC will look at remaining 2009 forecast and make a buy proposal for the two key components for those products	Lean Technologies and Supply Manager (ABC)	6/15
3. XYZ responds to 1 and 2 above	Business Manager (XYZ) responsible for the ABC business	6/22
4. XYZ determines what is needed for finished goods inventory build up	Business Development Manager (XYZ) and Director of Process Engineering & Lean Technologies (ABC)	6/8
5. ABC communicates to largest customer to confirm process acceptance	Business Development Manager (ABC)	6/15
6. Assess XYZ materials requirements planning and inventory management systems reliability. Pick randomly some items	Director of Purchasing (XYZ) and Director of Process Engineering & Lean Technologies (ABC)	6/8
7. XYZ will procure safety stock for the 64 critical items. Agree on the parameters and develop a plan for every unreliable supplier	Director of Purchasing (XYZ) and Director of Process Engineering & Lean Technologies (ABC)	6/8
8. Identify the one voice and propose a process to communicate and verify design and spec changes	Director of Research and Development (ABC)	6/15

The output from this session should be a set of action items that specify what is involved, who is responsible and when the item will be accomplished.

For example, this action plan states that in order to improve service to key customers ABC managers will look at the forecast for the remainder of 2009 and make a buy proposal for the remainder of the year.

In order to relieve financial pressures on the seller, ABC will commit to purchase key components based on their forecast.

The supplier will then set finished goods inventories and component inventories to match the forecast.

The action items may be very granular (specific activities by individuals or small groups) or they may be rolled up into complex initiatives depending on managements' choices.

Action Plan Template

From the drivers on each side of the relationship an action plan needs be developed. Actions items should include a brief description (What), who from each side are responsible for the item (Who), and when the next action is planned (When)

What	Who	When

The participant's packets should include a blank action plan form to record the specific action items jointly determined in the session.

Structuring Collaborative Relationships

Sustaining the Relationship

There are three major activities after the collaboration meeting. These activities are required to successfully sustain the relationship and their completion is an important part of ensuring the use of the Collaboration Framework is successful.

If timing does not permit, this content may covered by a conference call or by other means. However, these steps are critical.

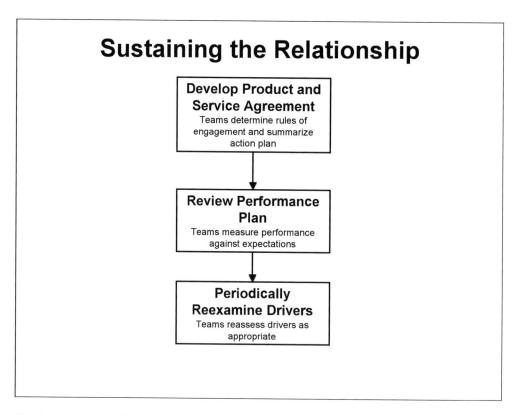

Sustaining the Relationship

Develop Product and Service Agreement
Teams determine rules of engagement and summarize action plan

Review Performance Plan
Teams measure performance against expectations

Periodically Reexamine Drivers
Teams reassess drivers as appropriate

Each one of the above boxes will be covered in turn.

Develop Product and Service Agreement

- Specifies the levels of performance and provides for joint improvement efforts
- Documents business goals
- Additional items that may be documented in the PSA beyond those in the action plan include:
  - Key contacts or relationship owners
  - Order acceptance guidelines
  - Credit terms
  - Planning activities
  - Returned products
  - Driver-specific commitments
  - Performance review process

The goal is to develop a working product and service agreement (PSA). While each party likely has their own format for producing such agreements and they may be known by different names, PSAs should specify performance levels for key aspects of the transactions as well as joint improvement efforts.

It is important to document the joint business goals. The documentation should capture commitments made by both sides of the relationship.

The list of items is not necessarily exhaustive. It is meant to capture most of the items present in typical PSA's.

Review Performance

- Performance related to the plan must be monitored
- Timing of reviews must be determined
- Methods of reporting must be specified
- Metrics must be based on the action plan
- Hard-to-measure action items should not be ignored

Depending on the specifics surrounding the relationship, progress reviews may take a number of forms and be conducted within a variety of timeframes.

The reviews can be performed monthly, quarterly or biannually.

The parties should consider what form the reporting process will take and who needs to receive the information.

The reporting should include references to the action items and the metrics specified in the action plan.

The reviews also need to address those items that defy simple quantification.

Periodically Reexamine Drivers

- Typically an annual activity
- Timing depends on volatility of the environment
- With good continuity of participants this may not require meeting facilitators for subsequent years

The two firms' representatives will develop a plan for initiating the next collaboration session.

In a volatile situation, the drivers may need to be reassessed more often. In the rare case where the drivers are quickly and substantially met, it may be worthwhile to revisit the drivers.

Author Index

Baba, Maretta L., 28, 29, 41
Benton, W. C., 41
Berry, Leonard L., 13, 14
Boyson, Sandor, 41
Bumett, Melissa S., 40
Burt, David, N., 21

Carter, Craig R., 41
Checkland, Peter, 41
Cho, Dong Sung, 16
Cooper, Martha C., 2, 33, 37
Corsi, Thomas, 41

Daugherty,Patricia J., 34
Dobler, Donald W., 21
Dresner, Martin, 41
Dudley, William N., 34
Dwyer, Robert, 36
Dyer, Jeffery H., 16

Ellram, Lisa M., 37
Emmelhainz, Margaret A., 2, 3, 27, 28,
    29, 32, 35, 36, 39, 48, 50, 52, 54,
    56
Erffmeyer, Robert C., 40

Foote-Whyte, W., 41
Frow, Pennie, 15

Gardner, John T., 2, 3, 27, 28, 29, 32, 33,
    35, 36, 37, 39, 48, 50, 52, 54, 56,
    58
Graham, T. Scott, 34
Gundlatch, Gregory T., 37

Harrigan, Kathryn Rudie, 38

Heide, Jan B., 38
Heskett, James L., 14
Holcomb, Mary C., 33

Jap, Sandy, 30
Jennings, Marianne M., 41
John, George, 30, 38

Kanter, Rosabeth M., 1
Ken, John L., 41
Knemeyer, A. Michael, 3, 27, 58
Kolbe, Richard H., 40

La Londe, Bernard J., 37
Lambert, Douglas M., 2, 3, 17, 19, 20,
    21, 22, 23, 24, 25, 27, 28, 29, 32,
    35, 36, 39, 48, 50, 52, 54, 56, 58
Langley, John C., 33
Lincoln, Yvonna S., 41
Lusch, Robert F., 15

Macneil, Ian R., 36
Maloni, Michael, 41
Mateus, Paula, 15
McAlister, Debbie T., 40
McCracken, Grant D., 41
McKeman, James, 41
Mentzer, John T., 2, 41
Min, Soonhong, 2
Moberg, Christopher R., 41
Mohr, Jakki, 33
Murphy, Patrick C., 37

Naslund, Dag, 40
Nevin, John R., 30
Noordeweir, Thomas G., 2, 30, 37

Company Index

Subject Index